55-99 BK Bud 9/99

THE
GOOD-BYE
WINDOW

THE GOOD-BYE WINDOW

A Year in the Life of a Day-Care Center

Harriet N. Brown

The University of Wisconsin Press

The University of Wisconsin Press
2537 Daniels Street
Madison, Wisconsin 53718

3 Henrietta Street
London WC2E 8LU, England

All photographs by James H. Young
"The Red Wheelbarrow," by William Carlos Williams,
from *Collected Poems, 1909–1939, Volume I.*
Copyright 1938 by New Directions Publishing Corp.
Reprinted by permission of New Directions Publishing Corp.

1   3   5   4   2

Printed in the United States of America

Library of Congress Cataloging-in-Publication Data
Brown, Harriet N.
The good-bye window: a year in the life of a day-care center /
Harriet N. Brown
264 pp.   cm.
Includes bibliographical references.
ISBN 0-299-15870-5 (cloth: alk. paper).
1. Red Caboose Day Care Center (Madison, Wis.)   2. Day care
centers—United States—Case studies.   I. Title.
HQ778.67.M33B76   1998
362.71'2'09775—dc21   98-17528

For Jamie, Anna, and Soleil—
my family and friends

Contents

ILLUSTRATIONS

ACKNOWLEDGMENTS

My grateful appreciation goes to everyone at Red Caboose. The board of directors took a chance on letting me into the center. The teachers allowed me into their classrooms, ignored my whispered notes into a tape recorder, and gracefully answered my questions. The parents opened their hearts and lives to me. A very special thank you goes to Wendy Rakower, who spent hours being interviewed, bringing me up to speed on crucial issues, and gently correcting my errors in perception and execution. I couldn't possibly have written this book without her help. Any remaining mistakes in the text are mine alone.

My thanks also to Gloria Jacobs and Marcia Gillespie at *Ms.*, who published an article on Red Caboose that later became part of this book.

A million thank yous to Rachel Pastan, Nancy Holyoke, and Michelle Watkins, each of whom generously took the time to read and critique the manuscript at various points. Some, heroically, read it more than once. Thanks go to my father, who encouraged my writing even though he wanted me to be a lawyer.

Finally I'm immensely grateful to my editor, Mary Elizabeth Braun, for believing in this project with all her heart.

AUTHOR'S NOTE

Most of the children and families in this book appear under their real names. A few asked for pseudonyms, to protect their privacy. To keep the narrative flowing, I decided not to mark these with an asterisk or note. There are no composites; everyone described here is real, every interaction did occur. No quotes were invented or "elaborated on" for the sake of a smoother narrative. But some names and identifying characteristics have been changed.

THE GOOD-BYE WINDOW

Prologue

At 6 a.m., the parking lot in front of Red Caboose is dark and empty. The chain-link gate that fences the playground from the parking lot swings open in the warm predawn breeze, whistling as it scrapes back and forth across asphalt. Inside the gate the wooden play structures are humped shadows, taking on fairy-tale shapes in the early morning darkness—a castle turret, a drawbridge, Rapunzel's silent tower. There are no ogres, no kings or queens, no wizards, but there is still magic here, waiting to be set free. Two hours from now the gate will be firmly closed, the playground alive with children crisscrossing the blacktop on tricycles, swarming over ladders and slides and ropes and tires, belly-flopped on swings, digging small feet into piles of wood chips, patting handfuls of sand into cakes and other offerings. Rush-hour traffic will trundle down Williamson Street, the steady *whoosh whoosh* of leavetaking and arrival.

And inside the gray stucco walls, a community will be reinventing itself, as it does each day—grown-ups chatting in the cluttered hallways, teachers setting out cups and plates of food, mothers and fathers blowing kisses, waving, sometimes turning away from a tearstained face. In the long days here, nothing much happens and everything happens. So many lives come together under this roof—parents, staff, and of course the children. Toddlers in tiny wooden chairs scoop eggs from paper plates into their mouths. Two-year-olds carom off the walls. A preschooler carefully carries a steaming bowl of oatmeal from the kitchen. Four-year-olds tell elaborate stories as they race up the stairs for breakfast.

Across the country, scenes like these are played out thousands of times a day, with infinite variations. In 1995 there were about 7 million children in center-based care—31 percent of all children under age six[1]—plus another 4 million in other forms of care.[2] Preschoolers—children ages three, four, and five—are more likely to be enrolled at centers than younger children.[3] But very few parents really know what goes on after they leave. Some are afraid to know, frightened of discovering that the people they entrust with their children are not as thoughtful and caring and warm as they wish. Separation is painful for parents, too; it's easier to blind yourself, to not know what happens after you say good-bye. Others don't have the time or energy to find out what their children do all day and how they do it.

As a society we don't talk much about what goes on in child-care centers. We seem to have decided that the day-to-day experiences of young children are not important or interesting enough to examine. This is wrong, and we are beginning to know it. More and more, the research shows that what goes on in the first few years of life sets the tone and timbre of what is to come. It may seem, after a long day with a young child, that nothing has happened, but that's not true. It's just that it's happening inside the child's brain, where we can't see it. Synapses are firing, wrinkles are forming in the cerebrum, the groundwork for intelligence is being laid. Language is developing, along with social and emotional abilities—all the tools for what we think of as a good life, a happy life, a useful life. The sudden leaps of cognitive ability, or language, or emotional maturity that all children make during their development are not really leaps at all but the most visible pieces of an internal puzzle in progress.

The poet William Carlos Williams wrote, "So much depends / upon / a red wheel / barrow / glazed with rain / water / beside the white / chickens."[4] For children, too, much depends on the simple details of living. What seem to us little things—a tricycle, a picture book, a blissful hug—are for young children the things that shape their lives. Anyone who's ever loved a child knows this, of course. As my older daughter, Anna, grew out of infancy, I watched her world take on meaning and form. By chance more than anything else my husband and I enrolled Anna part time at Red Caboose. She stayed there for four years, right up until kindergarten, and in that time we *all* got an education.

Our education began when we started looking at centers. I looked at many wonderful places, centers with new toys and carpeting and clean white walls, centers that boasted air-conditioning and bright new playgrounds and a kitchen in every room so kids could cook. But in some of those places I also saw things that puzzled and upset me: A four-year-old left to cry alone for half an hour to "teach him a lesson." Industrial-size packages of Stouffer's macaroni and cheese served for lunch. Three-year-olds expected to sit at little desks and pay attention to lessons. Preschoolers hitting one another while teachers looked on blandly.

And I looked only at the "good" centers, or at least the ones I had been told were good. I heard plenty of stories about the others, though. One woman told me about the licensed family day-care home she'd used when her son was an infant. "At three o'clock that lady went around and changed all the kids' diapers for the only time that day," she said, "doing a sweep for pick-up time." Another mother visited her son's center on impulse and discovered everyone, from the babies to the five-year-olds, glued to a giant TV—this after she'd been told the center didn't own a television. Another friend's placid eight-month-old began screaming whenever she tried to put him in a car seat. Later she discovered he'd been strapped into his car seat all day long at his provider's home.

Horror stories about child care abound. Exposing the horrors doesn't make them go away, because too many parents don't have real choices. So long as parents are forced—by poverty, by scarcity, by lack of information—to find the cheapest, most convenient arrangement for their children, there will continue to be a market for destructive, poor-quality child care.

Too often the horror stories function as a lesson in morality, an object lesson on the dangers of working mothers. (No one ever talks about the dangers of working fathers, of course.) But most families have no alternative; both parents must work, either for money or for their own sanity. Single parents must work. And all children must learn to be separated from their parents, whether it's for an hour or seven hours. The only way to avoid it is for parents never to leave their children—an undesirable solution for both parents and kids.

We know all too well what bad child care looks like, at least in its most extreme form. But what does good child care look like? Too many parents don't know. One of the most disturbing findings of a 1995 study done through the University of Colorado is that parents are the worst judges of the quality of their children's care. Ninety percent of the parents in the study rated their kids' programs as "very good"; trained observers, rating the same programs, found that most provided care ranging from poor to mediocre.[5] Take away the obvious forms of abuse and neglect, and most parents don't know how to judge what's left.

So this book is about one child-care center in America and what's right with it. In my year of observations at Red Caboose, I tried to analyze what makes the center as good and as special as many people feel it is. Much of the Red Caboose magic is ambience, a feeling of community, but there are specific things that go into making it a special place: It has extremely low staff turnover. It has a sliding-scale fee schedule, so wealthier parents effectively

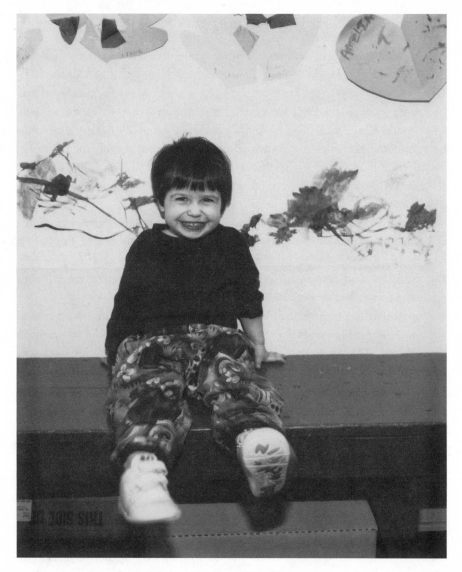

Soleil on the red bench outside the Elephant Room

subsidize poorer parents. In a state that is predominantly white, its population is reasonably diverse, both economically and ethnically. It has a proactive, parent-run board of directors and a philosophy that centers on fairness, egalitarianism, and compassion. It is accredited by the National Association for the Education of Young Children and certified by the city of Madison—two credentials widely regarded as marks of high quality.

Which isn't to say that it's perfect, or that my husband and I loved everything about it all the time. I've gone through periods where I worried deeply about whether my children were getting "good enough" care from Red Caboose. I considered other centers for Anna, but I never could bring myself to switch. Somehow Red Caboose always felt like home, for us and for Anna.

At 16 months, Anna was a timid child, easily frightened by other children. Smaller than the other kids, she was a perfect victim. But at Red Caboose she learned how to "use her words" to verbalize her feelings, how and when to go for adult help. She learned to care about the feelings of other children, to be compassionate. She began to have her own life, precious and independent from ours.

On Anna's first day of kindergarten, I watched her climb the steps to the school bus, her lower lip quivering. I was crying, too, as I climbed into my car and raced to school to meet the bus. But by the time she got off the school bus, she was so wrapped up in conversation that she walked right by me. By the end of that first day she was bubbly and excited, ready and able to deal with the ups and downs of public school. I think Red Caboose had a lot to do with that.

Now my younger daughter, Soleil, goes to Red Caboose. I'm less ambivalent this time around. Red Caboose provides a service to both of us: care for my child so that I can work, and an education for her, nurturing her physical, mental, and emotional growth. Which isn't to say that I don't worry about her, that I don't sometimes feel guilty about being apart from her. Worrying about our children—what I think of as informed worrying, not sensationalizing but an honest appraisal of dangers and pitfalls—is part of what makes us good parents.

Researching this book made me aware of how fortunate I am. I spent a whole year at my children's child-care center. I watched what happened after the other parents walked away. From talking with teachers and policy makers and experts, I gained a good idea of what's supposed to go on and why. I offer my experiences to other parents because I believe that the more we know about our children and ourselves, the better.

FALL
THE BUMBLEBEE ROOM

September

On a warm morning in early fall, the Bumblebees are sitting on the golden line, the metal strip where the sturdy brown carpeting meets the linoleum. Well, a few of them are sitting on the line; the rest are bouncing, rolling, pouncing, and jumping on the line. Most of these Bees are pretty new to the room, either because they've recently moved up from the two-year-old room or because they're newly enrolled at Red Caboose. While there is no official school year here, the center's rhythms tend to follow those of the public schools. Each year in late August a big group of five-year-olds goes off to kindergarten, making room for a group of four-year-olds to move up, and so on down the line.

So these three-year-olds are still learning the ropes in the Bumblebee Room. It shows in their restlessness and unwillingness to listen to teachers' directions. None of this is a surprise to the teachers, of course; they go through it every year, a kind of reverse honeymoon period, and they have ways of dealing with it—especially Clark Anderson, the lead teacher. A tall, lean man with shoulder-length hair and a drooping mustache, he works the room like the pro he is, using his voice and his physical presence to quench dissent in several different places at once. Now, for instance, he squats on the linoleum and begins his version of "The Itsy-Bitsy Spider," a favorite preschool song. In Clark's rendition, most of the words are replaced by a variety of grunts, hums, and sounds, and the kids are entranced. Shaunté, one of the most rambunctious of this year's Bees, stops wiggling and grins at the funny sounds. Another reason why these Bees are a little harder to control is that they're at the younger end of the age range for the room, most of them closer to three than to four. A year makes an enormous difference in a child's ability to control herself and her behavior.

This morning the kids are even antsier than usual because there's a treat in store: a trip to the public library—on a real live city bus!—for its weekly preschool video hour. While Clark entertains everyone, Carolyn Shields, the other Bumblebee morning teacher, finishes the breakfast cleanup. She carries the last of the spoons and plastic cups to a wheeled cart, stacks the used silverware in a dirty cup, and rolls the cart down the hall to the kitchen. She reappears a moment later to spray disinfectant on the two low tables, wipe them down with damp paper towels, push the red child-size chairs underneath. Then she checks the Bumblebees' traveling bag: a couple spare diapers, extra clothes, bandages, a list of emergency contacts for everyone. Finally she's ready to go.

The Bumblebees are more than ready. Coats on—it is fall in Wisconsin, after all—they're lined up at the door that leads to the hallway, chattering excitedly. Skye, an impish three-year-old with brown pigtails, lifts her voice to be heard. "Our sheep are getting winter coats," she announces to no one in particular. Her parents own a farm in Stoughton, on the outskirts of town.

"Coats?" asks Clark, lifting one eyebrow, not catching it at first.

"Like these," says Skye, fingering the vividly colored jacket on the girl in front of her. Carolyn smiles, imagining a herd of woolly pink and purple ovines.

Just as a case of terminal restlessness threatens to overtake the line, Carolyn, who's been keeping watch through a window, calls, "The bus is coming!" The Bees pour out of the building two by two and clamber onto a white and blue city bus. There are 12 kids and 4 adults this morning, counting the 2 teenagers who are here as part of an alternative high school program. Every adult has three kids to keep track of—not a bad ratio at all.

The bus lumbers down Williamson Street, known as Willy Street, and climbs the short hill leading to the capitol, rounding the square, passing a row of shuttered stores. Like many small cities Madison struggles to keep its downtown alive, and mostly it's succeeding. State Street, which runs from the capitol to the University of Wisconsin campus, is alive with upscale coffeehouses and head shops, with stores selling everything from used books to Lands' End irregulars to incense and futon covers. L'Etoile, Madison's best restaurant, looks out onto the great white statehouse dome from the second story of a building smack on the square. But most of the bigger businesses that once drew crowds to the square are boarded up, their customers lured to the west and east by the city's two malls and by scores of Wal-Marts and other discount stores.

On Saturday mornings from April to October the Farmer's Market takes over the square. By 10 o'clock the sidewalks are jammed with slow-moving, good-natured mobs drinking coffee, wearing babies in backpacks, buying bunches of carrots and bright showy flowers. But this Wednesday morning the square is all but deserted, its empty benches warming in the sun. As the bus turns down State Street, Clark and Carolyn get the children ready to go, prompting them about when to stand up and where to hold on. Carolyn gets off first and holds the back doors open for the Bees, counting them like pearls on a string as they carefully make their way to the sidewalk. Clark brings up the rear.

It's not just the Bees who are excited this morning; the teachers, too, are almost manic on this brilliant fall day. Everyone knows there aren't many nice days left before the cold comes. Luckily the library is only a block away. Some child-care centers use a rope to help keep the kids together on a busy street, each child holding on, the whole group moving together slowly down the sidewalk. The Bumblebees hold hands instead; they're old enough to listen, and the teachers are happy to spare them the indignity of the rope, at least for today.

Two by two, the children step through the automatic doors of the library. They file up the steps to the second floor and settle themselves on benches outside the auditorium, waiting to go in. Transitions are always rife with potential difficulties, and those that involve waiting are the worst. If there's one thing little kids don't do well, it's wait; left to themselves, they squabble, fuss, and fall apart. Part of what makes Clark such a good teacher is the way he handles transitions. Now he starts a song to distract them. "Let's do 'Open and Shut,' James Brown style," he announces. The kids look blank—they don't yet know Clark well enough to get his sense of humor, or maybe they're still too young—but they gamely sing along. "Open, shut them, open, shut them," sings Clark, holding his palms toward the children, winking them open and closed along with the song. "Give a little clap"—he claps, and then gives a loud, bluesy *UNH!* One or two giggles from the Bees. "Creep them, creep them to your chin"—suitable creeping of fingers up the body to the chin, where they pause dramatically—"but do not let them in, noooo"—the fingers scurry around to the back—"do not let them in, *UNH!*"

By now kids from other preschools are milling around in the hallway, plus a few moms with their children. Clark's unorthodox song attracts stragglers from other groups, who stare, openmouthed, at his long hair and mustache. A few teachers stop to say hi. At 9:25 the doors to the auditorium open. The Bees find a spot on the floor of the big room and sit down. Kenny, a handsome dark-skinned boy, snuggles in Carolyn's lap. A young librarian in a purple sweater welcomes everyone, and then the lights go out and the first video comes on. There must be a hundred kids sitting on the floor in the dark watching *The Lorax*. Judging from their reactions, most of them have seen it before. The Bees certainly have, since it's a favorite at Red Caboose's Friday afternoon movies. But here the picture is bigger, the sound is louder, and the room is darker, all of which help keep the Bees' attention riveted to the screen. The Super Ax Whacker decimates the truffula forest and the animals slouch away. The evil Onceler and the noble Lorax face off, and even the three-year-olds can see who the winner will be. "I speak for the trees," intones the Lorax, and somewhere toward the back of the room a child chants mournfully, "Mommy, Mommy, Mommy."

At movie's end the children clap enthusiastically. The next movie is *The Zax*, another fable from Dr. Seuss, this one about two Zaxes who come face to face on the prairie of Prax. Neither will budge an inch to let the other pass, so they stand nose to nose for 50 years while a whole city springs up around them. The adults in the audience laugh appreciatively and the kids follow suit, though the message is over most of their heads. Going to the movies is such a treat, they'd clap for anything bright and loud up on the screen.

When the lights come back on, the Bees stay on the floor until most of the other groups have gone. Clark counts and recounts noses — literally, asking the kids to lift their noses into the air — and the Bees head out. The bus ride back to the center is thankfully uneventful, and by 10:30 the Bees are upstairs in the Moonshine Room, one of the center's two indoor play areas. Normally they'd be outside at this time of the morning, but the playground is under construction, so they're up here instead.

Everyone loves the Moonshine Room, a big loftlike space dominated by a wooden play structure, the top of which is so close to the ceiling that grown-ups have to stoop. There are so many secret spots and ways to play here: a pair of steep slides, one carpeted, one metal; a built-in ladder; a cavelike tunnel; a long, railed wooden ramp; cutout windows to peek through. One wall of the Moonshine Room is painted deep blue, with swirls of planets and stars and rocket ships. Shelves house toys that move: airplanes, trucks, fire engines, big wooden blocks for constructing.

Along one side of the play structure, some of the Bees are setting up gymnastics equipment. There's a mini-trampoline and a pair of metal climbing ladders with a wide wooden plank that straddles them, a kind of combination jungle gym and balance beam with a thick rubber mat underneath. A group of

The Moonshine Room and its wheelchair-accessible play structure

Bees are already lined up, waiting their turns to climb a metal ladder and walk across the plank. Lydia stands watching in a black leotard with a sparkling black tutu, her black patent leather shoes buckled onto the wrong feet. "I want to visit my sister," she tells Carolyn; her two-year-old sister, Claire, is downstairs in the Elephant Room. Teachers encourage visits between brothers and sisters whenever it's practical. Now Carolyn tells Lydia she'll check with the Elephant Room teachers to see if Lydia can come down.

Clark helps Bruce clamber up one ladder, across the plank, and down the other side. At the bottom, Bruce races across the floor and, unseen by either teacher, whacks Kenny in the head for no apparent reason. Kenny bursts into extremely loud tears. "There's Kenny again," says Carolyn, and Clark lopes over to attend to him. This is one of Kenny's first weeks at Red Caboose. He's also adjusting to a new foster home. That's a lot of big changes for a kid who's three and a half, especially one who's been through what Kenny has.

Kenny was taken away from his parents when he was two. When his first foster mother gave him a toy, he didn't know how to play with it; he had never seen a toy before. He had very few words. He never questioned people or things, he wasn't oppositional, he didn't get wild and bounce around—all the behaviors you might expect from a healthy two-year-old. One day he was playing a game with another foster child, an older girl. She told him to put his arms up over his head and stay that way until she said he could move. Then she left the room and forgot about him. When she wandered back in 15 minutes later Kenny was still in the same spot, arms rigidly extended over his head.

Kenny was in that first foster placement for almost a year. His foster mother loved him, but she and her husband already had several other foster kids, and at some point the chaos and the dealings with various social service agencies got to be too much for them. So Kenny was placed with Jill and Dave, a couple in their early 30s with one other foster child. The transition, like all transitions for him, has been rough. Jill thinks that Kenny wasn't allowed to cry for his first two years, and so crying has become his reaction to stress. In some ways it's a good sign, because it means he feels safe enough to show his feelings. But in social situations like Red Caboose, Kenny's loud, near-constant crying can provoke aggression from the other kids and irritation from the teachers — even when, as in this case, it's triggered by something that's not his fault.

Now Clark sits with Kenny, whose face is distorted by tears, and talks to him in a low, soothing voice. Eventually Kenny gets up, wiping tears with the back of one hand, and slowly wanders across the room toward the shelves of trucks and planes. Shaunté whizzes past him, running hell-for-leather down the wooden ramp and across the room, an old brown purse looped over one arm. A few minutes later, Kenny comes tearing down the ramp behind Bruce, his eyes bright, his mouth curved in an infectious grin.

As the morning wears on, the Bees wear out — which is part of the idea behind large-motor areas like the Moonshine and Sunshine rooms. Kids need to exercise their muscles as much as their minds; they need to push themselves, to learn what it's like to feel tired, to get used to the rhythms of the human day. At 10:45, Clark announces cleanup time. By next spring the Bees will be pros at cleaning up, but now, early in the year, they require a good deal of encouragement. The teachers need to readjust, too. "I've been doing this 15 years," says Clark, "and I still can't understand every year — how come these kids are so much dumber?" His laugh defuses the meanness of his words. There's a big difference between a three-year-old and a four-year-old in terms of the ability to listen, self-control, and cognitive skills, and every year Clark and Carolyn and Crystal Betterley, the third Bumblebee teacher, reexperience that gap.

Eventually the Bees head downstairs to their room to get ready for lunch. The Bumblebee Room is divided into two halves by a lightweight, sliding, accordion-fold door, which serves as a boundary even when open. Kenny immediately hides behind the door and bawls. Carolyn tries to get him to tell her what's wrong, but he just keeps crying. The other kids wash their hands in the bathroom off the main room, two or three at a time at the two little sinks.

Because the Bees divide into two smaller groups for breakfast, lunch, and snack, there are tables and chairs on each side of the room. This early in the year, the groups are still evolving, the teachers still sorting out which kids do well together and which need to be separated, which kids do best with which teachers. The process is complicated by the fact that there are so many part-timers, so each day brings a different complement of children. Today's Rainbows, the group led by Carolyn, are Cathleen, Lydia, Skye, Kenny, Bruce, and Julie. As they get settled, Kenny finally stops crying and comes out from behind the door. "What's wrong, Kenny?" Carolyn asks again, but he still won't tell her, and eventually he sits down with the other children at her table.

Immediately Lydia announces to Carolyn in a singsong voice, "Kenny's kicking Julie." "I think Julie can tell us if that's true," replies Carolyn, and Julie is silent—not because she isn't being kicked, which she is, but because she doesn't like to stir up trouble. Earlier, in the Moonshine Room, Shaunté got hold of a hank of Julie's blond hair and pulled, *hard,* and Julie didn't say a thing. Carolyn happened to notice her big blue eyes filling with tears and brought the two girls together to work things out. She considered it a successful interaction because after much prompting, Julie actually said to Shaunté, "Don't do that!"

The Bumblebee teachers spend more time encouraging the three-year-olds to verbalize their feelings—"use your words"—than they spend doing just about anything else. Three-year-olds are beginning to make the long transition from acting to thinking, a transformation that will continue through adulthood. Some of the feelings they're used to acting out—anger, frustration, disappointment—they now must learn to sublimate, to put into words, to intellectualize. If they don't, they run the risk of being labeled troublemakers later on, and that's a label that can stick for a long, long time. Three-year-olds are still willing to give other kids a chance to back down and change directions, but five-year-olds are not so forgiving.

The lunch cart is rolled into the Bumblebee Room by one of the high school students, and Carolyn immediately begins handing out paper plates, silverware, and food. Today's spaghetti with meat sauce is one of the kids' favorites, especially the toasted garlic bread that comes with it. Carolyn serves each child noodles in sauce, bread, and salad. "Keep your bread to yourself, Bruce," she warns, and he freezes, one arm in the air, garlic bread poised to attack Kenny.

After that the children eat in a more or less orderly way, sopping up tomato sauce with hunks of bread, sucking pale orange dressing off the salad, gulping milk with much smacking of lips. Carolyn keeps a conversation going while the children eat, drawing them out one at a time, talking about what they've done thus far in the day. And because these are three-year-olds, after all, lunch doesn't last very long—maybe 15 minutes from start to finish, and then they're off again.

After lunch it's choice time, and the Bees gravitate toward their favorite spots and activities. An amazing amount of stuff is packed into the room in plastic crates and tubs. There's a kitchen area with wooden cabinets, a play stove, a table and chairs, all child-size. Brightly colored plastic plates are stacked where kids can reach them, their shelf in the cabinet marked by a cut-out drawing of a plate so the kids know where to put them away. There's a dress-up area with a bin full of fancy clothes, mostly donated over the years or scavenged by the teachers, including lots of hats. There's an art area with a couple of freestanding easels and containers of paint, and a loft area by the Bumblebee Room door, where kids can climb up a flight of wooden steps to use a train set. One of the parents last year donated a special train table, so now the trains have their own permanent landscape, with hills and tunnels, trees and houses.

Next to the loft is the good-bye window, where the three-year-olds say good-bye to their parents. When the weather is warm, the storm window is pushed to one side, leaving only the screen with its one strategically placed hole. The children stand on the wide windowsill and stick a finger through the hole to touch the tip of a parent's finger, one last brush of skin against skin, one last tactile reminder of family. Then they turn back toward Clark or Carolyn or whoever is helping them say good-bye, jump down from the windowsill and back into the life of the room. And even though there's a shelf of books nearby and a wide sill to sit on, very few kids come back to this spot to play.

Today, sun streams into the Bumblebee Room through the big windows that face Willy Street. Shaunté and Annie run around the room together, lost in their own game, a study in contrasts. Annie is pale, with curly blond hair, and Shaunté's skin is the color of rich toffee, her thick dark hair springing from her head in four or five neatly contained braids. Carlos heads straight for his beloved dress-ups and immediately pulls out his favorite item of apparel— a silky blue negligee, which he wears as often as possible. His parents are not happy with his choice of activewear, but they haven't gone so far as to make it off limits. There have been parents in the past who have issued difficult directives, like the father who insisted that his son not be allowed to play with dolls. Things like that put teachers in the awkward position of having to go against their instincts and knowledge. None of the Bumblebee teachers even blink at Carlos's negligee; nor do they think it portends anything about his sexuality. His choice is just that—*his* choice, his chance to explore the world, in this case through clothing.

Next comes story time, when the kids begin to wind down before nap. Carolyn sits on the woolly brown-and-white plaid couch with a pile of books at her feet, and the Bees arrange themselves on the floor in front of her in a ragged semicircle. She leans over and picks up the first book, called *But No Elephants*—a fitting choice for this group, many of whom have recently moved up from the Elephant Room. Most of the kids listen attentively while Carolyn reads, but Shaunté just can't seem to keep still. Carolyn interrupts her reading several times to ask the girl to sit down, and finally she puts the book down and says to her, "Shaunté, I saw what you did to Annie. Please go sit on the golden line. You have to leave now." Shaunté goes without a protest, as if she's been itching to be caught, and Carolyn picks up the book again and starts reading.

While she reads, Clark buzzes around the room, putting away stray toys, wiping down tables, sweeping up lunch detritus, setting up low purple cots for naptime. At the far end of the room, near the easels, Kenny crouches alone in tears. Clark spends a few minutes stroking his back, speaking softly to him, and then goes back to his duties. Carolyn puts down the last book, a story about trains. "Do you think that's why it's called Red Caboose?" she says to the kids. "Because we hear trains here all the time?" Her question is something of a non sequitur, but no one in this group is going to point that out. Lydia yawns and rubs her eyes, starting a rash of yawning. Carolyn smoothes her blond hair back behind one ear and gathers up the books, and the kids begin getting ready for nap. Many of these three-year-olds no longer take naps at home. But here at the center, they tend to nap more willingly and for longer than they do at home. Peer pressure has a lot to do with it, and so does lying in a dark room with soft music playing.

Upstairs in the office, Wendy Rakower, the director of the center, sits at her desk with a worried look. For weeks now she's been scheduling substitutes every day to cover Belindah Anderson's afternoon spot in the Elephant Room. Belindah has worked at Red Caboose for years. Clark says she's one of the best teachers he's ever seen. Of course, since he's married to her, he's not exactly unbiased. But Belindah's out on medical leave, and Wendy's been advertising for a long-term sub, known as an LTE, someone to do Belindah's job for a while for an hourly wage and few benefits. So far, no bites, not even a nibble. So Wendy's been scrambling to fill the slot with subs, which runs counter to the center's policy, but what can she do? She doesn't mind stepping in from time to time herself, but she can't sub for Belindah every afternoon—she'd never get her own work done.

Like so much here, it all comes down to money. Subs at Red Caboose make $6.00 an hour, and LTEs earn $6.80—less than some starting wages at McDonald's. You don't sign up for this work unless you really like taking care of kids. And you don't stick with it unless you love it, because child care is hard, hard work. It's physically demanding, with lots of lifting, carrying, changing diapers, and running around the playground. But in some ways that's the easy part. Each day also brings a continual series of emotional and intellectual challenges, figuring out how to care for and guide 4 or 6 or 12 kids, how to draw this one out and calm that one down, what to do in the face of temper tantrums, genuine distress, and high levels of mischievous, perfectly normal energy. You've got to think fast, be ready to scrap the sit-down activity planned and go with the flow, to pull the group together when you have to and let it out when you can. It's not the kind of work you can do on automatic pilot, at least not well, because this job requires a constant use of judgment. Kids know when you're not paying attention, and they're awfully good at forcing the issue.

All this for six bucks an hour. No wonder Wendy has a tough time hiring subs. The saving grace is the university, which over the years has provided a steady stream of young, mostly female students who love children. The two-year degree in child care at Madison Area Technical College (MATC) is a good source of temporary labor, too. But students come and go, and every fall brings a new crop of subs to Red Caboose. It takes a while to work out everyone's schedule—who has morning classes and who has afternoons, who's available Tuesdays and Thursdays but not the rest of the week—so Wendy has a lot to juggle.

Wendy's got other worries as well on this September afternoon—enrollment, for example, which is lower than she'd like. Right now the center has 53 slots, known as FTEs (full-time equivalents), which means that on any given day there should be 53 children spread among the four child-care rooms. About a quarter of the kids are part-timers, so all in all about 70 children spend some part of their weekdays at Red Caboose. It's very difficult to hit the magic number 53 on the nose, especially with all the part-timers, some

Wendy spends hours on the phone each day

of whose schedules change with their parents' class schedules. Over the year, enrollment tends to even out; the Turtle Room's down half a slot for three weeks, the Grasshopper Room's up a slot for a few days, and it all works out in the end. Which is good, because the margin for error is slim. Each FTE represents about $6,600 to the center, and every penny of that money is carefully budgeted by Wendy and Louise, the center's financial manager. It may not *sound* like a big deal to be down one slot, but if that money isn't made up over the course of the year, Red Caboose winds up with a $6,600 deficit.

Enrollment is the responsibility of the director and the lead teachers, and they take it very seriously. Now Wendy fiddles anxiously with her straight black hair, taking out her purple barrette, smoothing the hair, sliding the barrette back in. Her hair is waist-length, reminiscent of Cher's hair in her pre-*Moonstruck* days. In the 1970s Wendy was a hippie living on a farm in southern Wisconsin. Her looks are still hippielike—the long hair, the plain clothes, the clogs—but her attitudes are up-to-date: a thorough understanding of budgets and finances filtered through the social conscience of a left-wing New York Jew.

Wendy grew up in New Rochelle, New York, with her two younger sisters, one of whom lives in Madison, the other in New York City. Her mother, a sculptor, and her father, a retired oral surgeon, brought their daughters to peace marches in the 1960s. From an early age Wendy learned to take the concepts of social justice and equality more or less for granted, which partly explains why she's stayed at Red Caboose for 22 years. Wendy likes to joke that she's never had a job interview. She graduated from UW in 1973 with a degree in early childhood development, eager to work with young kids. Most jobs back then with preschoolers were at part-day nursery schools, where almost all the kids were from the white middle and upper class. But Wendy wanted to work with a more diverse group of children and families. She came to Red Caboose for a visit, and that was that. "I walked in the door and said, 'This is it, this is the place for me,'" she remembers with a smile. "I was offered the job almost on the spot. I didn't even have an interview."

Her first job was co-lead teacher in the Bumblebee Room. Fresh out of college, bursting with enthusiasm and all the latest educational theories, she asked to see the planning book, to check out what kinds of lessons had been planned for the Bumblebees for the coming week. "I was told, and this is a direct quote, 'We groove with the kids,'" she says with a droll smile. "I ran out and bought a lesson-planning book and said, 'We *plan* for the kids now!'"

Wendy taught in the Bumblebee Room for a couple of years, and then, in 1975, began teaching in the center's new kindergarten program. Throughout the late 1970s and early '80s there was no real director at the center. Certain pieces of the director's job were split among the lead teachers, and some were done by Alan Everhart, who was hired in 1975 as the center's financial director. While some people—notably Clark—felt that this division of labor worked well, many parents felt that things at the center were too chaotic.

So in 1983, Wendy was offered the job as director. She took it on a trial basis and she's still doing it. In an industry where centers often go through three directors in a year, Wendy's broken all the records for stick-to-itiveness. "The thing that's kept me here is that I feel like my work is effective," she explains. "Not that it will do everything I want it to do, and it's not going to change the world like I really wish I could. But I can say I did my best. And that's important to me." Some staff members have been known to grumble about Wendy's penchant for worrying, but no one denies that she's an excellent director. And it could be argued that worrying—and addressing those worries—is part of the director's job, along with troubleshooting, dealing with state licensing, sitting on half a dozen committees, subbing for sick teachers, doing the budget, redoing the budget, and a million other tasks.

For instance, low enrollment. At this time of year the center should be full. The mass exodus of five-year-olds over the summer means that kids all over the center can move up. The lead teachers are meticulous about keeping up their waiting lists, juggling full-timers, part-timers, and schedule changes to keep their rooms as close to full enrollment as possible. The fewer kids in a room, the less flexibility teachers have in making the numbers come out right. The Bumblebees have 16 slots, which gives them a fair amount of flexibility. Clark can ask one part-time family to switch a day, if necessary, to accommodate another family's needs. Often lead teachers work together to solve enrollment problems, moving one child up to make room for someone else.

Some months, everyone expects the numbers to be down—for example, in December or over the summer. Fall should be full up, but this year there have been some unexpected withdrawals. The waiting list is gone; everyone on it has either enrolled or made other arrangements. Wendy wants to have a sign made for the Bumblebee Room window, listing openings for kids of various ages. It's a good idea from an advertising standpoint, since anyone who walks or drives down Willy Street would see it. Lots of people in the community just assume that Red Caboose is always full, so a sign might actually help. Wendy will bring it up at the next board of directors meeting in a few weeks.

For now, everyone has to cope. Low enrollment is bad for the center, but it can be a relief for teachers and kids. Fewer children in a room means that each child gets more individual attention—which is especially helpful during the daily transitions. Wake-up time, for example, can be quite chaotic. In good weather kids who wake up early can go out to the playground and let off some steam. On this mid-September day, though, it's raining, and the playground's still under construction anyway, so the early risers are in the Sunshine Room, the center's other large-motor, indoor play area.

The Sunshine Room is indeed large, much of its space taken up by the same kind of wooden play structure as in the Moonshine Room. This one is designed on a smaller scale, with a canvas slide, little hidey-holes, and steps more suited to a toddler than a five-year-old. The play structure is no sleek modular wonder in brightly colored plastic but a funky and idiosyncratic wooden fantasy, painted with primary colors that were once bright and now could use a touch-up. Large red cube-shaped structures line one wall, with circles cut from their wooden sides so kids can climb in and over and through them. The near half of the room is fairly open, with toy shelves along some walls and a thick red mat in the center, where kids like to jump and turn somersaults and roll around.

Compare the Sunshine Room with a play area in one of the more corporate centers — Preschool for the Arts, for instance, out on the city's more suburban west side — and it looks untidy, even dingy. Some parents who visit here are clearly turned off by the center's shabby, less than perfect look. For other parents it's a plus, signaling hominess and warmth. To them Red Caboose looks like a place where children can shout and giggle and roll on the floor, let down their hair. And some parents put up with it. Maybe they'd rather have their children at a center with gleaming white walls, but they're not willing to give up what their kids get at Red Caboose for a spic and span unknown.

The kids who are in the Sunshine Room this afternoon are a mix of ages. Many of the older kids don't nap at all, but state licensing mandates a one-hour rest period for preschoolers, so they have to stay on their cots. By 2:00 there's a teacher on duty in the Sunshine Room to watch over the nonsleepers and early risers. By 2:45 there are two teachers in the room, Carolyn and Crystal today, supervising a mixed bunch of about 10 kids, two- and three-year-olds. Crystal sits on a set of three red wooden steps near the door, helping a Bumblebee in green sweatpants put on her shoe. The mood in the room is quiet, the kids still waking up. Kenny hangs by his hands from a wooden bar suspended over a mat, swinging his feet, testing his own weight. Bruce pushes a truck along the floor, pausing to bang it on the floor and holler with frustration. "What's the problem, Bruce?" asks Carolyn. Of all the teachers at the center she's the most glamorous-looking, with her neat blond hair, her polished fingernails, her slim elegance.

"It's too big!" yells Bruce.

The Sunshine Room in a rare state — empty

Carolyn crosses the room to see what's going on. It turns out that Bruce is trying to drive the toy truck in through the door of a plastic dollhouse. "Shall we build a garage for your truck?" she asks, smiling at him. She *could* remind him that the truck is too big for the dollhouse, and ask him to look for a smaller vehicle. But he already knows that; his problem is that he's feeling frustrated. So Carolyn chooses to distract Bruce rather than to lecture him.

The distraction works. Bruce, taking the initiative, piles several plastic cubes together to make a garage. He walks away for a minute, and one of the Elephants picks up the truck. "Hey, mine!" shouts Bruce with a wail, rushing over. "Bruce, once you leave a toy it's not yours anymore," Carolyn reminds him.

For a while a group of children take turns doing tricks on the red mat. Kenny is having trouble waiting his turn and following the rules, despite the fact that he's one of the oldest kids in the group. He tries to "budge" — push in front of someone — and when that doesn't work, he starts to cry loudly. "Kenny, you're being very uncooperative today," says Carolyn calmly. A few minutes later, when he manages to wait in line and then take his turn without incident, Carolyn rewards him with a one-on-one conversation. "Do you see the big UPS truck outside?" she asks, pointing out the window.

"Ye-ah," he says warily, not sure where this is leading.

"What do you think it's carrying?" asks Carolyn. Silence from Kenny. "Packages?" she prompts, and his eyes light with relief.

"Yeah," he says.

"A UPS truck came to my house this morning and brought me a package," says Carolyn, and they're off, launched on a several-minute conversation about presents and trucks—two of a three-year-old's favorite things.

Today was one of Kenny's visitations with his mother, which explains why he's especially emotional. A social service aide comes for him at naptime every week or so and takes him to see his mom and some of his brothers and sisters, all of whom are in different foster homes. Over the summer, when Kenny first came to live with Jill and Dave, he spent his days at a preschool close to their home on the north side of Madison. There he was the only African-American child, and one of only two foster kids. Some of the other kids picked on him for being different, and the staff wasn't very understanding. Kenny's teachers there hated having the aide come at naptime to collect Kenny. "They'd say, 'Can't you change the visitation schedule?'" says Jill in her no-nonsense, rapid-fire voice. "And I'd tell them, 'You know I have no say about when he goes for visits. He just goes.' They were very frustrated."

Jill and Dave understand that frustration; like other foster parents, they often feel helpless to change or even understand the rules that govern their child's life and therefore their own. Jill has short blondish hair, round tortoise-shell glasses, a wiry, athletic build. She wears several gold studs in each ear. She teaches second grade, so she's used to dealing with bureaucracy. She and Dave are also foster parents to a six-year-old girl, Celia, who came to them two years ago as an emergency placement. They've done the state's training for foster parents, a 16-hour course that teaches the basics, but it didn't come close to preparing them for working the real-life system. Twice in two years they've given the state a 30-day notice that they were ending the placement for Celia. The first time it was a last resort. "We just couldn't get the services she needed," explains Dave. Both Dave and Jill thought the girl needed therapy to help her deal with the fallout from the abuse she had suffered, but the state kept dragging its feet. "We've learned very unfortunately that if you're in a crisis where you think your kid really needs something, the issue is that you can't make a lot of decisions," says Jill wearily. "Ultimately you aren't the ones who get to decide." Ten days after Jill and Dave gave the state notice, Celia was in therapy.

It used to be that young children in Wisconsin could be placed in foster care for up to seven years, not sure when or whether they would ever go back to live with their parents. Thanks to a new law, children now stay in foster care for a maximum of two years, and their cases are reviewed every six months. At the end of two years they either go back to their parents or parental rights are terminated and the kids can be adopted. Celia's parents' rights were just terminated, but her mom asked for a jury trial, so the whole thing could drag on for months. Jill and Dave would like to adopt her, but they're not getting their hopes up; they've seen too many other foster parents get chewed up and spit out by the system.

Kenny's future is still officially up in the air. At the moment, the plan is reunification with his mother, but who knows? "Things may be going OK, and then two months before the six-month review things go bad," explains Jill. *Bad* can mean anything from a parent losing a job or apartment to doing drugs again. "Do you now change it to termination, or do you keep it reunification?" she adds. Kenny's social worker thinks he may have attention deficit disorder, or ADD, and wants to put him on Ritalin. "There are so many things that have happened," says Jill. "How can you tell if he has ADD? He's had increased visits with his mom, increased visits with a sister, he's moved to our house fairly recently, new day care." So when the social worker made the recommendation, Jill resisted it. "She spent maybe an hour and a half with him. How does *she* know what he needs?'" she explains.

Thanks to Jill's tenacity, Kenny will soon be starting a series of psychological evaluations to see whether he does in fact have ADD. Without Jill's assertiveness he might have been put on the drug on the social worker's say-so alone. The psychological evaluations will have to be fit into a family schedule that already includes meetings with both kids' social workers, visits to Kenny's first foster parents and their kids, meetings with judges and guardian ad litems, writing letters to various county agencies, and, of course, the usual ups and downs of living with young children.

In Kenny's case, these ups and downs include nightmares and flashbacks, common but devastating reactions to the abuse in his past. Sometimes he wakes up screaming in the middle of the night, and when Jill or Dave go in to comfort him he becomes infantile, bawling as a newborn might. Other nights, because of the nightmares, he doesn't get to sleep till 3 A.M., so he's exhausted all the next day. Dave tries to rearrange his schedule on those mornings and bring Kenny in to Red Caboose a little later, so the boy can get some sleep.

Now, in the Sunshine Room, Kenny seems tired and vulnerable. Carolyn is busy with a new Bee who's just woken up, disoriented and in need of comforting. She doesn't see Kenny drag a huge gray plush elephant out into the middle of the room, or what happens next. The elephant is very lifelike, with soft white tusks, and Kenny is obviously enthralled. He sits on its back and lovingly strokes its head. Another Bee, a boy named Paul, spots the elephant and purposely rides his plastic trike right over the elephant's trunk. Kenny is tremendously upset. "Don't!" he cries furiously, anger sharpening his consonants for once. Paul laughs and does it again. A husky boy named Joseph, his blond hair long on top and shaved near his neck, hears the commotion and rides over on another trike. Joining in the fun, Joseph starts mauling the elephant's big soft ears. By the time Paul and Joseph wander off, Kenny is so upset that he's weeping. His face working, he tries to gather the elephant into his arms. But it's too big; no matter how he maneuvers, he can't hold the whole elephant, he can't keep it safe. And no one sees him trying, no one notices and comes over to help. So Kenny gives up, sliding off the elephant's back and running, literally running, across the room and away.

A week later, on the last Wednesday evening in September, the board of directors assembles for its monthly meeting, 16 grown-ups sitting in red plastic chairs around a child-size table in the Elephant Room. For years everyone's been complaining about how uncomfortable the chairs are, but there just aren't enough adult-size chairs at the center to accommodate everyone. These 16 grown-ups spend hours each month fretting over ridiculously tiny sums of money. As one policy maker put it, "In child care, the root of much evil is not the love of money but the absence of it."[1] The board has been known to devote an entire evening to cutting $300 from the center's annual budget—the cost of a morning's photocopying at any midsize law firm.

The meeting starts on time at 6:45, in the unaccustomed hush of the closed center. The only other sounds are the janitors vacuuming in the halls and rooms outside this one. As usual, the first item on the agenda, after approving last month's minutes, is the program director's report. Wendy attaches a copy of her report to the papers each board member receives, and then takes a few minutes at the meeting to go over the salient points.

The first of these is enrollment. So far, the center's year-to-date enrollment is 52.34, about two-thirds of a slot down from the budgeted enrollment of 53. Normally this wouldn't be too bad, but the number is on its way down, owing to a number of recent withdrawals. There are five openings right now, which is unheard of; Wendy says she's never seen so many withdrawals at the same time. Most were the random, unpredictable kind: one divorce settlement changed, so the child is moving away; a couple of kids got into four-year-old programs in the public schools, which don't let families know until the last minute. One parent lost her public funding, and this is the one Wendy's most worried about. Funding comes and funding goes, fluctuating with the state's budget, the time of year, and political trends. But this loss may be ominous, thanks to the Wisconsin Works program, known as W-2, being debated in the legislature. W-2, the brainchild of Wisconsin governor Tommy Thompson, would replace Aid to Families and Dependent Children (AFDC), which provides income assistance and child-care funding to many poor families. It would also replace the county's child-care funding programs, which are numerous and confusing and which have various rubrics, among them Title XX, Transitional, and JOBS.

Wendy brings the board up to speed on what she knows about W-2. Its exact content is still being debated, but there's no doubt that some version of welfare reform will pass this year. The main thing that's clear at this point is that, unlike AFDC, W-2 would *not* be an entitlement program; parents receiving aid would have to work to get a check. Child care, then, will have to be an essential part of the package. Recently an ad hoc committee of women legislators and community leaders put out a paper on W-2, detailing some of its possible elements: Parents will be required to work when children are 12 weeks old. All families, even the poorest, will have to pay a percentage of the cost of their children's care. A new category of care, called provisional certified care, will be established.

All these elements would have far-reaching consequences, but at the moment Wendy's most worried about the second one. Right now the county decides every year what its weekly reimbursement rate will be, how much it will pay caregivers for kids on county funding. Red Caboose sets its lowest tuition for three- to five-year-olds at the county reimbursement rate, so parents don't have to chip in any extra. But the center *has* to charge more for kids two and under because their care costs more. Teacher-child ratios are lower: 1 to 6 in the Elephant Room versus 1 to 8 in the Bumblebee Room. This year, the lowest rate in the Elephant Room is $120 a week, which means that parents on county funding have to pay $10 a week. It doesn't sound like a lot of money, but when your family's monthly budget is only $800, and $550 goes toward rent, every penny counts.

Under W-2 as it is now being debated, all families would have a copayment, and those copayments would be pegged to the cost of care—10 or 20 or whatever percent of the total child-care bill. "If parents are required to pay a percentage of their cost of care, are they going to go to a $500-a-month center or to a $200-a-month person next door?" Bridget Timm asked me. Timm, who is program manager for the Dane County Department of Human Services, knows that all too often, cheap care is poor care.

In this scenario, Red Caboose's sliding-fee scale would give it a slight advantage over other high-quality centers in town, most of which charge a flat fee. But provisionally certified child care would make competition effectively impossible. Provisional caregivers would have to meet no training requirements and only the most basic health and safety requirements, and they could charge only $54 a week, about half the going rate for preschoolers. Red Caboose's lowest fee is $110 a week.

So the center could suddenly lose lots of kids—and not just any kids, but the poorest and most vulnerable, the kind of children Red Caboose has always worked hard to include in its programs. In mostly white Wisconsin, parents looking for economic and ethnic diversity for their kids have a hard time finding it. Diversity is a big part of Red Caboose's mission and philosophy, and the center has been moderately successful in achieving it. If the poorest kids are pushed out of licensed centers like Red Caboose, the center may either have to alter its philosophy—and prices—or close its doors.

The specter of W-2 looms especially large given the fact that enrollment is down five slots. "When people lose funding, people lose their jobs," Wendy tells the board. "It doesn't matter how good our reputation is. We can't *make* people get funding. We can't *make* people get jobs. No matter what I do, there's no way I'm going to be able to make our budget be a nice positive number. No way. And I just feel horrible."

The rest of Wendy's board report is standard stuff: The playground renovation is almost finished (at last!), including the new gate and toy shed; all that's left are the parking lot stripes and some work on the new back door, which now accommodates wheelchairs. The take from the face-painting booth at the annual Willy Street Fair was excellent—$200, minus the cost of the paints. Finally, Wendy has hired Calliope Linster, one of the center's substitutes, to take Belindah's place for now. "This has set a record for the most difficult hiring ever," she tells the board.

Staff turnover—the rate at which teachers and staff leave their jobs—is a huge issue in child care, for many reasons. The most important one is quality. The higher the rate of turnover, the lower the quality of care. Children aren't like plants, which need just water and sunlight to grow; they build relationships with their caregivers. "What we call turnover, they experience as loss," says Deborah A. Phillips, associate professor of psychology at the University of Virginia, who has researched the issue extensively.[2] In an article called "The Costs of Not Providing Quality Early Childhood Programs," published in 1990, Ellen Galinsky reviewed the research on quality care and concluded that the most important ingredient in good-quality child care is the relationship between the child and the caregiver.[3]

Nationally, the turnover rate in child-care centers is around 40 percent. In Wisconsin, the annual rate is around 25 percent.[4] Last year in Dane County, centers reported anywhere from 0 percent turnover to 183 percent.[5] Over the last five years Red Caboose's center turnover (the school-age program is higher) has averaged 8 percent; one year, 1993, the center had 0 percent turnover.

But no matter how loyal the teachers are, there will always be times when Wendy has to do a hiring, and the process isn't getting any easier. Clark, who is one of four staff representatives on the board, says things started getting tough about 12 years ago. "We've been darn lucky to retain staff for a long time," he tells the board. Two staffers, Wendy and Cheryl Heiman, have been at the center for more than 20 years; seven more, including Max the cook, for 10 or more years; another four, for 5 or more years. Wendy thinks part of the problem may be that it's an LTE position rather than a permanent one, though the fact that it comes with some sick and vacation time should make it more appealing.

Now, at the board meeting, Wendy wonders out loud for the umpteenth time whether raising base wages for teachers would make hirings easier. As everyone here knows, the answer is yes; the more money offered, the more people want the job. But the issue is more complex than it sounds, and the reason can be summed up in one word: negotiations.

Every year around October, the Red Caboose union begins negotiating the next year's wages and benefits with the board. To say that no one looks forward to the process is an understatement. Ever since the center was unionized in 1985, negotiating the contract has been like jumping out of an airplane without a parachute—everyone *knows* it's going to get ugly. What makes it particularly unpleasant is that for 10 months of the year, everyone here gets along so well.

Two years ago negotiations reached an all-time low. At several of the meetings between union representatives and parent board members, voices were raised and accusations were made that were better suited to three-year-olds than grown-ups. One parent quit halfway through because she found it too stressful to leave her son every morning in the care of a teacher she'd been knocking heads with the night before. At several points there was talk of a strike, something that had never come up before. Things were so acrimonious that the contract wasn't finalized until February. So tuition didn't go up until February, and teachers missed a month's worth of raises.

There is a cause-and-effect relationship between the two. It is parents, almost exclusively, who pay teachers' wages. Ninety-seven percent of the center's income comes from parents in the form of tuition. This isn't Denmark or Sweden or Germany or any of a dozen or so progressive countries; neither private employers nor the federal government (with the exception of the food program, which constitutes 2 percent of the center's income) contribute to Red Caboose's budget. In bureaucratese, there is no other revenue stream.

On the other hand, 80 percent of the center's annual budget is spent on wages and benefits to teachers. (Another 18 percent goes toward costs like the mortgage, insurance, food, utilities, and janitors, and 2 percent goes toward field trips and educational supplies.) So there's a direct link between what parents pay and what teachers get. Every child-care center struggles with the same dilemma: how to pay teachers adequately without raising rates beyond what parents can pay. The truth is, it's impossible. And the tension between those two irreconcilable goals can turn parents and teachers, who work together every day for the good of the children, into snarling adversaries.

Management is afraid that the union will muddy the waters by demanding unrealistic concessions. The question of whether to raise the base wage is a good example. Wendy has pushed repeatedly for adding the money available for raises onto the base wage, so that every employee, whether just starting out or a 20-year veteran, would get the same number of additional cents per hour. This would help attract qualified teachers to the center, Wendy argues, plus it's equitable. Instead, the union has often lobbied to put money toward seniority, to reward teachers who have been around longer.

This year everyone is hopeful that negotiations will be better. One of the parents on the board, Lynn, has spent months arranging for parents and staff to take a one-day training course in a technique called interest-based bargaining, given by the Federal Mediation & Conciliation Service. In early September a small group of parents and teachers, plus Wendy, did the training, the goal of which is to teach labor and management to come to consensus together on the basis of mutual interests. The feeling was that anything would be an improvement over the current adversarial negotiating style.

The best news at the board meeting tonight is that school-age enrollment is high. Red Caboose runs an after-school program in two local public schools,

Lapham (grades K–2) and Marquette (grades 3–5), as well as a full-day program (for days when the schools are closed) and a summer program. The school-age programs are by far the most lucrative part of the budget, carrying the center financially, making up for the money routinely lost in caring for the one- and two-year-olds. The reason: the older the kids, the more kids per teacher are allowed. Since staff costs are the biggest chunk of any program's cost, more money can be made on taking care of older kids.

Lee Lohr, the school-age program supervisor, reports that both the before- and after-school programs at Lapham are full. Marquette isn't quite as full, but that's to be expected; parents are less willing to pay for care for older kids, trying instead to find activities and friends to keep them busy for the two hours or so after school lets out. Lee and Wendy take this and many other factors into account when they try to guess what each year's enrollment will be in the school-age program. So far they've always been close, and this year looks as though it will continue to live up to budgeted expectations.

Next on the agenda is the treasurer's report. "For the month of August we lost $2,500," says David, better known as Rosebud. A lawyer specializing in tenants' rights, Rosebud has shaggy hair kept short in front and long in back, tied in a ponytail. Usually in early fall the center's bank accounts are swollen with the money from the summer program. "The finance committee wondered about this," admits Rosebud. "We've been back through everything to see where the loss is. It's not clear what exactly happened. Summer program enrollment was very high, which is good, but it was so high that we needed to hire extra teachers, which ate up some of the profit."

So far the center shows a loss of $12,615 for the year. Some of that is depreciation, which is a loss on paper only. Some is accrued staff vacation time, which is also not a real loss but which could be. The center's accountant has explained it to the board several times, but it's a complicated concept that comes up again and again. Basically it means that if Red Caboose were to close tomorrow, the center would owe its staff a certain amount of sick and vacation time, time that they have earned and not yet taken. Or if a couple of teachers were to leave at the same time, especially if they have a lot of seniority built up, then the center would have to cash them out, paying for any sick and vacation time they haven't taken. So this year the center has begun accruing money each month to cover those eventualities.

Wendy points out that the center lost money when the financial manager left earlier in the year. Louise came back after a couple of weeks, but her leaving still cost the center in temp wages and extra hours for the accountants.

That's not enough to explain the $2,500 loss, which, in the language of two-year-olds, is not OK. "We have money in savings to deal with a loss at the end of the year, but we don't want to keep eating up our surplus," warns Rosebud, shifting on his little plastic chair. "Plus the accountant keeps telling us we should have more in reserve than we do, just in case of a catastrophe. So it makes me nervous."

The meeting ends early, around eight. Clark, Gary, and Emily gather their things and leave, but the parents stick around for another meeting. For the next few months, this parent subcommittee will meet after each board meeting to discuss negotiations. Lynn opens tonight's session by describing the training. Interest-based bargaining sounds great in theory, finding a way to talk about issues without creating enemies and bad feeling. But the reality is that there isn't enough money to meet everyone's needs, and everyone here knows it. What good will fancy theories do when it's time to talk dollars and cents? "At some point you're going to wind up talking about 41 cents or 45 cents on the base," says Wendy.

"We don't have to use it for every point," argues Lynn. "We can use it to talk about noneconomic issues, and handle the money separately."

"I'm just not sure how much we have to talk about *but* money," says Wendy. In the end the parent subcommittee agrees to give interest-based bargaining a try. And soon, because the process promises to be long, and everyone wants to be done with it. The quicker the better.

October

A sunny day, warm for October, and the Bumblebees are out on the playground. Breakfast is scheduled from 8:30 to 9, but no way can three-year-olds sit still for half an hour. So by 9 o'clock they're rocketing around the new playground. It's a much tidier space than it used to be, with neat black rubber bumpers setting off areas of wood chips and play equipment. The asphalt has been fixed, all the dips and broken chips flattened and smoothed so that someone in a wheelchair, say, could navigate it. Clarks sits on a picnic bench with Lateef in his lap. When Lateef started here a year ago, he was often mistaken for a girl because his face had a feminine sweetness and his hair was tied into thick lively braids that stuck up from his scalp. Now he's lost some of that sweetness but he's still a beautiful child, his eyes wide and clear, his skin the color of espresso.

This morning Clark and Lateef are deep in conversation about a problem

Lateef has been having with some of the other boys in the room. This seems to be Clark's day for problem-solving; already in the last 10 minutes he had to move Kenny to three different spots on the playground, trying to get him calmed down enough to talk about why he was crying. The minute Lateef jumps down, Laila comes out of nowhere, wraps her arms around Clark's long lean legs, and begins crying. She's having an argument with one of the other girls, and Clark helps them resolve it, squatting between them with an arm around each of them, prompting, cajoling, facilitating. Afterward he stands up, brushing wood chips off his blue jeans. He's in a typical Clark outfit: long-sleeved white shirt, black leather vest, denim jacket over the vest. On his jacket Clark wears two buttons, reading "Families or Fight" and "Naptime's Over," both of them from the Wisconsin Childcare Union.

It's ironic in a way that Clark is so good at problem-solving with three-year-olds, because he's equally good at stirring things up among grown-ups. He sees both as necessary, and it's hard to say which he enjoys more. He's a curious mixture of provocateur and peacemaker. Or maybe it's not curious when you watch him at work. Clark is no make-peace, no pourer of oil on troubled waters; he doesn't pass judgment or solve problems for the children but gives them the tools to solve their own. The tools are words, and in the use of words Clark is certainly an expert. He's a slick talker, a big talker, a spinner of rhetoric and tall tales who believes in the power of words to change things and who's willing to talk till he's hoarse for a good cause.

Clark grew up in a blue-collar family, first in St. Louis and then Portage, Wisconsin, the oldest of three brothers who used to go hunting and fishing with their father. In the turbulent early 1970s he attended the University of Wisconsin–Parkside, majoring—as he says with his usual deadpan delivery—in English and alternative lifestyles. After he left school, just shy of graduating, he held every kind of job imaginable: longshoreman, cab driver, carpenter. In 1979 he was working in McHenry, Illinois, as a machinist on the American Motors assembly line when he got laid off. An old college friend invited him to come sleep on his floor in Madison, and he's been here ever since.

Like many people in child care, Clark fell into it. His girlfriend Belindah, now his wife, was doing infant care at a center called Freedom House, and he began subbing there for extra money. His only experience with kids before that had been working as a playground supervisor in Kenosha. When Freedom House closed, Belindah encouraged Clark to stay in the field. "She said it would be sad if I didn't commit myself to working with young children because

Kenny in a happy moment on the playground

I was good at it and I added something and I was able to provide something beneficial for children," he explains, the words tumbling out in a rush. Some of the "something" that he adds (aside from his own particular brand of humor and personality) is his male presence in a field where 97 percent of the teachers are female.[6] It's critical for young kids to have male teachers, to learn how to relate to both women and men, to have positive male role models. Many single mothers, like Patricia, Lateef's mom, choose Red Caboose because of its two male teachers.

One of the things Clark has liked about the job from the get-go is getting out from under the thumb of minute-to-minute authority. "I liked the freedom to plan the day's activities and the fact that whatever I did, as long as it was appropriate, was fine with whatever supervisors I had," he says. "So I didn't feel like it was a paternalistic kind of relationship with supervisors and management." The ability to be goofy appealed to him, too, because goofiness is one of the things Clark does best: loping down the hall, looking for an errant pacifier, singing, "A man needs a nippy" to the tune of Neil Young's "A Man Needs a Maid"; or telling Kenny, after warning the boy to settle down, "Kenny, I'm as serious as can be. I'm *Sirius* as the dog star!" "The freedom to behave in appropriate ways with children was appealing to me," he says. "And it still is."

Like Wendy, Clark also relishes the effect he has on kids, the difference he can make in their lives. Child care is a field where his iconoclastic personality and off-the-wall sense of humor are assets, not liabilities. "When I worked on the line," he says, "you had to put the hood hinges in in a certain way, and throw the brakes in, and grind the lead off in a certain way. And then a good car would be the end product. You created stuff to specifications, and if you did it perfectly to specifications, that was your goal. This is much more wide open. And it changes children, the way a doctor who practices her profession has an impact on her patients."

He certainly has made a difference in the lives of many children. And not just the Kennys, the kids who have been damaged. There are teachers who gravitate toward those children, who are best at "helping" the small unfortunates in their care. Clark is just as interested in the "regular" kids, and they adore him back. Years after leaving Red Caboose, kids come back to the Bumblebee Room to visit "Clarkie."

Clark began substituting at Red Caboose in 1980, when the center was bigger than most of the other child-care programs on the mainly residential east side. At the time he had no idea that child care would be both his vocation and his avocation. He worked in three of the four rooms at the center, first as a sub and then as a full-time teacher; the only room he hasn't worked in regularly is the Grasshopper Room, the four-year-olds. Then in 1989 the lead teacher in the Bumblebee Room left, and Clark got the job.

"I loved the performing aspect of working with two-year-olds. We did really silly, fun things together," he explains, hooking his long thumbs into his

Confidantes: Clark and Cory on the playground

belt loops. "But I feel more qualified to work with three-year-olds, because I've done lots of training and self-education, and I'm familiar with lots of theory on how best to create a program to benefit the development of three-year-olds."

Maybe it's because I've watched Clark only with the three-year-olds, but I can't imagine him working with any other age for long. Two-year-olds, in the words of child psychologist Jean Piaget, are "sensory motor," exploring the physical boundaries of their world. "Two-year-olds are learning how to take action," explains Clark. "In other words, how to lift my hand and push, and the focus is on the lifting and pushing." Three-year-olds are "preoperational," beginning to link cause and effect. "Preoperational is more about the effect of those actions, the relating of the effect of what happens when you push something or someone over," he says. Or, as he put it another day, "The job of the kids in the Bumblebee Room is to analyze the connection between acts and their consequences." Clark is skilled at facilitating these kinds of connections for kids, which is one of the things that makes him a good, even a great, teacher.

He's also good at helping kids make internal connections. Witness the impromptu lesson in sexuality he facilitated one afternoon this fall. The girls were in the hall at their lockers—really painted wooden cubbies, but everyone calls them lockers—getting their coats and shoes so the group could go outside. Clark turned to the three boys who were left and asked, "How can we tell the difference between girls and boys?" Three small faces gazed up at him blankly. Clark prompted, "The girls have—"

"Vaginas!" replied Joseph, light dawning in his eyes.

"And the boys have—" continued Clark.

"Penises," said Joseph, less certainly.

"And that's the *only* way to tell the difference between girls and boys," said Clark firmly. Later he told me dryly, "One of our children is concerned that when he turns four he's going to turn into a girl. We try to help with that."

What makes Clark or any other teacher good at what they do? All the training, education, and research in the world can't change a teacher's personality—and that personality is the essence of any early childhood program. An example: Clark is reading a book with Shaunté and Lydia. He points to a picture of a lollipop and asks what it is, and Shaunté answers, "A sucker."

Clark immediately snaps, "Who you calling a sucker?" and Shaunté runs off, giggling. The joke works because it is both parody and reality, the kind of remark the girl might hear in the real world, only in a different, more innocent context. Only Clark could or would have played it this way. Carolyn's a good teacher, but her style is completely different—less hyper, calmer, more tender. No one else would do things quite the way Clark does. The same, of course, can be said of every other teacher in the center. As a parent, if you like a teacher's personality, it's an asset; if you dislike it, it becomes a major liability, reason enough to take your child out of the center. Clark may be prickly with adults at negotiation time, but even his harshest critics admit that he leaves all that at the classroom door. To the kids he's always the same Clarkie, silly, loving, and wise.

Yesterday, Clark got a sub to cover his shift and spent the day down at the state capitol, at a public hearing for W-2. A bunch of Red Caboosers were there—even Wendy, who usually steers clear of politics. It's too removed from the day-to-day world she knows and thrives in, and it's also too depressing, constantly trying to change things that won't change. But this time she feels she has to get involved; too much is at stake for Red Caboose, for other centers, for families, for children.

The hearing is packed with legislators, parents, and child-care providers from around the state. The legislators sit behind desks on one side of the room, with microphones and glasses of water. They listen and take notes under a baroque ceiling painted with stars, patriotic motifs, and a banner reading, "Fraternity, Charity, Loyalty." The hearing opens with a long speech by Jean Rogers, an economic support administrator from the Department of Health and Social Services (DHSS), giving the state's version of how W-2 would work and what it would accomplish. The philosophy informing W-2 is popular right now with conservatives all over the country: No more free rides. No entitlements. No handouts. Under W-2, you work or you don't get benefits. It's the same principle behind the national welfare reform movement, a kind of theory of moral osmosis: the act of working will give people the courage, motivation, and ability to break the cycle of welfare dependency and become productive, constructive members of society.

According to Rogers, a single mother with two kids who's now on welfare would be better off by about $4,000 under W-2, even if she's working a minimum-wage job—and, Rogers insists, very few jobs pay that little. Wendy pulls out a pocket calculator to check the math. "She can't even multiply," she says, shaking her head in disgust. When the question period starts, Rogers deftly fields queries and squashes objections. "I feel like screaming," whispers Wendy. "This woman hasn't given one straight answer. It's disgusting."

There are a number of reasons why W-2 is of such concern to the child-care community. The first is that parents will have to go to work when their infants are 12 weeks old; under AFDC, they can stay home until their children are two. There's already a shortage of infant care, in Wisconsin and elsewhere; who's going to take care of all those babies?

The second reason for concern is the new copayments that would be required of families. Under the current system, families on county funding find out each year what the county is willing to pay for child care; if they choose more expensive care, they have to pay the difference. This year the rate for two-year-olds and preschoolers is $110 per week for full-time care—on the low end but not completely out of line. Under W-2, all families would pay a percentage of the cost of child care, depending on family size and income. The less their care costs, the less they'd have to pay out of pocket. Licensed nonprofits like Red Caboose, which tend to charge more, would be too expensive; for-profit chains like Kindercare and Bright Start—which charge less, pay their teachers less, and provide on the whole much poorer-quality care—would barely be affordable.

Actually, if W-2's legislative sponsors have their way, all licensed centers and family child-care homes would be at a disadvantage. If thousands more people suddenly enter the work force, there will be a tremendous increase in the need for child care, a need that can't be met by the providers that exist now. Hence the new "provisionally certified" caregivers, who will get $54 a week. George Hagenauer, a director at Dane County's Community Coordinated Child Care (4-C), calculates that provisional caregivers would earn less than inmates in prison work programs. No one at this hearing actually says the words *cheap care,* but that's what this is all about.

John Gard, the Republican representative from Peshtigo who's sponsoring W-2, says the idea is to give parents more choice. To prove his point, he reprises a famous comment made in the early 1980s by then President Reagan. "My mother raised eight children," Gard tells the hearing. "Are you going to tell me that she needs to go to school to learn how to take care of my son?" Under W-2, Gard's mother—and anyone else who can pass a criminal records background check—could set up shop as a provisionally certified provider. If all the women-next-door who now take care of babies and children under the table were to do the same thing, the number of child-care slots would go up and the state's share of reimbursement would go way, way down. There's nothing new here: during a 1973 congressional debate on child care, one senator proposed that welfare recipients be *required* to work in child-care centers.[7]

Advocates like Clark are afraid of what parents will get for $54 a week: custodial care, where the emphasis is on taking care of a child's most obvious physical needs—diapers, food, nap—and that's it. "Just because former President Reagan stated that 'mothers and grandmothers have been caring for children for thousands of years' doesn't mean that *anyone* can be entrusted with someone else's baby," says Nancy Balaban, director of the Infant and Parent Development Program at Bank Street Graduate School of Education.[8] In its 1991 report *Beyond Rhetoric: A New American Agenda for Children and Families,* the National Commission on Children pointed out that child-care workers who are trained in child development, health, and safety are more likely to provide care that fosters affectionate, trusting relationships, to structure activities in ways that support social and emotional development, to appreciate and reinforce kids' different heritages.[9] None of this is likely to happen in custodial care. Some advocates conjure a horrifying scenario: children parked in front of the TV or strapped into car seats, eating potato chips and bologna on white bread, getting into fights, victimizing one another. Even a trained caregiver might have trouble handling too many kids at once, and provisionally certified caregivers will have to take on lots of kids to make ends meet. Some might be wonderful with children; some will be awful. Many will be mediocre, able to keep kids from killing themselves or one another but not able to teach them social or emotional skills, to help them learn problem-solving or conflict resolution, to stimulate their natural curiosity, to open the world to them.

Ironically, Wisconsin has until now been a leader when it comes to licensing providers. Over the last 15 years the state has evolved one of the most rigorous and comprehensive licensing systems in the country. In fact, in 1993, *Working Mother* magazine recognized Wisconsin as one of the top 10 states in the country for child care because of its high level of regulation and because the state has consistently spent a lot of money on staff training and helping providers get accredited. Under W-2, this could all go down the drain.

And what affects poor children will affect all children. As 4-C's George Hagenauer explained to me, "There's not a separate marketplace for low-income child care. It's all one marketplace. It's all one care system. Anything that affects poor children will in the long run affect children from wealthy families as well." Red Caboose is a case in point. If W-2 goes through as proposed, the families who are now getting county child-care funding will have to pay a much higher share of their child-care bills. They will have to find care that is cheap enough—$54-a-week care, most likely. So Red Caboose could lose a third of its population. That's a huge hit for a little center.

"If we lose all those families, several things will happen," explains Wendy. "In real dollars, we won't get as much funding for the food program. And we also won't be as successful at fundraising. Because that's one of our selling points, that we serve a lot of low-income kids. People do not want to give to centers that serve middle-class people."

Even if those slots are filled right away, the center will almost certainly lose economic and ethnic diversity, will become more white and more middle class, which will be to everyone's detriment. And it's not just Red Caboose, of course; a proliferation of cheap (and therefore poor-quality) care will undercut every quality center and provider in town. "Anything that lowers the general quality of care," says Wendy, "brings everything down." So everyone's children will lose.

And there's not much room for loss. Right now the Bees are down almost three slots, with 13 or 14 kids each day instead of the usual 16. This is bad for the program but good for the three-year-olds, who soak up the extra attention. It's funny how the rooms often seem composed of mostly one gender or the other; right now in the Bumblebee Room it's boys, and they are—to put it in a positive light—very active. Out on the playground this afternoon, Paul, Zachary, and Joseph are at it again, arguing over the toy bulldozers in the sandbox, starting to get physical. "Zach needs to talk to Joe about getting pushed," says Clark, striding over to the scuffling boys. "Can you do that, Zach?"

Zach scowls at Joseph and says, "Joe, don't push me!"

"You need to talk to Joe about him pushing you," says Clark, doing his own brand of necessary pushing here.

"Stop pushing!" says Zach.

Joseph, in a high-pitched voice that belies his husky blond build, says to Zach, "Don't get in my hole!"

"If Joe doesn't want you in his hole, what should Joe do?" asks Clark. "Push you? No? Joe should do something else. What should you do, Joe?"

Joseph hangs his shining blond head and says meekly, "Use words?"

Clark doesn't exactly beam, but his eyes radiate approval. "And what would you say to him if you were going to use words? Don't get in my hole! Did you tell him that? And he didn't listen? Then what do you do, push him? Come tell a teacher he's not listening?" Joseph nods. "Can you remember to do that?" says Clark, winding down.

"I got sand in my eyes!" says Joseph plaintively, making a last-ditch bid for sympathy.

"Joseph, if we don't do any pushing, then we won't get as hurt around here," says Clark. "You know how it hurts when you get pushed sometimes, right? Always talk with words, and if someone's not listening, get a teacher to help them listen. Be a good talker, and you won't need to feel like you have to push, ever." With that the three boys go back to playing together. The incident— one of a dozen or more today—is more or less resolved.

Financially, having 13 or 14 kids in the Bumblebee Room is almost worse than having 9 or 10, because two teachers at a time are still needed. State licensing regulations require one teacher for every 10 three-year-olds, and one for every 13 four-year-olds. Clark makes it work by deftly juggling the numbers and the kids, having older kids "visit" the Grasshopper Room and younger kids visit the Elephants. If the numbers come out right, one teacher can work the room alone, with the help of the two high school students currently volunteering in the Bumblebee Room, without compromising the quality of the program. Carolyn will come in this afternoon. Crystal, the third Bumblebee teacher, is taking off a few days. And it's the same in the other rooms. The staff is pulling together to help lower the center's costs: trading kids from room to room, not getting substitutes, taking a day of vacation here or there. It takes coordination and people talking to each other every day, but it works.

Clark isn't fretting about the low enrollment. He stands on the playground in the autumn sun, watching Shaunté on a swing, throwing her head back, drinking in the air. "I'm really not worried," he says. "We can get creative. We haven't known a real crisis we couldn't handle." A few years ago, during a summer of low enrollment, the staff got together out on the playground and volunteered for layoffs or to take fewer hours, to help see the center through a hard time. It worked then, and it would work now if necessary.

Meanwhile, life goes on. On a brisk fall morning later in the month, the Bumblebees are getting ready to go outside. Once winter sets in, their visits to the playground will be few and far between, so at this time of year the teachers take them outside as much as possible. In the hallway outside the Bumblebee Room, Clark is patiently teaching Carlos—not for the first time—the easiest way to put on his coat. He talks him through the process: Lay the coat on the floor, inside up, upside down, with the hood closest to your feet. Stick your arms into the sleeves. Whip the coat up and over your head. *Voilà*—the day-care flip. Carlos grins, then bends his head to struggle with his next objective—zipping.

At 10:10 the Bees line up on the golden line. Clark layers a down vest under his denim jacket and leads the kids outside. Back in the Bumblebee Room, Carolyn helps the last few kids on with their coats. "Did you use the bathroom yet?" she asks Kenny, holding up his coat so he can slip his arms in. "Not yet," says the boy, and then, "Ooh! He farted!" He makes rude noises between his teeth, laughing at Bruce and Isaac, who are putting away the last of the toys they played with this morning. "I need help," whines Bruce, dragging a blanket toward Carolyn. "Lay it out on the floor," says Carolyn. She helps him fold it, matching corner to corner, stretch it out, fold it again. "You can do it!" she exclaims when he's done. "You didn't even know you could!"

When the three boys finally emerge into the sunshine, they head for the new toy shed, where another group of boys is futilely and happily trying to push over a tree. The mood on the playground is unusually peaceful. Maybe it's the foreknowledge of winter on this warm fall day, with the leaves turning gaudy. Everyone plays in relative harmony, 11-month-olds and 4-year-olds and their teachers out in the sunny yard. There are nine adults out on the play-

Clark believes in plenty of upside-down time. Here he flips Isaac on the playground.

ground: Cheryl and Ernie from the Turtle Room; Carolyn from the Bumble-bee Room; and an assortment of student teachers and high school students. The swing set is full, and elsewhere the playground is like a 12-ring circus, with something happening everywhere you look. Skye, Lydia, and Meghan hold hands, jump off the low rubber curbs, and run crazily around in a game that only they understand. Joseph and Isaac take turns coming down the metal slide attached to one of the big wooden structures, which is swarming with older kids.

There is a feeling of great happiness here, and liveliness too. Nothing feels unsafe, but it's not just about being safe. Put kids and play equipment together and anything might happen, any individual child might tumble off a ramp or fall off a slide, might get hurt. The sense of safety goes beyond the merely physical. These adults are known and trusted; these other children are known and for the most part trusted too. Isn't that a big part of what children of all ages need, trust in the grown-ups around them to help them and guide them and let them go?

One little girl, a Turtle, stands crying under a tree. She wants to touch its yellow leaves, but she can't reach. Ernie lifts the girl up and holds a branch down, and the toddler puts her hands on it in wonder. Near the sandbox Isaac waves a stick, which Cheryl promptly takes away from him. The back door of the center opens and the Elephants come out, a trickle of two-year-olds, along with Gary and Mary, their two morning teachers. Blond curly-haired Anna C. (to distinguish her from Anna H.-K.), a Turtle, sits in a baby swing, transported with delight. Beside her Ulric, another Turtle, and Shaunté swing too. Soon a line of trikes proceeds around the playground in a more or less orderly fashion, with Bruce in the lead. Next comes Kenny, in red sweatpants, a blue jacket, and sneakers. Todd is close behind him, in a turquoise jacket with a sailboat on it, then two-year-old Claire, Lydia's younger sister. And so the morning wears on, flows on, in hundreds of interactions, no one of them that important in itself but all of them adding up to make the quality of a child's day, day after day after day, constituting some of the most important years of a child's life. On the one hand, exquisitely boring; on the other, exquisitely fascinating. Both or either at any given moment.

In the kitchen, just inside the back door, Max is almost done making up the lunch trays. Today's lunch is salad, acorn squash, cottage cheese, cut-up cheddar cheese, chopped hard-boiled eggs, hot buttered bread, sliced pears, and milk. The three oldest rooms get a metal lunch tray on wheels loaded with paper plates, silverware, and cups. The Turtle teachers bring their food in on a tray, since they have at most only eight to feed.

Food is a crucial part of the day at the center, nourishing the body, providing opportunities for sensory adventures, smoothing social interactions. At many centers the kids bring bag lunches from home, which leads to a proliferation of less-than-nutritious packaged food. Everything served here is made in the kitchen by Max. Hot food in the winter, sandwiches in the summer, no potato chips or fluorescent candies. Because all the children eat the same food, it also serves as a kind of leveling factor, reinforcing the sense that, despite surface differences, everyone is of equal value.

Today the floor of the L-shaped kitchen is piled with boxes holding the raw materials of meals to come: bags of carrots, giant heads of romaine lettuce, three-pound slabs of cheddar and cream cheese, a crate of oranges. Silverware clatters to the floor. "Just what we need, more dirty dishes!" says Max with a laugh. She's been here 15 years, cooking two meals a day plus snack for 53 kids. She also makes snack for the school-age program, another 75 kids.

At 44, Max can still lift a heavy stockpot full of water onto the black industrial-size stove without straining. In a blue and red Indian-print skirt and T-shirt, wearing beat-up running shoes, her dark hair pulled back into a simple ponytail, Max looks like someone who would wear a black leather biker's jacket (she does) and call a spade a spade (which she also does). When all the lunches have been picked up, Max starts fixing snack for the after-school kids. Today it's blueberry yogurt, which she makes herself, blending fresh blueberries into plain yogurt, stacking each batch in a plastic container on the kitchen table.

By 11 o'clock the Bees are back inside, washing their hands for lunch. "I don't want to eat," announces Kenny. "Come and sit with us, Kenny," coaxes Carolyn. "You don't have to eat." The children sit around the kid-size table like grown-ups at a tea party, waiting patiently — well, pretty patiently — for everyone to be served before they eat. Carolyn narrates the meal as she serves it. Like most of the teachers at the center, she eats whatever the kids get. "Here's some squash," she says, making a plate for one girl. "With — brown sugar?" She lifts the plate to her nose and sniffs. "No, *cinnamon*. Yummy, yummy." When everyone is served, the three-year-olds dig in. Kenny eats hunk after hunk of bread. Bruce bounces in his chair until Carolyn puts one arm around him to help him settle down. "Know what I'm gonna be for Halloween?" he asks, pronouncing it *Hawoween*. "A Power Ranger!" Power Rangers are this year's craze, like Teenage Mutant Ninja Turtles a year or two back.

"*I'm* going to be a bus driver," says Todd in his slow, careful way. "I bet you'd be a really good bus driver," says Carolyn. "Because you're patient, and you're really nice to people. And I bet you know your way around, too." Todd beams. The red plastic bread basket is empty, and Carolyn sends Kenny to the kitchen for more. He comes back with the basket still empty. "No more bread," he says. "Really?" Carolyn says, clearly surprised. But she doesn't question him or double check. She puts the empty basket back on the cart. She trusts him, takes him at his word, a more satisfying experience than any amount of bread. Next she sends Bruce off for more cottage cheese. "More salad, please!" calls Meghan from one end of the table. "Can I get a glass of water?" asks Kenny. "Fill it up just halfway, to about here," instructs Carolyn, showing him on an empty cup. Bruce comes back with the cottage cheese. "There *is* more bread!"

he shouts. "Max said so!" "Really? Did it just come out of the oven?" asks Carolyn tactfully. "I'll get some!" offers Bruce at top volume. But Carolyn hands Kenny the basket. "No, we'll let Kenny get some," she says. Kenny comes back a few minutes later, carrying the basket of hot crisp bread reverently.

But the moment doesn't last. Kenny starts playing with the empty chair beside him, tipping it farther and farther back until it clatters to the floor. He squirms, leans from side to side, bangs his cup on the table, scrapes the empty chair across the floor. "Kenny, no spitting at the table," says Carolyn. "You seem to forget that rule lately." "Fire burns you up!" announces Isaac suddenly from across the table. "What made you think of fire?" asks Carolyn, not missing a beat. "Did you see a fire truck today? We saw an ambulance." She puts half an acorn squash on Todd's plate so he can eat out of it.

Kenny makes a gun shape with his thumb and forefinger and rises out of his chair, making shooting noises. "Kenny, I need you to sit in your chair, please," says Carolyn. Bruce, off to the kitchen for more pears, says, "Don't anybody touch my pears!" When he returns, the first thing he says is, "Are my pears still there?" "Nobody's touched your pears, Bruce," says Carolyn gravely. Kenny wiggles his chair away from the table. "Kenny, scoot your chair back to the table, please," says Carolyn. All through the meal, it's a running refrain: "Kenny, sit up in your chair, please. Kenny, put your chair on the floor, please." Now Kenny and another boy start tussling over the empty chair between them, struggling for control. Carolyn separates them and pushes the chair back in. Meghan digs the core out of a pear quarter with her fork. Bruce spears a pear on his fork and pretends to shoot it across the table. Kenny, finished, throws his paper plate in the garbage and carries his fork and cup to the cart. He hasn't cried all morning.

By 11:20 the meal is done. The table is littered with cubes of bread, chunks of fresh pear, grated cheese. Only Todd is left at the table, chewing distractedly. Bruce carries his plate to the trash at a run, spilling food everywhere, and sends it flying into the can just as Clark comes over to confer briefly with Carolyn. His group, in the other half of the room, is finishing up too. "I swear Bruce had chocolate," Carolyn says to Clark with a laugh. "He's real high today. Maybe it was all the honey in that rice pudding this morning. Max uses so much honey."

Some of the children help clean up, while others fan out and play quietly. Clark squirts water onto his table, and Annie runs a paper towel over it. Carlos and Shaunté stand at the sensory table, a kind of big low sink that holds various kinds of play materials. Today there is cornmeal inside, and the children run tiny trucks and cars through the soft yellow stuff. Lydia, in a pink dress with a cat ballerina on it, twirls barefoot near the couch. Most of the Bees have shed their shoes; the floor between the couch and the table is littered with small sneakers. Shaunté takes off her shoes, too, but Clark immediately lifts her onto his lap and puts them back on. "Nooo!" she cries. "It's just not fair," agrees Clark, "is it? Annie's mama says it's OK for her to have her shoes off. What does Shaunté's mama say? *Keep—your—shoes—on.*" He releases her and she scampers off, pouting. Carlos slips the blue nightgown over his head and turns back to the sensory table, engrossed in the miniature world he is making. Soon Carolyn will settle on the beat-up couch and begin reading to him and the other Bees. The mood in the room will quiet. Kids will lie down on cots with their loveys and blankets and pillows. Soothing music will begin. Clark and Carolyn will move among the cots, rubbing backs, settling kids for the sweet sleep that punctuates their long day away from home.

A Wednesday night in late October. At six o'clock, closing time for the center, parents and teachers gather in the Sunshine Room for a prenegotiations meeting. The street outside the window is dark, the room brightly lit. Parents trickle in, along with a handful of teachers: Gary Dosemagen, the lead Elephant teacher, a lanky Abe Lincoln look-alike, his light brown hair sticking up disarmingly in tufts; Amy Schuster, a Grasshopper teacher, her blond hair cropped short, a row of silver rings climbing the side of one ear; Emily Lyman, another Grasshopper teacher; Crystal and Clark; and Leah Donahue, one of the teachers from the after-school program. A good turnout, especially since no one really wants to talk about negotiations.

Everyone sits on the floor in a ragged circle. Amy wields red and purple markers, taking notes on big sheets of paper. As each sheet is filled, John, Todd's father, tapes them up on the wall where everyone can see them. Emily bends her head toward a white takeout container and scoops noodles into her mouth with chopsticks. Everyone is making a conscious effort to mingle, to blur the boundaries of the old adversarial relationship.

The meeting starts with a long discussion of procedures: who will facilitate meetings, what constitutes a quorum, setting the agenda, and so on. At one point Emily becomes impatient. "Why does everything have to be so formal?" she asks, wiping her mouth with a white paper napkin. "We've spent 45 minutes just talking about facilitators and quorums."

"I'm glad you asked that," says Clark, jumping into the breach. "It's like a free throw, you know? You have to bend your knees, hold your hands just so, squat, shoot—all of this is done quite formally. But next week you don't think about all that. You just shoot. We'll loosen up. I know we will."

Mitch, a short, slender man with a dark ponytail, leans forward and says, "We're laying the groundwork here, building trust." Or maybe it's *preserving* trust, because the trust is already there. Every time a parent stands outside the building, looking in through the big window in the Bumblebee Room— the good-bye window—she or he is trusting a child to the teachers. No matter how much that parent knows about the program, the center, the teachers, there is still an enormous amount of trust involved, a leap of faith that the teachers, too, have the child's best interests at heart. Maybe that's one of the criteria of a successful negotiation process, to get through it without rupturing that trust.

The subject most likely to cause a rupture is money. Everyone here is aware that virtually every penny of the teachers' raises comes out of parents' pockets. These parents aren't greedy or selfish, and they're quick to acknowledge that teachers are grotesquely underpaid. But no one here is rich; many parents at the center work for the state, which raised salaries about 2 percent last year. They earn good salaries for Wisconsin with top-notch benefits, so they're not in the same boat as the teachers. But even if the parents at the center right now were able and willing to pay, say, another $15 a week for child care, there are all the other parents to consider, whose children might come to Red Caboose in the future, who will keep the center going after this batch of families has passed through.

That's one of the issues that make discussions about child care so difficult, the fact that it's part of a family's life for a relatively short time. A couple of years, and the child is off to kindergarten. There's after-school care, of course, but that's in a different league, less threatening and less expensive. School-age children are older and less vulnerable, and they spend less time in child care, an hour or two a day compared with seven or nine hours a day for preschoolers.

So the center has to stay marketable. For most families, fees at Red Caboose and elsewhere are barely affordable—and they *still* don't cover the cost of good child care. Barbara Willer, who writes extensively on the cost of child care, estimated that in 1990 parents paid an average of $4,900 a year for each child enrolled in an accredited center. But the *real* cost of providing that care, she wrote, was close to $8,500, taking into account the poverty-level wages paid to most child-care workers.[10] The $3,600 difference comes out of the pockets of teachers and staff, in the form of the money they should be earning to make a living wage but aren't. Economists call this forgone wages, meaning the wages that child-care workers forgo in order to stay in the field. In the United States, forgone wages subsidize every family who buys child care.

Why do people who work in child care put up with such low wages? For a variety of reasons: because child-care providers are almost all women, who tend not to be as assertive as men about money; because there are few education and training requirements, which leads to the perception that "anyone could do it"; because the vast majority of providers love children and love their work, and simply accept the conditions and wages as they are. The annual median salary for an early childhood teacher in this country is $14,100, compared with $28,900 for a public school teacher. Is it twice as hard to work with six-year-olds as it is to work with five-year-olds, or three-year-olds, or infants? Is that why we pay early childhood teachers half what we pay kindergarten teachers?

Forgone wages are the single biggest reason for high staff turnover. Many teachers who love kids and enjoy working in early childhood programs get to a point where they just can't afford to stay in the field. When Clark and Belindah first started teaching at Red Caboose, they needed food stamps, city day-care funding, and housing assistance to help raise their daughter. Not everyone is dedicated enough to do that.

The problem of forgone wages is less acute at Red Caboose than at many centers because the pay scale is more generous and because many of the teachers have been here for so long. Each year on the anniversary of their hire, employees at Red Caboose get a raise of 19 cents an hour, on top of whatever raises are negotiated. So a teacher who's been at the center 10 years earns $1.90 more per hour than a teacher who's just been hired. Teachers like Cheryl Heiman, who have been here 20 years or more, make pretty good money— for child care. Rewarding seniority helps the center retain good teachers and reduce staff turnover. It also counterbalances the extremely low pay scale for management. The director's job, for instance, has a base wage of $9.95 an hour, $1.00 less than the average at other nonprofits in Madison.[11] Because Wendy's been at the center for 22 years, she earns an extra $4.18 per hour. Imagine paying a top executive—even at a nonprofit—less than $10 an hour!

But just as the center has to charge less to stay attractive to families, it has to pay more to be able to attract new teachers. Even Red Caboose has to hire new teachers from time to time, especially in the school-age programs, which have much higher turnover than the center. So the base wage, the rate at which teachers are hired, has to be competitive. Many centers set up a strict, bottom-heavy hierarchy among employees: aides, teaching assistants, teachers, lead teachers. Traditionally the aides and assistant teachers make minimum wage and do most of the grunt work. That kind of arrangement would be considered exploitative here. Red Caboose has only two categories, teachers and lead teachers. Lead teachers are responsible for the room's enrollment. They get subs when their teachers are out sick, and they're generally responsible for the well-being of the room. For this they earn a base wage of $8.23 an hour, 50 cents more per hour than the other teachers. Egalitarianism has always been part of the Red Caboose philosophy.

At the board meeting the following week, everyone seems hopeful about negotiations, which is lucky because the center's finances haven't improved since Rosebud's report last month. Louise is at the meeting to talk about the third-quarter financial report. She perches on a stool in the Elephant Room, towering over the parents who are scrunched into the child-size chairs. A stylish, grandmotherly woman in her 50s, Louise lets everyone absorb the bad news on paper first—the center has a deficit of $11,000, and the year's not over yet—and then begins to speak. "To give you some perspective," she says, "in '93 the deficit was even bigger. So we've certainly been in worse shape. However, we'd all like to see a positive number instead of a negative one." Around the table, heads are bent over copies of the report. This is one of the most important and grueling meetings of the year, where the board votes on a preliminary budget and FTEs for the coming year. The numbers agreed on tonight will set the framework for negotiations.

Wendy's in a black dress, a departure from her usual blue, though she is wearing navy tights and clogs. Her long black hair is streaked with barely visible lines of silver. Around her neck gleams a silver Star of David, several silver loops, and a pendant with a dark blue stone, which she fingers now, glancing down at her papers. She doesn't need to study the numbers; she and Louise work together on the budget, so she practically knows them by heart.

Finances are the toughest thing to understand on the board, unless you happen to be an accountant or a lawyer or a numbers whiz. Newer board members get confused and overwhelmed the first few times they look at a profit and loss statement or a financial report. "As a general rule," says Wendy now, speaking to the newer parents, "if you look at salaries and tuition, and they're pretty close to where they should be, we're doing OK. If we're 500 percent over on snowplowing charges, that's only a couple hundred dollars."

"We're on budget for most things, though we're high on repairs and equipment," adds Louise. "And by the way, thank you for the new printer. My ears thank you!" The board recently voted to buy Louise a laser printer to replace her old dot matrix. The laser printer is about a million times quieter, and faster too; documents that used to take two hours to print now take about six minutes.

For the next hour or so the board goes through the financial report, line by line. It's a tedious process, but by the end even the newer members are beginning to get a feel for the center's finances. Rosebud works his pocket calculator as the discussion slides from bad debt to late fees, from the county's reimbursement schedule to principles of accounting.

After that, Wendy gives her report. Enrollment is still low, but she's been taking a lot of calls from parents looking for care. "The real problem is how the openings are spread," she says, lifting a long loop of hair off one shoulder. If they were all in one room, the center could temporarily lay off staff in that room until things pick up. But they're spread across the center, one here, two there—not enough to justify cutting staff. "We can't go on being six FTEs down, and I hope we're not going to," she continues. "I have a full-timer and a part-timer starting next week, and some calls to return. I don't think we need to do more than we are right now."

"You mean we don't need to panic?" asks Maria, only half joking.

"Not yet," says Wendy, allowing herself a smile. "If this keeps up through next month, then we might need to think. There's a feeling among staff—how shall I say this?—of not wanting to ever be over the ratio, and I think if we're going to be under, then we're going to have to push sometimes harder and *have* 13 in the Elephant Room one day a week for some period of time." What Wendy's talking about makes sense, and is possible because Red Caboose's internal teacher-child ratios are well below what the state requires. The Elephant Room, for instance, could legally serve 14 children with two teachers, but the center's own ratio caps the room at 12. Two extra kids can make a huge difference in the stress levels of both teachers and other kids. Even one aggressive or especially needy child can turn a room upside down.

A few years ago, for instance, there was a particularly aggressive Elephant named Hal. Hal was a hitter and a biter, a child who expressed his frustration by lashing out physically and emotionally at other kids. The other two-year-olds quickly learned to avoid him, which added to his sense of isolation and rage. The teachers devoted a lot of time and energy to teaching Hal more acceptable ways of expressing his feelings and to integrating him into the group—time *not* spent with the other 11 kids in the room. The more kids in the room, the less time teachers have for the Hals and for everyone else.

Sometime around eight o'clock the board finally gets to the budget. Wendy and Louise have put together a draft budget, and now Wendy explains some of the trends she's seen at the center in recent months. "We have more part-timers," she says. "Last year 34 percent of our FTEs were part time, and this year it's 40 percent. That's good because we have more revenue, but bad because it's harder to schedule everything." For teachers trying to coordinate 8 or 12 or 18 kids, each with a different schedule, part-timers can be a major headache. But part-timers pay 10 percent more than full-timers, and those extra dollars add up. Part-time care is becoming the norm all over the country, not just at Red Caboose, as more and more parents work part time and juggle their schedules to cover the kids. Some of the centers that haven't traditionally accepted part-timers are beginning to come around. It's either that or go under.

Another issue to watch is the food program, the other main source of revenue besides parent tuitions. Each year the center gets between $15,000 and $20,000 in federal money from the Child and Adult Food Care Program (CAFCP), so much per child per meal, with the amount depending on how many children are at each meal and how many of them are from poor families. The more low-income children at the center, the more federal money the center gets. "The CAFCP helps to redistribute income by rewarding centers that care for a relatively large number of disadvantaged children," wrote William T. Gormley, Jr., in his book *Everybody's Children: Child Care as a Public Problem.*[12]

Earlier this year, the CAFCP was scheduled to be slashed as part of the Republicans' Contract with America, and it's still not clear whether that will happen. If it does, Red Caboose will be in trouble. Luckily for tonight's board, any cuts enacted won't take place till 1997, so they won't have to play guessing games about how much projected income to cut from next year's budget. In fact, Wendy and Louise have upped the food budget for next year; school-age enrollment keeps rising, and kids at after-school eat a lot of fruit, which is one of the more expensive food items.

This whole budget process is a big guessing game, of course: Guess how many full-timers and part-timers will enroll at the center next year. Guess how many kids will sign up for after-school and summer programs. Guess how many of them will be from low-income families. Guess what each program will spend on food, educational supplies, field trips, toilet paper. Guess how much utilities will go up. Guess how much it will snow, and how much the center will need to spend on plowing. The amazing thing is that most years, the projected budget is within 1 percent of the actual budget—a testament to Wendy's business sense, experience, and hard work.

Next Wendy brings up tuition. The board won't actually decide on 1996 tuition increases until the union contract has been negotiated and the budget finalized, but Wendy likes to get people thinking about it ahead of time. Every year around this time she calls around to other centers in Madison and gets their new rates. University Avenue Day Care, which is usually the most expensive center, is raising its rates to $141 a week for full-time preschool care. Red Caboose is currently charging between $110 and $141 a week for preschool care, depending on family income and size. Any increase—and there will have to be one—will make Red Caboose the most expensive center in town. "Of course, only 18 percent of our parents pay our highest rates," points out Wendy. But that 18 percent subsidizes the other 82 percent who can't afford to pay full price, and the center needs them badly. Would a family paying $141 a week balk at paying $148 or $150 a week? "The people who are already here don't leave because the rates are raised too high," says Wendy, swinging her dark hair back off her shoulders. "It's the ones who call up and ask what the fees are, and who never even come to see it. Those are the ones we need to worry about."

Another complicating factor is the county day-care rate, which isn't going up at all. So once again, families with two-year-olds at Red Caboose have a weekly copay—a fact that definitely discourages Elephant Room enrollment. "It kills me when we're low like this to turn two-year-olds away," says Wendy. "If you're on county funding, you can't find care for that amount for a two-year-old. And I have to tell these people they have to pay. They say, 'The county told me they'll pay,' and I have to tell them, 'You have to go find cheaper care, and they *will* pay for it all.'"

Of course, by next year this may be a moot point. If W-2 goes into effect, every family on funding will have a copay, not just those with two-year-olds. And what happens then is anybody's guess.

November-December

Friday's breakfast is the most popular meal of the week: toasted bagels and cream cheese. No one makes bagels quite the way Max does, slathered with butter and then toasted in the oven. Delicious, unless you're worried about cholesterol, which the kids aren't. One of the first sentences my daughter Anna ever said was "Yay, yay, bagel day!" Now the Bumblebees take up the chant as Carolyn wheels in the breakfast cart.

Even bagels can't hold a roomful of three-year-olds for more than a few minutes, though. By nine o'clock the Bees have split into small groups for the morning. Clark leads his group, the Stars, to the Sunshine Room for a musical interlude. Denise, a student teacher in the Bumblebee Room this semester, follows along, watching and occasionally jumping into the fray. Each semester the Bees and other rooms get one or two students who are either in the two-year child-care program at MATC or studying early childhood education at UW. The student teachers learn a lot, and the center gets extra hands — an even trade.

Lydia sits on the floor with a plastic xylophone, winding the toy's string around its stick. Lateef has the other xylophone, and he's banging away with enthusiasm. Joseph strums a plastic guitar while he and Clark sing his favorite song. "Born on a mountaintop in Tennessee," they sing. "Kilt him a b'ar when he was only three." They swing into the chorus. "Davey, Davey Crockett, king of the wild frontier," they sing, and then dissolve into giggles, the man along with the boy. "Shoot me five," says Clark, and Joseph does, beaming.

Zach, hearing the usually forbidden word *shoot*, picks up a xylophone stick and play-shoots it at Clark, who sobers instantly. "No, I don't like to be shot," he says. "Don't shoot at me." He pulls a tambourine out of a plastic laundry tub and hands it to Zach, who briefly accepts the substitution. Lateef jogs around the room, pulling a xylophone behind him; luckily it's on wheels. Zach throws down the tambourine and snatches a pair of metal cymbals, which he uses loudly and enthusiastically. "Jungian instruments," mutters Clark. "Man and his cymbals." Annie picks up a set too, and she and Zach stand face to face, alternately clapping them together and putting them over their ears.

Wendy comes in to go over a timesheet with Clark. As the lead teacher Clark oversees the Bumblebee staff, all of whom have schedules and time-sheets to fill out. Annie and Zach, clapping their cymbals, zoom right between Wendy and Clark, making a deafening noise. But it's happy noise.

Lydia pushes a doll carriage with one hand and pulls a xylophone with the other. "I want to play with it, Clark," complains Lateef, pointing at a drum on a shelf high over his head. "No, the one thing I won't have today is the drum," says Clark. "If you want to bang on something, bang on the xylophone." Lateef sets to with gusto. Lydia puts a doll's head up to her shirt and says, "I'm nursing my baby." Clark picks up the plastic guitar, abandoned on the carpet, and strums a satirical version of "Davey Crockett" that begins, "Bored on a mountaintop in Tennessee . . ."

After a minute, Clark puts down the guitar and calls the kids into a circle on the floor. "Let's do a song together, like a band," he suggests. "I'm gonna be the bandleader." He picks up a xylophone. Zach and Lydia crowd him, each with his or her cymbals. Lateef has a little drum and two plastic drumsticks. Joseph has cymbals, Carlos a xylophone. "OK, now listen," says Clark with relish. "When you're 18 and you live in a village, you learn how to play in a band together, OK? Because it takes a heck of a village to make a band. Now watch carefully. When I go like this, then we play." He waves his hands as if he's conducting a symphony orchestra. "When I go like this"—he points both index fingers downward—"then we stop. When I go like this"—he lets his hands rise through the air, palms to the floor—"we play louder and louder. You ready?"

They're ready. At Clark's signal cacophony begins, the volume swelling with his gestures. "Louder, louder!" he prompts, lifting his hands. Joseph looks as though he might explode if he bangs the cymbals any harder. "Now softer, soft," says Clark, dropping his hands. "Now louder and louder." His voice rises to illustrate the concept. "You gotta watch my hands, or you won't know the signals." The children's eyes are glued to his hands. They follow along devoutly as he has them play louder, then softer, then louder, then stop, then start again, over and over, for what seems like a very long time but is really only about five minutes.

Finally Clark stops the game, his eyes alight with pleasure and mischief. He suggests a song instead. Joseph wants, of course, "Davey Crockett." Lateef preempts him by picking up a plastic stick and banging on a little drum, singing, "Little Bunny Fufu." Soon they're all singing with Lateef. "Down comes the fairy godperson," sings Clark. The only one who doesn't join in is Lydia, who sits on the bottom step of the climbing structure with a doll. Clark asks Carlos to bring him a small toy piano, which he uses to pick out the melody of "Freres Jacques," leading the group.

At 9:25 Clark announces, "One more minute till cleanup time!" Lydia is now pushing a doll in a plastic stroller around and around the music makers on the floor, watching them with interest. Despite the fact that it's a very cold day, Lydia's purple pants are pushed up past her knees and her calves are bare. "Let's do 'She'll Be Comin' Round the Mountain,'" says Clark. "Ready?" Annie lies down, clapping her cymbals rhythmically. Lydia finally joins in, sitting down and patting her doll's head in time to the music. At the end of the song, Clark gathers the instruments. "I'm going to count to 33," he tells the children, "and I want everybody to sit by me." He counts in a breathless, rushing voice, and the kids respond to his urgency, plopping down around him by the door of the room. Lydia and Joseph roll around, tickling each other. "Now listen," says Clark. "Denise is going to precede us into the room and pick out one really really super good book to read for group time. In the meantime, while we're waiting, I'm going to remind you what we're going to do. Every single one of us is going to sit on the bench. Is it going to be a good story?" A chorus of *yeahs* goes up. "Will it be a scary monster book or will it be exciting?" "Scary monster book!" cry out a couple of kids. "Joseph, I want you to stop pushing Lydia," says Clark. Lateef offers, "Snakes coming out of a box! It happens." "Yikes!" says Clark. "Pigs come out too," adds Zach. "Do they fly?" Clark asks drolly. "Nope," instructs Zach. "They don't fly. They go oink, oink, oink." He leans forward to demonstrate.

Back in the Bumblebee Room, after Denise has finished reading, it's choice time. Clark asks each child in turn to make a plan for the next hour. Lateef and Joseph and Zach decide to play in the child-size kitchen. Lydia chooses puzzles. Annie joins the boys on a cooking spree. Making a plan is a key element in the Bumblebee curriculum, which is based on a program called High/Scope from the Perry Preschool Project in Ypsilanti, Michigan. The program is based on Piaget's theory that children learn differently from adults, and emphasizes child-directed and -initiated activities as opposed to the curriculum units favored by many preschools. Amy Schuster, who uses the program in the Grasshopper Room, explains it simply. "Children learn by doing," she says. "Telling a kid, 'This is white,' isn't enough. They have to *experience* white. They have to touch it, taste it, smell it, feel it. They have to immerse themselves in white."

Before High/Scope, kids at Red Caboose—like kids in centers all over the country—moved from one planned activity to another, in 20- or 30-minute blocks. Crystal recalls the way it used to be: "It was, 'Now we're going to do a project for 20 minutes. Then it's group time. Then we're going to sing for 20 minutes. And then it's time to switch sides. We've been there for an hour, that's long enough. For the next 20 minutes we're going to do art. And then we have 20 minutes more till lunch, so we're gonna have another group time, because you don't want to get everything messy, do you?'" Give the kids a chance to focus on something they really want to do for more than 20 minutes, says Crystal, and behavior problems go way down.

In a High/Scope curriculum, children make their own plans, carry out those plans, and review what they did—Plan, Do, Review, the cornerstone of the program. Clark believes it helps empower children. "Our job is to facilitate children's development by supporting their play," he explains. That means letting kids choose what to play, not forcing them to color turkeys at Thanksgiving and shamrocks on St. Patrick's Day.

Some parents worry that "child-directed play" is a euphemism for unsupervised play, for letting kids just run wild. And there are times in the Bumblebee Room when that appears to be true. It depends somewhat on each teacher's personal style. Carolyn, for instance, tends to sit and watch quietly. Clark tends to involve himself in the kids' play more often, but only when he feels he's welcome or when a child invites him directly. He calls this "validating" children's choices rather than the more traditional teaching and directing.

Once all the three-year-olds are settled, Clark will leave for a meeting with some local children's advocates who are lobbying hard to change W-2's most egregious provisions. Last month the group met with John Gard, the bill's legislative sponsor. "We gave him some good arguments he could use as ammunition in talking to his fellow Republicans," explains Clark. He lifts his voice in mocking imitation. "He'd *like* to be able to help us out, but those dog-gone fellow Republicans don't know what he's talking about." He grins. "So we gave him some good arguments to use."

In the play kitchen area Kenny and Bruce crouch under a child-size picnic table, each wearing an animal pot holder on one hand. Kenny has a brown and white cow, Bruce a duck. They're doing a puppet show, the plot of which is intelligible only to them. Carolyn, sitting on the couch, claps as Meghan approaches them. "Yay!" she calls over. "Are you going to have a puppet show with Meghan?" The boys instantly adopt her idea, rummaging through a pile of animals for a puppet Meghan can wear. Soon all three children are under the table, waving their puppeted hands at Carolyn. Kenny's attention quickly lapses and he climbs out from under the table, using his cow pot holder to pull all the books off the bookshelf in back of the table. "I want one more puppet show," says Carolyn, trying to rein him back in. "Nope! A couple more!" says Kenny, and grins.

From the loft comes the sound of loud, hysterical sobs. Denice Watson, an Elephant Room teacher, is subbing for Clark, and she goes up to investigate. A small woman wearing round silver glasses, her brown hair hanging in unruly ringlets, she comes down the steps with Zach beside her. At the bottom she lifts him into her arms; Denice may be small, but she's sturdy, tough even, in her habitual T-shirt and ripped blue jeans. "Annie yelled at me!" Zach cries, outraged. "Oh, that must have hurt your feelings," says Denice, not so much soothingly as encouragingly. "What could you have done?" Zach keeps crying. "You could have told her you didn't like it," continues Denice. Zach's face is red, the fingers of his right hand in his mouth. "She pushed me over!" he says finally between hiccups. "She pushed you over," repeats Denice, nodding her head. "You need to remember to tell Annie to use words."

Slowly, Zach calms down. "Should we find something else to do?" Denice asks when he's more or less rational. He nods. "Look, we have Lydia here. Maybe she wants to do something with us." "I want to do Play-Doh!" announces Lydia. "I don't know if we have any Play-Doh on this side of the room," says Denice, searching the cabinets.

She finds some, though, and she and the children begin setting it up on the tables near the loft. Meanwhile Kenny, still wearing his cow puppet, is arranging a row of little red chairs facing the picnic table, an audience. "Everybody sit down for a puppet show!" he announces. His pronunciation is garbled, especially the consonants, so "puppet show" comes out sounding like "bubbed dough." Luckily the other kids don't seem to have any trouble understanding him. Bruce and Isaac pop under the table with Kenny, puppets on their hands, and begin goofing around. Carolyn watches from the couch, making notes in the Bumblebee log, a notebook that parents can read each day. She tries to write down at least one thing each child has done, so parents have a way to find out what their child's day was like. It's no good asking a three-year-old, "How was your day?" It's more constructive to say something like "Did you put on a puppet show today?" Specific questions tend to elicit specific answers, and most parents are grateful for any cues they can get.

Now Denice unearths a huge lump of homemade orange salt dough and a bunch of toys to go with it: scissors, a tiny rolling pin, cookie cutters, a plastic pizza cutter, little animals. Annie and Carlos run over and sit down at the table, Carlos still wearing his negligee. Lydia takes the pizza cutter and begins making shapes from a flattened chunk of dough. Annie rolls hers out with the rolling pin. Joseph walks a plastic polar bear across his piece of dough. "Ooh, polar bear footprints," says Denice, picking up another polar bear and walking it across her dough. "Look at those shapes!"

Gradually, the other Bees drift toward the table. In his hurry to sit down, Bruce trips over a chair and stubs his toe. "Ow!" he yells, and starts to cry. Lateef throws an arm around him and rubs his head, to comfort him; it works for a second, then Bruce resumes crying, heading for Carolyn. Carolyn rubs his stomach, which does the trick, and he's off again toward the table. He watches for a few minutes, then loses interest, heading back toward the other side of the room, where he takes a tubful of little plastic vehicles from a shelf and hauls it over to a play mat marked with drawings of a road and city. Kenny sits down beside Bruce with another tubful of vehicles. Isaac joins them a few minutes later, drawn by the irresistible pull of moving wheels. His hair is short, except for one long skinny braid trailing down the back of his white hooded sweatshirt.

The three boys incorporate more and more toys into their game—a plastic dollhouse, more cars and trucks, a tubful of plastic airplanes. Kenny uses a toy tow truck to move a car back and forth, back and forth, patiently and carefully. Bruce hands him a pink airplane, and Kenny accepts it, puts it down, and continues with the tow truck. Isaac watches, waiting for his chance.

When Kenny unhooks the car from the tow truck and drives it over to a picture of a house on the play mat, Isaac reaches for the plane, but Kenny is faster. He grabs it before Isaac can and flies it over to his car, making loud airplane noises. He lands it with one wing resting on the car. "Uh-oh!" he says. Now the car takes off, chased by the plane, both of them pulling up to the dollhouse. "It's a barn!" cries Kenny. "No, it's my house!" says Isaac, desperate to break into Kenny's game. "No, it's a barn!" insists Kenny. Isaac parks his airplane in the dollhouse. "Don't get my airplane out!" he instructs the other two boys. "Don't get it out," agrees Bruce, adding, "Let's go!" "No!" says Kenny sharply. "We've got to stay here. Right?" "Yeah," agrees Isaac. Now two green plastic airplanes are parked in the dollhouse. "We could sleep at an airport," suggests Isaac. "Yeah!" say Bruce and Kenny, and the game goes on, evolving for the most part peaceably and dramatically. When a crisis comes up — Bruce pushes all the toys away from the dollhouse, to the others' consternation — the boys resolve it by themselves, negotiating terms and compromises remarkably well.

Outside, the gray wind-whipped waters of Lake Monona are just visible through the Bumblebee Room windows. Denice has seven Bees ranged around the table. "This looks kind of like the squash Max makes for lunch sometimes," observes Denice, looking at her pile of squishy orange dough. Joseph is still making polar bear footprints. Lateef, watching, decides it looks like fun and grabs Joseph's bear. Joseph shrieks. Denice calmly takes the bear away from Lateef and gives it back to Joseph. "I think you did not ask for that," she says to Lateef. "You need to ask if you want to use the polar bear." Carlos scoops up a wad of dough on one finger and wiggles it thoughtfully. Lateef pushes his chair away and crosses the room, where he joins a nerf ball game already in progress.

The nerf game gets wilder and wilder, with the soft missile hurtling around the room, chased by Lateef and Meghan. It crashes into Isaac, who tosses it back. "Keep it over here, please," says Carolyn, anxious to protect the game still evolving on the play mat. But the damage is done; the spell has been broken. Or maybe it was cracking already. Kenny, whose attention span is the shortest, calls out, "Let's get a horse!" He grabs a big teddy bear and hugs it to him, its legs dangling from between his, and starts hopping across the room.

"Giddyap, giddyap!" he shouts. Isaac and Bruce are still on the floor with the dollhouse, the toy people, the airplanes and cars and horses. "You don't want to play cars anymore?" Carolyn asks Kenny. "I am!" says Kenny, hopping the bear back over to the dollhouse. "We're going to be in a barn. We're horses!" Bruce hugs Kenny from the back and gets on the bear with him. In his excitement, he jumps up and down and slaps Kenny on the back. "No hitting!" Kenny says firmly, staring out the window toward Willy Street for a minute. Two months ago he would have burst out crying at the insult. He's come a long way since September.

Upstairs, Wendy stands by her desk, conferring with the fire inspector, who's just finished touring the building. Her half of the little office room is filled with prints and posters of flowers. Her desk faces a wall, which is decorated with color photographs from trips Wendy and her husband, Warren, have taken to the Southwest, framed in clear Lucite and hanging from straightened paper clips. And everywhere there are childish drawings, some yellowed with age, some new.

The fire inspector is telling Wendy that the emergency exit in the Bumblebee Room doesn't work, and neither does the one in the Turtle Room. After promising to come back on Monday, he leaves. Wendy sighs. One more thing to take care of, and she's already in the middle of several other crises, including negotiating with the contractor who worked on the playground. Somehow, during the renovation, the sand in the sandbox was contaminated by oil. The old sand had to be hauled away, the sandbox cleaned, and new sand delivered. The contractor insists it's not his workers' fault. "They still swear they didn't spill any asphalt," she says. "I think they must have spilled some along a tree root, which is probably a lucky thing, or else it would have spread out and contaminated a lot more sand."

Next Wendy puts on her coat, heading out to the playground to consult Amy about a confidential phone call from a parent. Louise giggles as Wendy pulls on her hat. It's a very Wisconsin hat, made from close-fitting black Polartec with a blue lining, tying snugly under the chin. "It looks ridiculous!" says Louise. Wendy keeps tying, unembarrassed. Dressed for the chilly playground, she sighs again. "I couldn't get anything done this morning," she complains to Louise. "I don't know what I would have done if I had something I actually was *supposed* to be doing today. I thought it was gonna be a nice quiet day." Louise says, "Well, that's the reason you don't have big routines to do every day. You could never get them done. Your job, Wendy, is to be a fire-

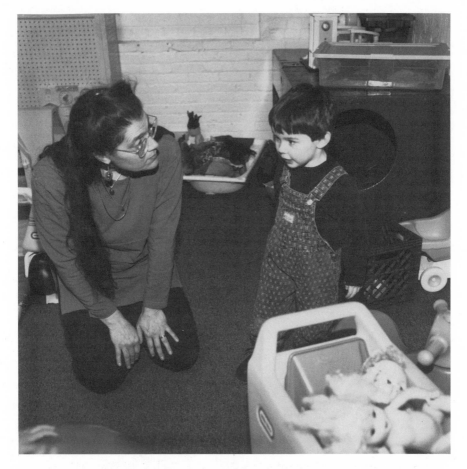

Wendy and Lexie discuss dolls in the Sunshine Room

fighter." Wendy laughs. "Me and Mirko," she says, referring to a Grasshopper who constantly draws, talks, and plays firefighter. "It's true," Louise goes on. "That's why managers like you are not supposed to have routine things they get done every day. You never could do it, and you never would get it done."

Like every financial manager the center has ever had, Louise wishes she didn't have to share an office with Wendy, not because she doesn't like her but because it's hard to concentrate in a small room with the phones ringing and the constant sound of Wendy's voice. Louise has to keep track of a lot. She does the billing, figuring out what each family owes, depending on how many kids they have enrolled, which tier they're in, and whether they're full- or part-time. Her biggest headache, though, is dealing with the government.

Each month, Louise has to keep her eye on every Red Caboose family on any kind of funding—county, city, whatever—keeping track of who pays a share and how much, whose share is going up, whose funding is being cut, and so on. Each family on funding has its own bulging file folder, paperwork galore. The center is reimbursed in the form of one big check, which is supposed to cover everyone. Many centers, and especially family child-care providers, don't track the funding reimbursements as closely as Red Caboose, and they wind up losing money; mistakes are common, and, like bank errors, they're rarely in your favor.

By 6 P.M. the center is usually quiet, the last child gone or going, the last teacher closing up. Tonight, though, a Wednesday night in mid-November, the center is packed for the annual Open House. For half an hour families eat popcorn, drink cider, and talk while their kids run wild, made bold by the novelty of being here after hours. Only a handful of families shows up, this year as other years, and it's almost always the same ones. No matter how much Wendy and the staff encourage everyone to come and talk with their children's teachers, to have a voice here, the reality is that the most disenfranchised families don't. Maybe they don't have the time or energy to spend. Or maybe, as Lateef's mother, Patricia, puts it, they feel out of place.

Patricia is a single parent, African American, with seven children, who overcame drug addiction and reunited a family split into foster care. She works two jobs to make ends meet, earning about $22,000 a year. She's got plenty to say and she knows how to say it; at the public hearing on W-2 in October, Patricia gave a moving speech about how much child care and Red Caboose mean to her. But she rarely if ever shows up at gatherings like this. "What do I have in common with the other parents at the center?" she asks flatly. "The majority of the parents are white two-parent families, double income, a house, two cars. What would I talk to them about?" Her voice sharpens into a mocking parody of yuppie-speak. "We're not going to talk about our vacations. We're not talking about flying into or out of anywhere, unless we're on drugs. We're not going to talk about how we support one another or how we wind down at the end of a day."

In reality, about a third of the kids at the center live in single-parent homes, and a quarter are on some kind of public assistance or funding. Considering Madison's small minority population, Red Caboose is pretty diverse. But it's true that it's the white middle-class families who are the most visible tonight. Only a few Bumblebee families have showed up: Todd's parents, Donna and

John; Carlos's parents, Mary and Roger; Meghan's dad, James; and Annie's dad, Mitch. Patricia is not here. Neither are Jill and Dave, or Shaunté's family, or Bruce's foster parents. They don't get to know the other parents. They don't get a chance to talk with their kids' teachers outside the harried morning drop-offs. They won't hear the presentation on High/Scope that Amy and Crystal are giving. Not that the Open House is the only way to participate, the only chance to find out more about how their kids spend their days. But it is a missed opportunity.

The Open House is over at 7:30, but not everyone gets to go home then. The negotiating teams are having their third meeting tonight. They gather in the Sunshine Room—Lynn, John, Maria, Mitch, and Val from the parents' subcommittee, and Clark, Amy, Gary, and Crystal for the union. Val holds her 10-day-old son, Aden, in her arms. Lynn facilitates, in her after-work blue jeans and a sweater. She stands by an easel in her socks, wielding a black marker, ready to write.

Wendy pokes her head into the Sunshine Room, wearing her bike helmet. "Goodnight, I'm locking up," she calls into the room. Despite the good reports she's been getting, she wants to keep her distance from negotiations. As the director she has to be able to advocate for both teachers and parents. Ever since the center unionized, she's felt tension about her role—a management person in the trenches with labor, a spy in the rank and file. It's especially uncomfortable because she was a teacher herself for so many years. As director, her pay is linked to what teachers get, so she has a stake in the outcome of negotiations. But part of what she's paid for is to take a broader view, one that encompasses the interests of everyone at the center, not just her own.

So far, interest-based bargaining has proven to be a time-consuming process. The first thing the negotiating teams did was come up with a list of issues to be settled. It's a short list: the length of the contract; whether to close the center for the Martin Luther King holiday and for Worthy Wage Day, a national day of advocacy for child-care workers; health insurance; and wages. Each team identifies its own interests on every issue and any mutual interests, and then they brainstorm together. Any and every idea, no matter how off-the-wall, is considered seriously. Then the teams analyze each idea in terms of agreed-upon standards (Is it fair? Is it feasible?). Out of this should come consensus.

Even on a seemingly minor issue like the length of the contract, the discussion can get heated. There's a lot of old history to work through. The first few union contracts were for one year, and then there were several two-year contracts. At the last meeting, Amy was given the job of finding out why the switch occurred, to see if the reason has any bearing on this year's decision. Since she's been at the center for only five years, and Clark has led all the other negotiations for the union, Amy has asked Clark to tell the group about the history of the two-year contract.

He begins in his usual blunt, provocative way. "The purpose of the two-year contract," he announces, "was to keep the union from making proposals to improve language throughout the contract." In other words, to give the union fewer chances to agitate for improvements. Silence greets this announcement, and dread. This is the kind of inflammatory remark that has derailed past negotiations, causing tension and angry feelings, putting the subcommittee instantly on the defensive. Is this session going to degenerate into the kind of name-calling and resentment of other years?

Into the breach steps Lynn. "Was that a stated purpose or an assumed purpose?" she asks. "Highly assumed," says Clark, and everyone starts breathing again. He goes on. "We didn't know why else they would not want to talk about it. The union was always against the two-year. The only thing the union ever proposed a two-year contract on was wages and economic items, in situations where we weren't getting what we wanted. But the employer wanted two-year contracts on everything."

More silence, then Clark continues. "The union has been adding noneconomic clauses year after year, trying to improve the contract," he says. "One that comes to mind is health and safety. We got beat out of the standard health and safety clause two or three times. The employer cannot promise that we're gonna have a healthy, safe place for the union. They didn't want to promise — what if something goes wrong? We said, 'Well, we'll file a grievance.' They said, 'But we don't want to have a grievance filed.' I think the employer was getting tired of all these new ways to make life better when it could just say, 'Let's set a two-year contract and we'll only do wages and economic issues.'"

"Can I take my facilitator's hat off for a minute?" asks Lynn calmly. "From the parents' perspective, I've talked to a few people about this. The only reason that I ever heard that we wanted a two-year contract was that negotiations were so awful, nobody wanted to go through it again. And I don't think that's an issue any longer."

"So where does that put us now?" adds Amy. Between them, she and Lynn defuse the tension and get the discussion back on track—the first of many close calls to come. By 8:30 the teams have come to their first TA, or tentative agreement, subject to ratification by the union and the board: the 1996 contract will run for one year. They also agree that each side will appoint a liaison, and that the liaisons will meet several times a year. The idea is to break the tightly segregated nature of negotiations, to keep talking about issues all year long, to integrate the negotiation process into the basically good relationship between staff and parents.

As John tapes the last sheet of paper onto the wall, everyone relaxes a little. It's been a long day. "I've been here 12 hours," says Amy, allowing herself a laugh. "Oh, I had a break," says Clark, not missing a beat. "I went home and dealt with my teenage daughter for a couple of hours." The room explodes with laughter, all the tension of the night and the process set free.

The next day, Wendy is upbeat about negotiations. When things don't go well she's the one who hears about it, from *both* sides. Now she can save her pessimism for the really important things, like W-2. She sits at her desk, legs crossed, reading a report written by 4-C's George Hagenauer. Even without W-2's new, higher copayments for child care, 95 percent of the centers surveyed in the county had trouble getting families to pay their share on time. More than three-quarters of the centers lost money because some families never did pay their share, and almost half said that collecting copayments caused chronic and ongoing problems. Losses averaged $3,100 a year per center, and would have been higher except that many centers drop children immediately when their parents miss a copayment.

So what will happen when copays rise precipitously under W-2? Hagenauer has two theories, which he presented to the City Day Care Advisory Board in mid-November. "First," he told the Advisory Board, "there may be an increase in the number of centers that will not accept any publicly funded clients." This is bad news for a number of reasons, but especially because under W-2, *more* poor kids will need care, not fewer. To some degree it's already happening; Wendy has heard about centers that theoretically accept kids on funding but in reality find ways to discourage their families from enrolling. Second, said Hagenauer, centers like Red Caboose serving low-income kids stand to lose a lot of money. Too much money. "Child care programs work on very tight profit margins," he explains, "and can easily go out of business with major changes in the child care market like those proposed by W-2."

This year especially the center can't afford to be caught by surprise by low enrollment. By the November board meeting, the year-to-date enrollment is 51.51 — still 1.5 slots down from the budgeted 53. The weekly numbers are beginning to rise, which is encouraging, but since December is traditionally a low month (student parents often withdraw their kids between semesters), Red Caboose isn't out of the woods yet.

The changes that might come when W-2 is enacted—and at this point it's *when*, not *if*—will have other repercussions as well. Teacher turnover, for one. Imagine you're a professional, trying to do a professional job. Now imagine that the government decrees that *anyone* can do your job, without training or experience—and because your job requires so little in the way of know-how or education, those who perform it will be paid only half of what you make. How do you feel now about yourself and your work? Does this make you want to keep doing child care? Or will this be the straw that breaks the camel's back, the one that pushes you over the edge of burnout?

Everyone doing negotiations is aware of the calamity waiting in the wings. Both sides know that the center is vulnerable, now more than ever. And that, too, contributes to the wary goodwill at the meetings.

By the fifth negotiating session in early December, the teams are working well together, and it's a good thing, because this is the big one, the night to talk about the toughest economic issue on the table: wages. The teams are under a lot of pressure to come up with an agreement tonight; once wages are negotiated, tuition raises can be set, parents can be notified, and the 1996 budget can be finalized. But they also want to do it right.

The group gathers in the Sunshine Room, as usual. By now everyone has his or her favorite spot. John, who's facilitating tonight, stands by the easel. Clark sits with his back to the door—a statement? or just a statement of purpose?—in his usual boots, leather vest, and jeans. Val holds Aden on her lap, pulling a blanket over him to nurse. Crystal sits crosslegged on the floor, in jeans and a pink sweatshirt. Mitch, Maria, and Gary slouch or sit on the floor. Lynn perches neatly on a red wooden block.

Silence falls, uncharacteristically, as everyone settles in. Clark breaks the ice by passing around a 1994 study on child-care staffing in Wisconsin, done by the National Center for the Early Childhood Work Force (NCECWF) and the Wisconsin Early Childhood Association (WECA). "This has some intriguing summaries, which I'll make available to anyone who's interested," he says. According to the report, staff turnover in the state is still high—25 percent for teachers, 40 percent for assistants—and no wonder. Child-care teachers in Wisconsin made an average of $6.50 an hour in 1994, for an annual income of $11,375—less than half the state median income. More than half of all centers offered teaching staff no health insurance benefits at all.

Red Caboose is hardly typical of centers in Wisconsin. The base wage, $7.73, is much higher than the average, and the 19 cents per year seniority benefit helps boost wages. The center even has a pension plan—a *tiny* pension plan, but it's more than most places offer. Looking at the report should make everyone in this room feel proud of Red Caboose for doing more than the minimum, being better than most—which is probably not what Clark had in mind. His role is to push, push, push for more, not to congratulate the board for what the union's already getting. So this report makes the parents here nervous, especially those who have been through other negotiations with Clark. What does he have up his sleeve this time?

John leads off the discussion by asking the staff to list their interests on wages, their underlying concerns on the subject. He towers over the easel, a permanent marker uncapped and poised in his hand. He's a tall man with lots of wavy black hair slicked into shape, a square jaw, big hands and feet.

"Staff want to be able to afford to work here," begins Amy. "To continue to afford to work here. I can afford to work here right now." John writes as she talks, taking notes on everything that's said.

"Fairness," adds Clark. "To make the equivalent of teachers in the public schools in this area."

John writes "Approaching comparable worth" on the staff's list of interests. "Other union interests?" he asks in his deep, resonant voice.

"Maintain a wage where we are able to attract and keep qualified staff," says Amy. " 'Cause there's places out there that can't attract and maintain their staffs, because they don't pay. I think Red Caboose is lucky to have this staff."

Clark adds, "Wages that will inspire other programs to try and improve theirs through unionization. If I want to go out there and organize day-care centers, and if I tell them that we're making less money than them and we've been unionized for ten years, I can't inspire them. The more workers at other day-care centers in the community that can be organized, the better it's gonna be for employees here at Red Caboose. And it serves our union interests."

In a neutral voice, John says, "Sounds to me like your interest is in organizing, and wages are the tool. Is there a way to put that so it's more of an interest?"

Clark thinks for a minute. "Raising wages sufficiently to enable future union organizing in our community," he says finally. "Wages that encourage, enhance, and support union organizing. And that's overriding and important, despite the fact that it doesn't put food on the table for our members here. It will in the future."

Gary speaks up next. He's been known to infuriate his fellow union negotiators because of his willingness to play devil's advocate. Now he says, "Here's one that I've heard expressed before. To raise wages to the highest level we can and still keep Red Caboose marketable."

"How high can we go with these wages before we start losing parents?" asks Amy.

"How about raise wages to the highest level while maintaining competitiveness?" puts in Lynn.

"I've got one more," says Clark. "Wages that will improve the perception of the importance of the profession. Society really does judge the importance of a profession based on the wage."

John finishes writing and turns to a clean page, which he heads "Parents' Interests."

"Keep day care affordable," says Mitch promptly.

"Wait a minute," says Clark. "Are we talkin' about parent interests or the corporation's interests here? Or am I confused? Are they the same thing?"

"The way I look at it," says Gary, "parents bring in a set of interests, staff bring in a set of interests. You hope by hearing both sides that they're all part of the corporation's interests, because the corporation *is* parents and staff." A point that's very well put.

Going on, Lynn suggests, "Reducing turnover, particularly as it relates to the school-age programs. We don't seem to have that problem at the center." Her daughter Ramona goes to the after-school program at Marquette Elementary.

"It's a problem here, too," says Amy. "We just haven't had that many situations where we've had to hire people. I was hired five years ago, and the only person who's been hired since then is Emily."

"But at school-age it's continuous," says Lynn.

"If you retain 'em, you don't have to attract 'em," says Clark. "Increasingly we're retaining them at after-school. It's difficult, but we've got Laura. We've got Leah. Both of them have been around for a while."

Maria raises the next interest, maintaining enrollment, and John dutifully writes it down.

"I've got one," says Lynn, looking down at a list in her lap. "Maintaining a diverse parent group. There's a direct relationship between wage increases and fee increases. We don't want to price county-funded parents out of the ball game here. We want to make sure we have parent diversity. Economic diversity."

"That's important to us, too," says Clark, and John adds it to the union's list.

"What about being competitive?" asks Maria. "I'm thinking about being competitive with other child-care centers." Silence, while everyone thinks about how to phrase it as an interest.

"Paying staff as highly as possible while remaining competitive," offers Lynn, and John writes it down. "This is one I'm not sure how it fits," she continues. "Retaining service and convenience to families. Quality child care."

Clark jumps in. "There's only one thing you can look at in the budget vis-à-vis the program that equates with quality and it's not ratios, it's not group size, it's not levels of teacher education. The only thing you can look at in that budget to see if the program is of high quality is how much the top-paid staff in the program are making. This is from a huge study done in three states."

John carefully tears off the list of parents' interests and tapes it up beside the page of union interests. "Let's look at these and see if we can find mutual interests," he says. Amy and Crystal lie on their stomachs on the floor, looking up at the wall. Mitch leans against a big red wooden box, eating Doritos out of a bag. Only Clark looks energetic, leaning forward, his face alive with light and interest.

There are plenty of mutual interests, it turns out. Both teams want to attract and retain quality staff. Both want to raise wages as high as possible while keeping rates competitive and maintaining enrollment. Both want to keep staff turnover low and wages as high as possible. In fact, pretty much all the interests overlap to some degree.

Now comes the hard part. "OK," says Amy bravely, "we've worked out our interests on wages. Now how are we supposed to start talking about raises?"

"The way I see it," says John, "while we're brainstorming options, put up everything that comes into your head, and hopefully that will generate some that are viable. Just be as creative as possible."

"There can be a million options for solutions for raises," says Amy. "Start with one penny, two pennies . . ."

"But we don't need to think just in terms of dollars," puts in Lynn. "We can talk in terms of percentages. You could come up with ideas like tying it to the cost-of-living increase, tying it to inflation. There're lots of options other than just saying, 'I want ten bucks.' "

Another small silence falls while everyone considers. Maria begins the brainstorming. "I'm looking at 'Keep staff turnover low,' " she says. "How about raising base wage?"

By seven o'clock the negotiating teams have come up with a number of possible solutions. Some are silly, some are offensive, some are practical, some are off-the-wall. All of them go onto a list as part of the brainstorming process, neither judged nor commented on, where they will serve as jumping-off points for the nitty-gritty of negotiating. The ideas include a modest raise with a guaranteed bonus at the end of the year; raising tuition the same percentage it's been raised in the past and computing wage increases from there; not increasing wages at all; expanding the center's cafeteria plan for pretax benefits. The most interesting discussion comes in response to a suggestion from Gary. "Everybody agrees that child-care workers are underpaid," he says. "The question is, How do you get more remuneration in here?" One possibility, he says, is to establish some kind of barter system. A parent who's a lawyer might offer legal services to staff at a discount; likewise auto mechanics and anyone else whose field might be of use.

"I don't think—," begins Mitch in response to this idea, but Lynn cuts in, "Hey, killer phrase!" Knocking down ideas is not allowed at this point because it inhibits creativity and brainstorming. Lynn laughs to take the sting out of her words, and Mitch accepts the rebuke good-naturedly.

Gary goes on. "Another thing I thought is, How do you make use of Red Caboose facilities here during off-hours? I would really like to brainstorm that. One idea I had is you rent out the kitchen to a group when Max isn't there."

"Or run a catering business," says Lynn, catching his drift.

"I'm not sure I feel comfortable that negotiations is the place for that discussion," says Amy.

"But it could be up there as an option," says Maria.

"How does that reflect on options for wages?" asks Amy impatiently.

Clark, who has been following the conversation with interest, says, "In generating income in ways that don't increase tuition." In fact, Gary has hit upon an essential point. So long as teachers' wages come directly out of parents' pockets, so long as the economics of child care remains a closed loop, teachers will never make as much money as public school teachers. So Gary's ideas are deeply interesting. The teams agree that it would be great to come up with alternative ways of raising revenue.

Meanwhile, though, they still need to negotiate the 1996 contract—but not tonight. There's only so much tired parents and teachers can do in one night. The group meets again two weeks later, on a Monday in mid-December, in the Sunshine Room. Mitch tears into a package of cheese puffs and pops open a can of Coke. Lynn looks businesslike, as usual, since she comes straight from her job at Madison Gas & Electric, in an olive suit and silk shirt. After some preliminary banter and discussion, the group gets down to business.

"Do we want to start throwing around some numbers?" asks Amy. "We've got to do it sometime." But no one wants to be the first to actually mention a number. If it's too high the parents might respond with sarcasm or ridicule;

too low, and the union will be offended. At least that's the way it's happened in the past.

Finally a number emerges from someone on the parents' team: 50 cents an hour. As a starting point. "Yeah, let's look at what a 50-cent raise would be!" says Amy with a laugh. "Let's look at that real seriously!" Last year's teams settled on 40 cents an hour, plus one extra sick/vacation day for staff who have worked 13 years or more, plus extra money from the center toward health insurance. So 50 cents would be terrific.

Each penny added to the base wage will cost Red Caboose $446.40. Amy, who has looked it up, reports that last year's contract was worth about $19,000. To raise that kind of money this year, the center would have to raise fees about $8 a week across the board, a little higher than last year's tuition increase. This would make Red Caboose far and away the most expensive center in Madison for many families. Amy points out that money can be raised by increasing the rates at the after-school and summer programs too. But, she adds, Lee called her today to tell her that he had serious concerns about raising the rates at after-school. The older the child, the less willing most families are to pay a lot of money for child care. Play dates and relatives become more viable options.

As the parent of a school-age child, Lynn is familiar with this phenomenon. "I can see for myself that I'm finding other options for Ramona," she says. "There's Spanish class after school, there's Brownies, and these get out at 4:30, so she spends 30 minutes at after-school. I'm starting to think, Why am I paying for this? Maybe I can come up with some alternatives."

Crystal suggests that this year's raises should at least cover the raises in health insurance premiums, which are going up about $11 a month. Since some teachers work only half-time, that means raising the base wage at least 25 cents an hour. "I think 25 cents should be a minimum anyway," says Amy. "The feeling is that anything less than 25 cents is insulting. That terrible year" — she's referring to two years ago, when negotiations broke down completely — "the first board offer was 20 cents, and the feeling among staff was, 'I can't even believe it.'"

The teams agree on 25 cents as a floor and 50 cents as a ceiling. Raising the base wage 50 cents an hour would cost about $22,000 — $3,000 more than last year's contract. Everyone agrees that any increase should be added to the base wage. "Seniority raises sound really nice on paper," explains Amy, "but it costs a heck of a lot more than adding money to the base wage. Somebody who's been working here 20 years is going to get a *huge* raise compared to somebody who's been here five years." Like Amy herself.

A lull follows while everyone doodles over figures and looks through papers. Gary clears his throat. "I just want to say this," he announces. "Under normal negotiations, my team would have shot me for saying this. But I think an end-of-the-year bonus is the best thing we could come up with. Amy will remember conversations I've had with her in the past year, when we were doing really lousy. And I was saying, 'Hey listen, I don't even know if we can expect *anything* this year. And I don't know if I would want the board to stick its neck out.' I'm a fiscal conservative. I carry no debt other than we're buying our house, so I owe something on that. But if you guys said you wanted to give me a dollar an hour or two dollars an hour, I'd be sitting here really sweating, 'cause I'd be saying, 'How are we gonna pay for that?' When you say that 25 cents is the minimum, I go along with that. But if you're talking about a lot on top of that, I would want it to go into a contingency fund, a bonus. What if it's a lousy year? How many lead teacher meetings did we sit through this year saying, 'My god, what are we gonna do? What if we lose the food program?' That's where my conservatism comes in. But I do believe that if we have a good year the staff does deserve it. That's why I would argue, 'Give us a raise we can live by, but also, man, I know everybody would love a Christmas bonus next year.' You're going to argue with me, I know."

A small respectful pause follows this speech. But not for long.

"Yeah, I am gonna argue with you, Gary," says Amy forcefully. "Because part of the reason we unionized was so that we would get a guaranteed raise every year. And if we do something where we just get a small raise and then everybody hopes for the bonus, then we get into a situation where we're not in control of our own wages anymore. This way, we know what we're getting." She turns to the rest of the group. "I have the same concerns as Gary. When I say 50 cents would be really great, I know it's not going to happen. We need to keep this place in business. But at the same time, I *work* for a living. We all do. And we all need to make as much money as we can. I think part of our job being the union is trying to find that point where we can make the most possible money and still do our jobs."

"Did we find it last year?" asks Gary. "Did we push Red Caboose to the furthest we could last year?"

"We try the hardest we can," answers Amy.

"Rather than creating an automatic system of bonuses," says Lynn, "consider that an option when we might have a not-so-good year. Let's say they wipe out the food program next year and we lose $20,000. Then next year we know things aren't going to be the same, and maybe staff can be satisfied with a lower increase and a bonus from the profit if there is one."

"So let me just pick a number," says Gary. "Say, 40 cents, which might be stretching parents. So you would say, 'OK, we're gonna go for as much as we want to give the staff, and if it's a lousy year we'll go into the red, and then next year staff might have to make it up'?"

Mitch says, "If it gets really bad, we'd have to lay people off."

"To me that would seem more palatable to staff, to go with wage increases in a so-far OK year and then have to eat the problems when they arise," says Lynn.

Gary considers. "OK," he says finally. "I can live with that."

"Another way to look at it," says Mitch, "is if we take a $20,000 hit on the food program, a couple of nickels on a raise aren't going to make a difference. We're not going to have a *little* disaster." He laughs. "We're going to have a big disaster or we're probably going to be OK."

"If we have a big disaster there's going to be a lot of other people that are going to be in the disaster too," adds Gary.

Now the group begins to seriously try to find the magic number, the number of cents per hour that will be added to the base wage next year. In past years the negotiating teams didn't talk about raising tuitions or how the money could be raised; the parent subcommittee simply said yes or no to union offers and made counteroffers of its own. But it's impossible to talk about raising wages without some idea of where the money will come from, and so the teams discuss tuitions along with everything else.

Amy has the figures for what percentage of Red Caboose's families fit into each tuition tier. Only 18 percent pay full price; 24 percent pay the next highest, then 21 percent, and 37 percent pay the lowest rates, Tier C. What will happen if Red Caboose's tuition goes up the way it did last year, $7 or $8 or $10 a week? Gary, for one, is worried.

"This is the part that frightens me," he tells the group. "How many people are we gonna lose by going up? Right now the Turtle Room is full, but for about six months they were low, and Cheryl swore it had something to do with rates. So I don't know. That question is always there."

"But if you look at our lowest rate, which is $110, that's way lower than other centers, because they don't have a sliding fee," points out Amy.

"If we raise the rates and most people are in Tier C," asks Val, "and these are mostly people I would assume are on aid, are they gonna get that made up? Are they gonna be able to stay?"

"There isn't competition for that group of people," says Mitch. "W-2, of course, screws that all up. Because if the state starts allowing them the use of that money for noncertified care, that's the disaster where it doesn't matter if we raise wages 25, 30, or 35 cents."

"And it wouldn't matter if we lowered our tuition, either, by 40 percent," says Crystal. "Nothing is going to matter with that."

Especially for the parents of two-year-olds, who already struggle to make up the difference between what Red Caboose charges in the Elephant Room and what the county reimburses. "What if we add it up as $5 for everyone but the Elephant Room and the after-school program, and raise that only $1," suggests Val. "Add that up, see what it'd be."

"Look at it this way," says Amy, the veteran of several negotiations. "If there's a $5 increase in tuition, that generates $14,000. That's just for the center. A dollar in after-school adds about $1,500. So it comes up to around $15,500. Three bucks to the summer program is about $1,700. That gives us $17,200. A 40-cent raise is $17,800."

"We could go to 38," says Mitch.

Lynn says carefully, "I went back and looked at all the averages, and the average raise has been 32 cents." There's silence as everyone looks down at his or her paper. At this point, an offer of 32 cents would almost certainly be seen as insulting.

Mitch takes the bull by the horns, pointing out that because of increases in food and other costs, the projected budget already has a deficit of about $7,000, which also has to be covered by any tuition increases. But is that really true? No one seems sure whether that money has already been accounted for in the projected budget. Lynn gets up to call Wendy, who's at home, and comes back a few minutes later.

"Here's what Wendy said," she says. "We were originally at nearly a $6,000 deficit, but there have been some changes in the budget that made it look better. We are at a $2,800 deficit right now for the 1996 budget, which we will have to make up with tuition increases."

Val starts working her calculator. "A 35-cent raise would cost $17,600," she says, "and the number we came up with before was $17,200."

Mitch, with relief and joy in his voice, crows, "We're pretty close!"

But there's one more thing to consider: raises for substitutes and LTEs. Subs earn $6.00 an hour, and LTEs, who have all the responsibilities of regular teachers but none of the benefits, make $6.80. Wendy thinks that raising these wages will make it easier to find subs and LTEs when they're needed. Every teacher at the center has struggled to find subs, and most have had the unpleasant experience of working with a sub who's less than ideal. So the union knows that raising subs' wages is in its interests, too.

Amy suggests 34 cents, with a raise for subs and LTEs—which the union can't legally negotiate, only suggest. "I'm going to say this even though I've heard people scream when it was said," she begins, "but we also get a 19-cent seniority raise. So you're getting 34 cents on the base, and when your anniversary comes up you get another 19 cents. Some people are really lucky, like me. My anniversary is the 14th of January. So I get a raise, and then two weeks later I get another raise." She laughs. "The union likes to think of those things separately, you know, that base wage is one thing and seniority is another. But when it comes down to dollars . . ."

The union decides to caucus, to debate privately over whether or not to agree to the standing offer of 34 cents on the base. After they leave the room, the parents turn to one another.

"Will our people hack it?" asks Mitch anxiously.

"I think so," says Lynn, unruffled as usual. "I got the impression they're not real happy with it. But it's nice that we went through this process."

The thing is, the two sides still had to play the same game as always on the numbers—this costs too much, this is too little, let's try to find a number in the middle that everyone can live with. At least this year the discussions are taking place in an atmosphere of trust and goodwill. "I still think it's a much better process," says Lynn later, "because we're problem-solving together. We understand each other."

After about 15 minutes the union members file back into the room and solemnly seat themselves on the floor. "You ready?" asks Amy, deadpan. She's not giving anything away. The parents nod. Mitch, unable to bear the suspense, blurts out, "You OK about it?"

"I think we've reached a tentative agreement," says Amy, and everyone in the room laughs in relief. "I think one thing we wanted to express, though," she goes on, "and you can do this when you go back to the board, is that we think it's really important that the sub and LTE raises are in here. Whatever is possible."

"I think that should be a condition," says Val. "Otherwise it's 35." The difference between 34 cents and 35 cents is $446.40—enough for a 20-cent raise for subs, with some left over for LTEs.

So the deal is struck. Four hours after the meeting begins, the teams agree it's time to go home. There are still a few things to work out, but for tonight, at least, they're done.

A week later, before the last board meeting of the year, the full union meets to ratify the agreements reached by the negotiators. The parent subcommittee and Wendy meet at the same time to do the same. The parents and Wendy seem pleased with both the process and the outcome. Rosebud looks over the numbers and nods. "This is less expensive than previous years, so that's a big plus," he says. "Luckily that's what we need."

"I think the union recognized that too," says Mitch. "This is not a cash cow year."

"They really worked hard at this," says Lynn. "We talked a lot about marketability and competitiveness, and they clearly understood that issue."

Wendy, poring over a page that shows the last few years' raises, lifts her head and says, "It's not totally out of line. It's not even the lowest raise."

"It's the lowest in terms of dollars," says Lynn, referring to the total package.

"I like it," says Rosebud, giving the agreement his seal of approval.

"Well, you've been around the longest, Rosebud," jokes Mitch.

"Well, Wendy has," counters Rosebud with a laugh.

A few minutes later the union meeting breaks up, and Gary, Amy, and Crystal come through the Bumblebee Room door. The parents begin to clap, and the teachers acknowledge the applause shyly, sitting down, ducking their heads. Amy blushes bright red. When the clapping dies down, Wendy says, "That was for a job well done!"

"It was fun," says Gary, half-amazed. "It was really fun!"

And the board meeting begins. Tonight's agenda is short but time-consuming: to finalize the 1996 budget and tuition. Wendy begins by talking about some of the political issues coming up.

"It'll be a miracle if W-2 doesn't affect us," she says, shaking her head. "The child-care food program, the latest I hear from Washington is that centers may be safe this year, but family day care won't be. The last I heard about W-2 is that they're trying to pass it in the first two weeks of January, and it'll go into effect in 90 days."

Then what? No one knows for sure. Pat Mapp, a longtime children's advocate who does community outreach through the University of Wisconsin Extension, has followed W-2 from the beginning. "We think in Milwaukee there will be a decrease in the inner city of 40 to 47 child-care providers," she told me in early December. "They will simply go out of business because low-income women will take their kids out. And that's a significant chunk of the Milwaukee capacity right where you need more child care." Mapp also thinks that staff turnover will worsen. "There's going to be a huge exodus from the child-care profession," she explained. "People will find that they cannot make a living running centers or caring for children."

In a field where it's already tough to make ends meet, W-2 has the potential to be devastating. Mapp and others are working to oppose W-2, but it's a losing battle. "We got the Catholic bishops to object to the plan because there's no safety net," she said. "Families will be thrown onto the grates, and the churches are expected to pick up the slack. There is no safety net for a percentage of people who are not going to be able to function, for whatever reason." She paused, then added slyly, "Maybe because of poor early childhood education!" For now, all that centers like Red Caboose can do is keep their slots filled and their ears to the ground.

Meanwhile, there are other problems to solve—like how to fill the financial manager's job. Louise has quit for the second time this year, this time to work for the Nature Conservancy, which can pay considerably more than Red Caboose. It's agreed that the job description will be changed, with some of the more complex accounting tasks done out-of-house by the center's accountants and a business coordinator hired to do the day-to-day billing and other tasks.

Next comes the issue of FTEs for the coming year. Should they remain at the current level, 53? Clark has told Wendy he wants to cut it to 52.5, to take pressure off in a time of low enrollment. But it's not so simple. Cutting half a slot means a loss to the center of about $3,300, with no corresponding reduction in expenses. Wendy would rather see if the center can maintain 53 slots this year. The board can always cut FTEs next year.

The 1996 budget has been gone over line by line; there's not much money to be squeezed out of it at this point. Wendy found out a few days ago that Belindah is officially leaving, trying to get medical disability. It's sad to lose a longtime teacher; the only consolation is that it saves the center money—Belindah's seniority pay, plus her pension. Wendy has hired Lauren to replace her—the first (and last) hire this year. Wages for subs will go up 25 cents, to $6.25; LTEs will go up 20 cents, to $7.00. So the board passes the budget.

Now comes the dirty work, figuring out exactly how and how much to raise tuition for 1996, to cover the projected deficit and raises for teachers and cost-of-doing-business increases. All told, that comes to $19,424—petty cash for a company like Oscar Mayer but a big piece of Red Caboose's annual budget. In the wrangling and debate that ensue, two major questions must be answered:

How much money should come from the center and how much from school-age programs? How should the tuition hikes be broken down by income tier?

After hours of discussion (including a few last-minute cuts), the board finally passes tuition increases: $1 a week at after-school (but only at Lapham, where the kids are younger and the parents more reliant on the care), $1 a day for the full-day program, $2 a week at before-school, $7 a week at summer program. At the center, the full-fee rates will go up $7; Tier A, $6; Tier B, $6; and Tier C, $5, except for two-year-olds in Tier C, whose rates will not go up. Exhausted, relieved, sore from sitting on little chairs, the parents pack up and head for the parking lot, glad to forget Red Caboose and its problems for a while.

WINTER
THE TURTLE ROOM

January

People coming in the back door of Red Caboose and looking down the hall can see straight into the Turtle Room—and the Turtle Room teachers can see them, which means that they pretty much always know what's going on in the center. And parents often peek into the Turtle Room to say hello, even those whose children have long ago grown out of the toddler stage. The babies, as the Turtles are known, are an appealing sight, especially at mealtime, ranged around the kidney-shaped table in tiny wooden chairs, brandishing spoons and bottles with varying degrees of facility.

This morning there are only three Turtles at breakfast, spread out like royalty at a banquet table. Ernestina Gonzalez, one of the teachers, presides from a grown-up-size seat at the center of the table. Next to Ernie sits 11-month-old Tom, the youngest Turtle, a small innocent-looking boy with a large, sweet face. Considering that this is only Tom's second day at Red Caboose, he seems remarkably calm. The other two at the table—Anna H.-K., who's skinny, with curly hair, and Moser, a sturdy blond boy—spoon bread pudding into their mouths like the veterans they are.

The Turtle Room is quieter than the other rooms, partly because it has fewer kids (up to eight at a time) and partly because those kids are so much less verbal than the older ones. Between ages one and two, children are just beginning to make the transition from communicating with their bodies to communicating with their words. In Piagetian terms they're still in the sensory-motor stage, still in the process of naming things, still without much in the way of concepts or logic. What they *do* have are plenty of opinions and feelings. During the year they spend here, the Turtles begin the long process of learning to express their feelings with words rather than by hitting or throwing things or having tantrums. They begin to learn the lessons that will help

them become functioning adults: how to postpone gratification, how to con-
ceptualize, how to leap from the specific to the general—all the same things
the Bumblebees are learning, just at an earlier stage.

On this cold January morning *right now* is what counts, and right now the
room is cozy and mellow. A ceiling fan sends warm air around the room. Paper
snowflakes, hanging from the ceiling tiles, dance and spin. The toddlers sit at
the table, drinking milk from plastic sippy cups. Steven, a small dark-haired
boy, comes in with his father. At 14 months, he's just beginning to walk. Caetano comes in with Emily Lyman, his aunt, who teaches in the Grasshopper
Room. He sits down with his coat still on and the smell of poop wafts over the
table. "Sorry," says Emily, and gives the boy a quick kiss before heading upstairs. Ernie takes charge, helping Caetano off with his coat, carrying him into
the tiny bathroom to be changed.

After breakfast the Turtles migrate downstairs to the play area. Like the
other rooms in the center, the Turtle Room has two distinct halves. But here
the halves are divided by a flight of stairs, a relic of the time when the Turtle
Room was a loading dock. Upstairs, at the table, the Turtles eat, color, do
puzzles. Most of the play happens downstairs, where the big toys are. The
stairs connecting the two levels are wide and easy to navigate—four steps,
then a square landing, then three steps at right angles to the others, so it's impossible to fall down the whole flight. Still, those stairs are the main reason
prospective parents don't enroll. Some parents take one look at them and walk
out. Others watch the toddlers skillfully negotiating the stairs—the littlest
ones crawling down backward, the older ones holding the railings and walking
down—and are reassured. A few years ago Wendy met with a building inspector, to see if the room could be renovated to one level. But because the room is
more than 25 feet long it has to have two exits, and both have to be level with
the ground, so children wouldn't have to go up or down steps in an emergency
evacuation. The way the side street slopes, that would be impossible.

So the Turtle Room will keep its stairs. The kids seem to like them, anyway; as they get older and more independent, they enjoy the effort and ac-
complishment of traversing the stairs on their own. And the teachers are used
to them. Cheryl Heiman, the lead Turtle teacher, sits downstairs now on the
floor, surrounded by buckets of toys. In black pants and a blue sweatshirt,
with blue slippers on her feet, she looks—well, the word is *motherly,* a blend of
soft and comforting and down to earth. Cheryl has worked at Red Caboose
for 21 years. She came to the center as a high school senior and she's been here
ever since, first in the Bumblebee Room, then in the Elephant Room, and for

the last 15 years with the Turtles. She has two children of her own at home—Kari, who's 15, and Casey, age 11. The years of experience sit lightly on her.

Moser—his real name is Brandon—catches sight of his blankie, which he left lying on the floor before breakfast. He heads straight for it, clutching it in one hand and asking Cheryl hopefully, "Nukker?" *Nukker* is his word for his pacifier, derived from the brand name Nuk. "Nukker was put away," Cheryl informs him. "It's time to play. We'll get nukker a little later." The teachers encourage the Turtles to leave their pacifiers in their lockers, except at naptime or if they get hurt; it's hard enough to understand what an 18-month-old is saying without a big rubber nipple in his mouth. Some kids are adept at talking around them or even taking them out, saying their piece, and popping them back in.

Kanna arrives, wearing black leggings and a black hooded sweatshirt, and joins the Turtles downstairs. Tom sits on the floor near Cheryl, gumming a white plastic fence. Teething is currently his main activity, and he spends hours each day exploring variously shaped and colored plastic objects with his mouth. Anna H.-K. carries a bucket of Duplos over to Cheryl and dumps them onto the floor. The two of them start putting the colored blocks together, building a mysterious shape.

Like the other rooms, the Turtle Room has a play structure. A couple of ladderlike steps climb to a wooden shelf running the length of the big window downstairs. A small wooden sliding board leads back onto the floor. The kids can stand up here and look out the window at the traffic on the side street. The really agile ones can smush their faces flat against the glass, turn their heads, and catch a glimpse of the freight trains rumbling down the tracks a block away.

At the moment Moser wants to climb the steps and go down the sliding board, but Kanna, standing at the top, blocks his way. He puts one foot on the bottom step and she pushes him in the face. When that doesn't stop him she kicks him, hard, which halts him long enough for Cheryl to catch on and intervene, holding Kanna back so Moser can get up the steps. As he brushes by he returns tit for tat, giving Kanna a little shove so she stumbles down one step, shrieking. "Kanna, are you OK?" asks Cheryl calmly from the floor. "Do you need help?" She goes over to Kanna, sets her on her feet again, and leads her away from the play structure. "I think Kanna and Moser need some distance from each other," she says diplomatically. "Kanna, what would you like to do? Would you like to build with Duplos?" The one-year-olds have few if any inhibitions about hitting or stepping on other kids, so the Turtle teachers have to intervene much more than the other teachers. The Turtles can and do hurt one another without meaning to, and they don't yet have the words to work things out themselves.

Meanwhile, Ernie finishes cleaning up from breakfast, wiping down the table, stacking the chairs, sweeping the remains of bread pudding off the floor. When she's done she calls the kids upstairs one by one for new diapers. She used to change them right after breakfast, but now, she explains, she gives them a few minutes to "do their business." Otherwise she winds up having to change half of them twice in a row.

Some teachers are good at leaving their personal lives out of the child-care room. Ernie isn't one of them. When she's depressed or upset, she shows it. This has been a rough winter for her, but now that things are looking up, she's back to her usual wisecracking self. Last month Ernie's grown daughter, Maria, had brain surgery for epilepsy and suffered a stroke on the operating table. For the last few weeks she's been in a rehabilitation home an hour away, learning to walk all over again. Ernie doesn't have a car, so she hasn't been able to see Maria much. Cheryl took her for a visit last week, and the news was good: the doctors say Maria will come back all the way, and she hasn't had a seizure since the surgery. Ernie is happier than she's been in months.

Downstairs, Stephen leans into Cheryl, cooing gently. She lifts him up and he lays his head on her shoulder, and for a moment they rock in the age-old way, Stephen curled into Cheryl with every bit of himself. "Snuggle friend," murmurs Cheryl. Then Stephen climbs down and is off again, refreshed and ready for action.

Last year, for some reason, the one-year-olds were almost all white, but this year there's more of a mix: Caetano, who's half Brazilian; Stephen, whose dad is from the Philippines; Kanna, who's half Japanese; Roberto, whose mother is Italian and father is Turkish. Caetano's about to move up, though, so Cheryl's looking for someone to fill his three-day-a-week slot. All fall, while the rest of the center was underenrolled, the Turtle Room was full. Cheryl would like to keep it that way, despite the steep tuition: a full-time slot here now costs between $138 and $171 a week.

This morning every single one of the Turtles has snot leaking unattractively from the nose. Cheryl makes frequent sallies around the room with a box of tissues. "Today is a Kleenex nightmare day," she says, and laughs. She has an easygoing air; her eyes crinkle up at the corners when she laughs, and her smile is wide and generous. But there's iron behind that smile.

Now Anna H.-K. scampers across the room, holding a yellow plastic plate

Ernie and the Turtles return from a walk as Nicholas pedals by

with a blue cup balanced on top. "Look at that!" exclaims Cheryl. "You can carry a cup without touching it!" She lifts the cup and pretends to drink, then sets it down, laughing. Anna H.-K., clearly proud of herself, puts the plate away in the toy kitchen and closes the cupboard door. Then she pushes a big floor pillow over onto its side and sits on it. Moser comes over with his own pillow and two plates, and the two of them get into it, bouncing face to face on their knees, shouting, "Whoo! Whoo!" at each other, consumed with joy. Tom, on the floor, gums a Duplo. Anna H.-K. grabs a plate from Moser. "Mine!" she says triumphantly. Tom catches sight of Ernie upstairs, fixing his bottle, and begins to cry hysterically. "Ma! Ma! Ma!" he sobs. Cheryl says to him, "Ernie's working on your bottle." She knows better than to try to pick him up to comfort him; from his first moment here Tom clearly preferred Ernie, and won't accept comforting from Cheryl if Ernie's around. It's common for one-year-olds to have a strong preference for one teacher over another, and those preferences are honored whenever possible in the Turtle Room. Some centers divide toddlers into groups where they're always with one teacher, but Cheryl deliberately mixes the kids up—so, for instance, if Ernie is out sick, Tom will know Cheryl and Sue well enough to let them take care of him.

Building this kind of independence for the one-year-olds is a big part of the Turtle Room's mission, and a big part of the reason why caring for someone else's children is emotionally different from caring for your own. "We try to help them learn that they're a person and not just somebody bonded to a mom or whoever drops them off in the morning," explains Cheryl. "To be somewhere they feel happy, safe, where they feel loved, to be able to be with their friends, to hang out, to play, to socialize. And to know that we're there for them." To begin, in other words, the sometimes painful process of growing up that every parent both longs for and dreads. This part of a child-care teacher's job is rarely if ever acknowledged by parents and by society at large. "Caregivers must be invested in children's welfare and development," write Edward F. Zigler and Mary E. Lang, "and yet be willing to release children to the care of their families at the end of the day and at the end of months or years of caregiving with a minimum amount of strain on themselves, on their charges, or on parents."[1]

Of *course* we want our children to go boldly into the world; of *course* we resent feeling like animated pacifiers, security objects loved for our symbolism rather than ourselves. And of course we want our children to love us and to need us. The one-year-old who waves good-bye without a backward glance brings both pleasure and pain to her mother's heart. The one-year-old who must be pulled, screaming, from her father's arms brings a different kind of gratification, a different pain. So much is written about how parents affect children, mold them emotionally and otherwise, about the power parents have over their young children. And they do. But we rarely talk about how children change us, their parents, the power they have over us, the corollary to our deep and abiding love.

For the moment, though, only Ernie can console Tom, who sobs bitterly in Cheryl's lap. "Hurry up, Ernie!" calls Cheryl. "You don't have that bottle warmed up yet?" She grins, which Ernie can't see, but that's OK because this kind of teasing is a regular part of the Turtle Room repartee. After a minute that feels like eternity because of Tom's escalating cries, Ernie starts downstairs with the bottle. As soon as Ernie's near enough Tom grabs the bottle and starts sucking like a drowning person whose salvation is finally within reach.

Many new parents would not be happy to watch a scene like this, especially if they have a child Tom's age. Infants and toddlers are so tender, so new, and so are first-time parents, who don't really know their children that well yet, who don't have the perspective and experience of years to tell them when to worry and when to let things go. Is it worse when the baby cries at Red Caboose than when he cries at home? Is he being ignored, neglected, let down in some critical way?

Tom's parents, Megan and Dave, seem largely unafflicted with this kind of worry. The way they tell it, anything Tom goes through here has to be better than what he experienced at home with the nanny. Dave, 37, is an engineering consultant who travels the world for weeks and months at a time, on assignment for oil companies. Megan, 35, is a forecaster at Madison Gas & Electric. The couple met on a drilling rig in the Arctic Ocean.

Megan went back to work when Tom was seven weeks old. She could have taken more leave, but, as she puts it, she got antsy. "I'm the only woman in my group," she explains. "No one put pressure on me to come back early, but I felt it was best not to highlight the biological differences." The couple found a nanny through a service, but they were unhappy from the start. "She was young and lazy," says Dave. "It was a catch-22. You get her to the house, and the service said call if you're not satisfied, so we'd call and they'd send some more résumés out, and you realize they're sending you more people just like the people you have." By the time Tom was eight months old, says Dave, he was so bored at home with the nanny that he was sleeping most of the day and staying awake most of the night with Megan. "Nannies look good on paper," says Dave, "but ours was a very lazy young lady. When you pay all that extra money you expect to have a lot of problems eliminated. You expect not to have to worry about her showing up. You shouldn't have to worry about her falling asleep on the job, which she did."

Megan had heard of Red Caboose from a colleague whose children had gone there. She looked at a couple of other centers, but she took to Red Caboose instantly. "I liked the organized chaos there," she says. "I walked in there and said, 'This is it!'" And so far, so good. Tom's first day went well, and this morning, when Megan asked Tom if he wanted to go see Ernie, his tiny feet started waving in excitement. Those feet kicked aside any little leftover worries Megan might have had about whether Red Caboose was the right place for Tom.

Infant care and toddler care have always been in the forefront of the debate over child care, a debate that has been framed in terms of "mother care" versus "other care." In the 1960s, some states actually outlawed child care for the three-and-under set.[2] Thanks to the successes of programs like Head Start, even skeptics now acknowledge the benefits of child care for preschoolers. But the years up to age three are still controversial.

The controversy centers on whether child care harms the smallest children. The key word is *attachment,* which refers to the attachment of a small child to its primary caregiver—usually the mother. One of the biggest arguments against infant care is that it threatens this bond. This argument was popularized in the 1950s and '60s by British psychiatrist John Bowlby, who had studied British children separated from their parents during the bombing blitzes of World War II and sent to live in institutional settings. Many of those children experienced emotional and psychological problems as a result of their separation. Bowlby based much of his theory of attachment on their experiences.

Bowlby's theories helped reinforce the notion that the mother-child bond is sacred but vulnerable to outside forces, a conclusion that fit with the prevailing social views of women of the time. Attachment theory is often cited as an explanation for how child care (i.e., separation from the mother) damages young children. But as psychologists and others are coming to realize, the analogies Bowlby constructed are problematic. The children who were evacuated during the war were *completely* separated from their parents for weeks and months during a stressful, dangerous, fractured time. Kids in child care, even full-time care, live with their parents and spend many waking hours with their families.

In 1991 the National Institute of Child Health and Human Development (NICHD) began a long-term study of close to 1,300 families and infants at 10 sites around the country. One of those sites is Wisconsin, where Deborah Vandell, Ph.D., is the principal investigator. The Study of Early Child Care is designed to answer, among other things, the question of whether and how child care affects a baby's attachment to her mother, using what researchers call the Strange Situation. In the Strange Situation, babies are separated and reunited with their mothers twice in the space of 25 minutes. Their reactions are used to gauge the degree and quality of their relationships with their mothers. Secure infants tend to seek comfort from their mothers and then return to play; insecure infants show a range of reactions, including ignoring their mothers, clinging to them, and showing ambivalence when reunited.

So far, the study shows that child care alone does not affect a baby's attachment to its mother. At 15 months, infants who had already been in a lot of child care and infants who had had little or no child care reacted similarly in the Strange Situation. The babies who were most insecure—those with the weakest attachment—were those at "dual risk"; not only were they in poor-quality child care, but their mothers also provided poor, insensitive care. Infants with only one risk factor—those in poor care or with unresponsive mothers—were not affected.[3]

The news that good child care doesn't hurt young kids is great, but it's not enough. Most parents also want to know if child care is *good* for kids. The answer: it can be. One group of studies done in Canada, England, Sweden, Czechoslovakia, and the United States showed that children in center-based care score better than children at home on tests of verbal fluency, memory, and comprehension. They copy designs made with blocks, solve problems, string beads, write their names, and draw circles, squares, and triangles earlier than children at home. Their speech is more complex, and their IQs are 20 to 30 points higher. By first grade, though, the other kids have caught up, leading researchers to suspect that good child care can speed up intellectual development rather than change it permanently.[4]

The benefits of preschool—ages three through five—seem to last longer. A long-term study of the High/Scope Perry Preschool Program showed that kids who had been in good preschool programs were better off as young adults than a control group who hadn't gone to preschool. Fifty percent held jobs, compared with 32 percent of the control group; 45 percent supported themselves, versus 25 percent; 18 percent had been on public assistance, compared with 32 percent of the control group. Of the preschool kids, 31 percent had been arrested for criminal acts, and 64 percent had had children; for the control group, those numbers were 51 percent and 117 percent, respectively.[5]

Other studies show that good child care can improve kids' social skills. Children in centers can identify other people's feelings and points of view at a younger age than those at home. They're more outgoing and less timid with kids they don't know. They're more helpful and cooperative, and their interactions with peers tend to be more complex, reciprocal, and mature.[6]

These social gains are understandable, considering what goes on in the Turtle Room in the course of a day. When Moser deliberately pushes Kanna off the sliding board, it's as if he's conducting a scientific experiment, studying cause and effect. The results of his experiment are immediate. "No pushing Kanna!" says Ernie to Moser. "Pushing is a no-no. That hurts your friends." She lifts Moser off the play structure and puts him on the stair landing, where he starts to bawl. After a minute he makes his way back up the steps and over to the slide, where Kanna, turning to go backward down the slide, kicks him in the head, perhaps by accident or perhaps not. Either way, Moser sits down and starts crying. "Come here, baby," says Cheryl, gathering him into her arms. "Kanna, you need to come down now. Kicking is not all right." See-ing Moser's distress, Anna H.-K. comes over to hug him, but Cheryl deflects her for a minute, giving the boy time to recover. "Anna, can you bring me the box of tissues?" she asks, and the girl goes obediently to fetch it. "This is why Ernie and I ask you guys not to hurt each other," says Cheryl, wiping away Moser's tears. "It really does hurt."

Both Cheryl and Ernie have noticed that Moser seems unlike himself this morning. "I wonder if he has an ear infection," says Ernie. The two of them watch Moser for a minute, looking for the telltale signs: ear-pulling, banging on the head, green runny nose. Ear infections are the great catchall for one-year-olds; there's always *someone* in the room who has one or is getting over one or who may be coming down with one. But there's no way to diagnose them except with a visit to the doctor.

Tom crawls over to Cheryl, looking longingly at the play structure steps. "Can you go up the stairs?" she asks him. He brings his finger gently to her mouth, and she kisses it. He pokes at her nose shyly, without force. "Are you finally going to be my friend?" she asks him. But the minute she turns her at-tention away—sorting out a disagreement between Moser and Caetano, both of whom *must* have a certain plastic truck—Tom breaks down. Cheryl lifts him into her lap, where he stands crying until Stephen, too, crawls into Cheryl's lap. Then he drops to all fours and crawls away, sniffling. "Stephen's the most huggable baby," comments Cheryl. "It's nice to have one who has time for it." Tom crawls back to her, his tears forgotten. "Here's one for you," says Cheryl, handing him a purple plastic Duplo. Tom kneels in that pose only babies and young children can manage—legs bent at the knee, splayed out on either side under the body, flat to the floor. A pose that makes most grown-ups cringe in imagined pain.

The teachers at Red Caboose, like all child-care teachers, spend a certain amount of their time taking care of kids' bodily functions. Caring for one-year-olds can sometimes seem like an endless round of changing diapers, washing

sticky hands and mouths, wiping runny or crusty noses—plus all the annoy-
ances that go with such tasks. The smell, for instance. The Turtle Room bathroom has no windows, and the ventilating fan doesn't help much. Some days,
like today, the smell is worse than others. Either someone has a poopy diaper
or the smell is wafting in from the open bathroom door.

At the top of the sliding board, Stephen suddenly starts to cry. Moser
and Caetano, standing on either side, accidentally smushed Stephen between
them. Tom sits on the floor, puffy blue slippers on his feet, chewing placidly on
a plastic cup. Ernie, seeing twin streams running from Moser's nose, attacks
them with a tissue, and the boy cries bitterly. "Mose, are you having a bad
day?" asks Cheryl from the floor. Moser points forlornly out the door of the
room, toward his locker. Cheryl knows exactly what he wants. "Oh, we don't
need nukkers," she says cheerfully. "We can't talk with nukkers in our mouth."
"I had to take mine out so I could talk," pipes up Ernie in a spirit of camaraderie. Cheryl laughs. "Nukkers is only for ni-ni now," she explains to Moser, who
has been told this before, both here and at home. A moment later he seems
to have forgotten it, absorbed by a battered doll in a high chair. One-year-olds
are still essentially preverbal, thinking in images, not yet bound to the logical
thought patterns that are shaped by language. Has Moser forgotten his lost
pacifier? It's impossible to know.

By 10 o'clock all the Turtles except Stephen are ranged once more around
the table upstairs, for what Ernie refers to as a little snackie. Lunch is served
at 11, but the teachers have found that a few crackers help the morning pass
smoothly. Out in the hall, Ernie walks back and forth with Stephen—a little
entertainment on a long cold day. January in Madison is famous for breeding
cabin fever; the holidays are over and the coldest part of the winter stretches
endlessly ahead. The Turtles don't go outside when it's cold. Ernie says it's because some of them don't have warm enough clothes, which isn't the whole
story, because Red Caboose has over the years built up a collection of clothes
in all sizes and weights. But it's hard to bundle up kids this little. Their tiny
hands slip out of mittens, they pull off their hats, they cry (and who can blame
them?) at being stuffed like sausages into stiff, bulky snowsuits.

So the Turtles stay inside all winter. What saves them and the teachers
from going crazy is the Sunshine Room, where they spend an hour most
mornings. This morning Ernie takes them down the hall after snack, leaving
Cheryl behind to sweep up cracker crumbs. The Turtles spread quietly around
the Sunshine Room. Tom crawls over to a baby carriage. Moser heads for the
Sit and Spin, twirling himself around and around. Stephen crawls over to the

back wall and pulls himself up to play with a hanging busy box. Caetano goes up the stairs into the big wooden play structure and Moser follows him, climbing all the way up into a little tower, peering down through the round opening at the teachers below and saying, in a hopeful voice, "Hi? Hi? Hi?" waiting for someone to pay attention.

Anna H.-K., all in purple, capers around the room. Evan arranges dolls in a straight line on top of a set of three red wooden steps. He's almost two, but his verbal skills are so precocious and his walk so full of swagger that he seems a full year older. When Cheryl, reading a book to a group of Turtles, asks Evan if he brushes his teeth, he points into his mouth and says distinctly, "My top molars and my bottom molars!" Cheryl cracks up. "Evan, you're too much," she says affectionately.

Most of the Turtles are enjoying the Sunshine Room, but not Tom. The morning routine is proving too long for him, and when Cheryl wipes his nose yet again he begins crying and can't seem to stop. Ernie, leaning over to scoop him from the floor, is waylaid by Moser, who inserts himself between them. Tom cries harder. By the time Ernie sits down on the floor with Tom in her lap, he's inconsolable. Kanna starts to wander out the door of the room, but Ernie retrieves her with one well-directed "Kanna!" Tom continues to cry. Nothing helps, not even Ernie's dancing, twirling him around and around the room in her arms. "Is our baby getting tired?" asks Cheryl kindly. "Mama!" he sobs, his face crumpling.

At 11 months Tom still has the soft, downy look of a duckling. The swirl of hair on the back of his head, so prominent in babies, is still easy to see. In Ernie's arms now, he begins to scream. When Ernie has to put him down for a minute the screams escalate, until he's producing shrill, ragged cries that sound as if they're coming from a frightened horse, not an angry baby. Cheryl, watching, says unflappably, "Maybe he's ready to go down." Ernie carries Tom out the door toward the Turtle Room, their progress marked by the level of screams coming down the hall. The screams get louder for a minute—Ernie has to put him down to fix his bottle. Then abruptly they stop; the bottle is inserted. Peace reigns.

The group in the Sunshine Room is getting rowdier; the morning is long for them, too. Stephen, trying to escape out of the room for the umpteenth time, is caught again by Cheryl and lifted back into the room. "Pretty soon, Stephen, you'll catch on that I keep bringing you back," says Cheryl good-naturedly. In almost the same breath, and without turning her head, she says, "Kanna, get down!" And Kanna, climbing a book rack across the room, climbs down.

At 10:30 Roberto and his mother appear at the door. He's a small boy, oddly adult-looking, his elfin face half hidden by a large pink pacifier. Anna H.-K. immediately crosses the room to greet him. "Hi!" she says brightly. She and Roberto grin at each other in the doorway, and then she leans forward and gives him a little hug. Roberto's mother, Marina, says, "I think she likes him." "Anna's our social one," says Cheryl. "She greets everyone in the morning. But she likes him, too, maybe because they sleep in the same area. They do a lot together." Stephen takes advantage of this interchange to wander into the hall again. Cheryl puts down the book she's reading to Moser and Caetano and gets up to retrieve him yet again. "Stephen, you are going to give me many gray hairs," she says, lifting him back into the room.

Tom, on the floor by Cheryl—having been soothed by his bottle—begins once more to howl. "Tom, what's the matter?" asks Ernie anxiously. "It's right here." She tries to hand him his bottle, but he screams frantically. Roberto watches curiously, his mother crouching beside him. Marina is slender and dark, with a heart-shaped face that brings to mind the young Audrey Hepburn. "Book?" she says to Kanna in her melodious Italian accent, drawing out the o's. She almost always stays with Roberto for a while in the morning, so she knows the Turtles and they know her.

Most parents, after the first few weeks, spend less than five minutes saying good-bye in the morning. Many are rushing to work, and even those who have time to linger are often relieved to go. The process of saying good-bye isn't only stressful for kids; parents suffer, too. A crying or clinging child can bring to a boil a parent's simmering guilt and ambivalence about day care. A child who turns away easily can trigger the same feelings: Is Janey attached enough to me? Does she prefer her caregivers? So the quicker the drop-off, the easier on everyone.

When Roberto started here a month ago, Marina was very protective of him. She stayed with him for half an hour or more in the morning and made sure she was back within six hours. Gradually she's relaxed; now she stays because she enjoys spending time with the children.

This morning Marina is translating a bit of Kanna's chatter for Cheryl and Ernie. "She's always saying 'Ga-ga, ga-ga,'" she tells them. "I asked her mom why, and she said it's what a duck says in Japanese." "Ohh," says Cheryl, comprehension dawning. Her attention is immediately diverted to Evan, who's climbing up the book rack. "That's only for books, it's not a ladder," says Cheryl. When he doesn't get down she adds warningly, "Evan, it's not a choice. I have to keep you safe. Ernie and I promised to keep you safe." He clambers

down one step and looks at Cheryl—bargaining. She gestures him all the way
down and then laughs. "It's hard to get the last word," she says. "Evan, take
your feet off the bookshelf please, or I'm going to come and help you. Should
I come and help you take your feet off the bookshelf?" Evan, watching her,
moves one foot very slowly toward the floor. "OK, I see one is down," says
Cheryl patiently. "Can you put the other one down please? Thank you. *All* the
way on the floor, Evan. OK, then I'll give Tom to Ernie and I'll come and help
you. OK, I'm glad you could do it on your own." Evan has stepped away from
the bookshelf at last, his testing—for the moment, anyway—done.

Marina stays about 10 minutes, watching Roberto slowly dip his toe and
then his whole self into the social waters. When she leaves at last, Roberto's up
in the tower, peeking down. "Bye-bye!" he calls, waving cheerfully. He rarely
has trouble saying good-bye in the Sunshine Room. If his mother has to leave
him in the Turtle Room, the separation is much more painful.

Wendy steps into the Sunshine Room, a prospective parent in tow, doing
the grand tour. "Oh, this place is big!" exclaims the parent. "How many kids
do you have?"

"We only have 54," says Wendy, leading her back out the door. "But we
have enough space that state licensing would let us have 145." It's hard—no,
impossible—to imagine that many kids at the center.

By 11 o'clock the Turtles are back in their room, eating tostadas. The one-
year-olds are tired and hungry, focused on the task at hand. Halfway through
the meal the third Turtle teacher, Sue Rosenbaum, arrives to help with the
transition to nap. Music plays from a boom box perched on a shelf above the
table. Ernie runs the show like a queen from her adult-size chair in the center, refilling cups of milk, dishing out crackers and beans, chips and lettuce and
carrots, while Cheryl sets up cots downstairs. When Ernie's in a good mood,
as she is today, she's wonderful with the kids, warm, vivacious, funny. Her
wavy hair is pulled back into a barrette. It's a youthful style, and she carries it
off even now, in her 40s, her dark hair spilling onto her shoulders. She wears
a large sweatshirt over dark pants, to disguise the extra weight she complains
about from time to time.

Now she leans forward to feed Tom with a spoon. His bottle lies in front of
him, within easy reach. Moser dips a stalk of broccoli into a puddle of beans
on his plate and sucks off the beans. "Acker, acker!" he demands. "Look on
your plate, what do you find?" asks Ernie, gesturing to a cracker. Tom starts to
fret, and she lifts him onto her ample lap, bouncing him gently to the music.
He gums a chunk of banana—dessert—holding it up to his mouth himself.

Ernie's best feature as a teacher is her warmth, her love for what she calls "my babies." In this she is different from, say, Clark, who is typical of a newer breed of caregiver: the articulate, college-educated professional. Ernie works in child care because she knows and loves children, and because it gives her and her family a better, more comfortable life than the one she had before she came to Red Caboose.

Ernestina Dias Gonzalez was one of 16 children born to a Mexican mother and an American father. Her parents were migrant farm workers, picking tomatoes in Florida and Ohio, sugar beets in Minnesota, cucumbers and potatoes in Wisconsin. Ernie didn't go to school much, and she quit for good when she was 11 to work in the fields with her parents and siblings. Her parents earned very little, maybe $7 a day, but Ernie and her brothers and sisters always had a place to sleep and food on the table.

When she talks about her childhood and her parents, both of whom are dead, her voice takes on a dreamy quality. Those years seem to represent a kind of Garden of Eden, a lost paradise, despite their hardships. "I treasure my life when my parents were alive," she says in English that is expressive if not always grammatical. "I'm not gonna complain because we never had a toy, we never had one, no. We didn't care for any of those things because we had Mom and Dad with us, and we were happy." Ernie adored her father, but he wasn't always around or sober. Her mother was the emotional mainstay of the home, Ernie's number one role model. "My mom was never a person who would stay home and sleep or watch TV," she says proudly. "I remember her working at the sugar beets in Minnesota. She had these sores under her armpits. Her white shirt would just be full of blood, and I would say, 'Mom, go home,' and she would say, 'No, we have to finish.' She was always strong. She took everybody else's problems. She always had something for us. Never that I remember that I went to my mom and say, 'Mom, can you help me?' and she say, 'No, I don't have time.' Even if she was doing supper or whatever, she would always stop and help." On Christmas, Ernie's mother would make a big bowl of popcorn and tell the children stories about when they were young, about their grandparents, about happier times.

Despite the family's closeness Ernie was a wild, rebellious child. At 15 she defied her mother and eloped. Five years later she was living in Florida with five children and a husband who had grown steadily more abusive. While he was in prison—for assaulting someone else, not her—Ernie's father and brother-in-law drove to Florida and brought her and her children back to

Madison, where most of the family had settled. The family closed ranks, protecting Ernie; her husband never saw her or the children again.

Ten years ago, Ernie walked into Red Caboose to apply for a job as janitor. Wendy, seeing her potential, encouraged her to start subbing and then to take the courses she needed at MATC to become a child-care teacher. Ernie's grateful to be working here, taking care of her babies, instead of dying the way one of her brothers did, with white spots all over his body from the chemicals sprayed in the fields. Her children—Pablo, Juan Antonio, Appolinaire, Maria, and Daniel—are grown now, but she's very close to her grandchildren, who spend many nights and weekends at her apartment. Red Caboose, too, has become part of her extended family, especially Cheryl and Sue. This spring will be nine years the three of them have been a team.

"We stick together like glue," she explains. For a moment the girl she was— slender, fiery-tempered, fervent—shines from her dark eyes. "When we have a problem we talk about it. We give each other comfort, say, 'If you don't feel so good I will work for you,' or 'I'll help you get a sub,' or whatever. And I think that's the way it's supposed to be." This camaraderie evolved slowly over the years. "When I started here I felt out of place," says Ernie. "I felt like everybody looked at me like, a *Mexican* here? But now I think it was just me, I was feeling so insecure."

The Turtle teachers complement one another well. Cheryl, as lead teacher, takes responsibility for the well-being of both the children and her staff. She often speaks for Ernie and Sue, neither of whom is very assertive, and they look up to her and her opinions. Ten years ago, for instance, when the teachers at Red Caboose were talking about unionizing, Ernie asked Cheryl how she should vote.

Of the three Turtle teachers, Sue is the most private. She keeps to herself, tending the kids with a rare attention. She's not an easy person for most adults to talk to, but when it comes to children she is right on the money, bringing an uncanny level of perception and insight to her care. Ernie is the joker; her humor has a sarcastic edge, which is often directed at herself. One Friday morning, for instance, she sits at the breakfast table holding a sobbing child on her lap. Natasha, the newest Turtle, is just one, and she's having trouble adjusting. Clark pokes his head into the Turtle Room on his way back from the kitchen and calls, "Hey, what a cute babe!" "Thanks!" says Ernie, not missing a beat. "He means the little one," says Cheryl, and they laugh, their repartee an old chestnut of a vaudeville routine, corny but comforting.

Stephen makes a basket — with a little help from Sue

The teachers at the center have always been close, even back in 1972, the year Red Caboose officially opened its doors. Before that the Volunteers of America ran a day-care center in the building, with two rooms of about 15 kids each. In those days Madison's east side was home to fewer students and businesses and more families. Even then the neighborhood was diverse, and so were the kids who came to Red Caboose. One parent from the early days, Lori Hayward, drove her sons every day from the far west side to Red Caboose, through the congested isthmus that connects east and west. "I didn't want them to be in those neat, tidy centers," she remembers. "I wanted something where there was some diversity."

In the early 1970s, about 6 million kids under age six had working mothers,[7] compared with close to 13 million today.[8] For the most part back then, the parents who sent their kids to full-day centers, as opposed to part-day nursery schools, were the ones who *had* to: divorced moms, single mothers, two-parent families too poor to make it on one salary. Anyone who fit into one of these categories was less than popular, even in progressive Madison. Nadine Walston, whose children Aaron and Miriam went to Red Caboose in the 1970s, remembers a neighbor who knocked on the door about two weeks after Nadine's husband moved out. The neighbor asked whether the couple was planning to get divorced. "I said, 'I don't know. That might happen,'" remembers Nadine. The neighbor asked whether Nadine was planning to stay in her house if she got divorced, and then said disapprovingly, "You realize that a divorced woman is going to make property values drop." It sounds funny now, but it wasn't then.

Nadine also remembers running into a male friend in the park shortly after her divorce. As the two of them stood chatting, catching up after months of not seeing each other, his wife — also a friend of Nadine's — stomped into the park and said, "Just remember, he's taken." "And I said, 'What the hell are you talking about?'" recalls Nadine. "And she said, 'Well, what the hell are you doing out here?' And that was it. I never spoke to them again. Divorce was just not a cool thing to do."

Day care was not a cool thing to do, either. Annie Habel, whose son Joseph started at the center in 1972, remembers one Red Caboose field trip to a fire station. As the kids watched the firefighters demonstrate various pieces of equipment, she overheard one of them saying, "Oh, the poor sad little things." Kids in day care were perceived as orphans, deprived of their parents' love and attention. They were objects of pity, walking advertisements of their parents' inability to cope. On the plus side, this perception was helpful when it came to fundraising. Nancy Burke, whose son Michael was a Red Cabooser, remembers standing in a room full of west-side types, "folks who felt terribly *sorry* for us," she says, and laughs. "I distinctly remember attorneys who wrote out checks for $50 out of pity for the poor children who had to go to the day-care center."

In the 1990s, the concept of child care is much less threatening. The vast majority of parents work because they must, and their young children must be cared for somewhere and by someone. But as a society we are still struggling with our definition of child care. Is it a service to working parents, a kind of organized babysitting? Or is it an early but essential piece of a child's education? "Traditionally, child care and education have been viewed as separate and distinct services," writes Barbara Willer, the public affairs director of the National Association for the Education of Young Children. "NAEYC believes that for young children, care and education are integrally related. . . . For very young children, all learning is embedded within a caregiving function. . . . The basic components which define high quality in a program designed to provide a good 'educational' experience to a young child are the very same qualities needed to provide a high quality experience for children while their parents are employed."[9]

Over the last 170 years child care has at various times been seen as one or the other, either babysitting or education, but rarely both. The first child-care center in this country opened in New York City in 1825, as part of educator John Griscom's experimental high school.[10] This and other "infant schools" were set up to take care of poor children whose mothers had to go out to work, and their function was largely custodial. Academic and social skills were not part of the curriculum, though infant schools did try to give poor children a "moral" education, to save them from the poverty of their parents.[11]

In the 1830s infant schools became popular with middle-class parents, and their curricula expanded to include more academic subjects like reading. But by the 1840s a number of converging ideas had lessened the prestige of and demand for infant schools. A Connecticut doctor named Amariah Brigham wrote a popular book claiming that children could be permanently damaged by "early mental excitement." Brigham believed that children were not ready for intellectual learning until age six or seven—which may be part of the reason why our public school system begins at age five. The middle-class parents who had clamored for places in infant schools withdrew their young children and their financial support.[12] And the cause of early childhood education suffered a blow from which it has yet to recover.

But by the mid-1850s the issue of child care had once again become urgent. For the first time many mothers were working outside the home or farm, in factories and mills. Day nurseries sprang up around the country. Like infant schools, day nurseries were meant as a service to working parents, a bow to economic necessity.[13] What little education they provided was aimed not at children but at adults, in the form of self-help skills that might lift families out of poverty.

It wasn't until the 1920s, when college-educated nursery-school teachers began to replace untrained caregivers in day nurseries, that education again became a priority for preschoolers. Even then there was dissent in the ranks. Infants and toddlers didn't do well in nursery schools, where teachers concentrated on academics and paid little attention to emotional needs. Gradually the youngest children came to be excluded, a trend that persists today, when many preschools have a minimum age of two and a half.

During World War II, the federal government stepped in for the first time to encourage child care. Women were desperately needed to work in munitions factories and shipyards, and as usual, the economic imperative drove social and political change. The Community Facilities Act of 1941, known as the Lanham Act,[14] funded more than 3,000 child-care centers around the country. Some of those centers provided around-the-clock care, freeing women to work swing shift and overtime. Some centers even sold cooked meals for working mothers to take home.

The quality of care in the Lanham Act centers was monitored locally, which meant that child care in the 1940s was as variable in quality as it is today.[15] Some of it was excellent. The Kaiser Day-Care Center in Portland, Oregon, was established for the children of shipyard workers. It was open around the clock, 364 days a year, and served a record 1,125 kids every day. Teachers at Kaiser were required to have a bachelor's degree in child development *plus* three years' teaching experience[16] — incredible by today's lax standards.

By 1945, more than 1.5 million American children were in child care. But the federal subsidies ended with the war. Many women went back to being homemakers, but some continued to work. By the 1960s more than a third of American women worked outside the home, but public consciousness ignored them, focusing instead on the "feminine mystique," a byword for the Victorian notion that a woman's place is in the home.[17] "When women were needed to work the fields or shops, experts claimed that children didn't need them much," writes psychologist Sandra Scarr. "But when men left home . . . to work elsewhere . . . the cult of domesticity and motherhood became virtues that kept women in their place."[18] Day-long child care was not a national priority because half the kids under three with working mothers were looked after by grandmothers and other relatives.[19]

The 1970s, when Red Caboose was established, represented a turning point. Child care—or day care, as it was almost always called then—was beginning to come out of the closet. The 1970 White House Conference on Children chose day care as the most serious issue confronting American families. The next year, one of the most progressive pieces of child-care legislation ever was passed in the House and Senate. The 1971 Comprehensive Child Development Act (CCDA) was initially a key piece of President Richard Nixon's welfare-reform legislation. The CCDA set aside $50 million for new child-care facilities and another $700 million for high-quality child care for women on welfare, including money for health and nutrition programs and neighborhood outreach. A whole new system of child-care centers was to evolve, into which existing federally funded programs like Head Start would be incorporated.

In the end, Nixon vetoed the bill, saying it would cause the "sovietization" of the American family. His veto became the keystone of a peculiarly American policy stance toward families, one that subsidizes neither at-home parents nor high-quality child care.[20] It was also a bitter disappointment to advocates for children. Still, one good thing did come out of the battle over the CCDA: child care became part of the national consciousness.

The proof was in the mainstream press, which began to debate the subject in earnest. The August 1971 issue of Reader's Digest included an article called "Day Care: How Good for Your Child?" "Long thought of as either the self-indulgence of neglectful parents or a politically suspect undermining of the father-mother-child family unit," wrote the author, James Daniel, "organized care for preschool children . . . has suddenly picked up considerable prestige."[21] More and more educators, continued the article, were endorsing child care "because of its benefits to the children themselves." The author detailed the various kinds of child care available to working parents, and came to the conclusion that large numbers of children got inadequate care, for reasons that sound eerily familiar today. Children were at risk, he wrote, "primarily because day care is expensive. It costs an estimated $1,600 a year to look after a small child in a center during a normal working day. . . . And demands that day care be improved to levels substantially beyond custodial care threaten to make it even more expensive."[22]

Two years later, Margaret Steinfels wrote a seminal history of child care that clarified the connection between social policy and reality. "Throughout its history, day care has been linked with welfare and social deviancy," she wrote in *Who's Minding the Children?* "In our society, services thus linked are almost inevitably substandard. . . . The danger of day care 'ghettos' or purely custodial institutions will be minimized if day care . . . is perceived as a normal part of the social scene and not as a 'benevolent' service oriented toward categories of families seen as especially in need of help." A page later, Steinfels pushes the point further. "Day care must be more than custodial," she wrote. "It must be developmental and educational. This point is obvious except to those who see day care primarily as a means of reducing welfare rolls."[23]

Which, of course, includes most of the legislators who support Wisconsin's welfare reform. W-2 goes even further, though, by not only sanctioning but deliberately setting up a second tier, a network of purely custodial care. In their book *Starting Right: How America Neglects Its Youngest Children and What We Can Do about It*, Sheila B. Kamerman and Alfred J. Kahn point out that the United States has always had a two-tiered system. For kids ages birth to three, child care has been linked to welfare and seen as a service to working parents; from ages three to five, it's been more generally accepted as a way to socialize children and help them get ready for school.[24]

The educational view of child care got a push in the 1960s, thanks in large part to the United States–Soviet space race. The launch of *Sputnik* sparked an American rush to catch up to the Russians in a myriad of ways. Between 1967 and 1970, enrollment in nursery schools — not to be confused with day-care centers — doubled, from a quarter to half the eligible preschoolers in the country. Programs became more academic, increasingly geared toward fostering intellectual growth. This trend was carried through by Head Start, established in 1965 to give poor children the kind of nursery school education that middle- and upper-class kids enjoyed.[25]

The terminology of child care conveys a lot about our attitudes toward other care. At the bottom of the heap in terms of prestige are day-care centers, which are seen as primarily providing a service to parents. Next come preschools, a name that implies that educational concerns are primary. Preschools have more limited hours than day-care centers, though more and more are offering "extended care" to cover a working parent's day. At the top of the heap are nursery schools, a term that usually signifies a sense of privilege and an academic focus. Traditional nursery-school schedules — two or three hours, morning or afternoon — reinforce that perception. For parents who work full or even half time, nursery school is not an option.

Right from the start, Red Caboose was clearly a day-care center, not a nursery school. One difference was the hours; it was open all day, to serve working parents. But there were other differences, too. Alumna parent Lori Hayward remembers visiting nursery schools "run by middle-class women who wore skirts and sat in big chairs." At Red Caboose, by contrast, teachers sat on the floor with kids. The unofficial dress code included tie-dye, not girdles. Cheryl Heiman came to Red Caboose as a high-school senior in 1974. A sheltered girl from rural Wisconsin, she was shocked to discover that some of the female teachers didn't wear bras. Not only that, some of the teachers were men. When Nadine Walston was looking for day care for her children after the divorce, a professor friend suggested she look for a place with women *and* men on staff. "It was a long list," she says ironically. "This was it."

Of course, there weren't many day-care centers, period, in the early 1970s—about 6,800 licensed nonprofits nationwide. About 600,000 children were in licensed centers, and of those centers only a quarter or fewer provided quality care, or anything beyond feeding kids and keeping them safe.[26] Middle- and upper-income parents tended to send their kids to nursery schools or for-profit centers; poorer families used nonprofits. Almost all the nonprofit centers were subsidized in some way through Head Start or other public funds, private funds, hospitals, philanthropic agencies, and churches. Independent centers like Red Caboose were rare.

With no educational requirements, day-care work in the 1970s was even less prestigious than it is now. "I used to get it a lot from my parents," Cheryl Heiman remembers. "They'd say, 'When are you gonna get a job that's not just babysitting?'" Male teachers were especially vulnerable to scorn. Clark's parents asked him over and over when he was going to get a *real* job. Maybe that's one reason the staff here has always been close-knit—a kind of us-against-the-world attitude. "That was one of the things you felt when you walked into the place," recalls Nadine. "There was a real sense of family."

Parents were part of that family, especially early on. Red Caboose was organized by a group of parents; the board of directors was mostly parents, as it still is. Parents stepped in to substitute when teachers were out sick (before state regulations made this illegal), painted walls, built playground equipment, and were generally involved in the day-to-day affairs of the center. They also formed lifelong friendships that crossed ethnic and class lines. The father who was a bank vice-president, the single mother on AFDC, the hippie mom who lived in a commune—they all were part of the Red Caboose community. "The unspoken rule here was that who you were as a person was what was important," says Nadine. "That meant there was all this room for people of very diverse opinions to somehow have a sense of shared life that we called Red Caboose."

One apocryphal Red Caboose story dates back to this time, about a little girl at the center whose mother had just given birth. The girl was called to the phone to hear the news. When she hung up, everyone wanted to know whether her mother had had a boy or a girl. "This was at a time when feminism was very much in, and the word *girl* was out," remembers Nadine. "So this little girl started to say, 'She had a baby —,' and then she stumbled a bit, and finally she said, 'She had a, she had a, she had a baby woman!' That just summed up Red Caboose."[27]

The times were different, but the big issues facing the center were the same as they are today: How to give staff more money and benefits. How to attract and retain good teachers. How to keep parent tuition as low as possible. How to provide top-notch child care. In a memo dated February 1974, board member Charles Gregory outlined the number one issue facing the center: "At present we are on the verge of paying $33 per week for day care, making Red Caboose the most expensive day care place in the city."

Many of the less crucial issues are still the same, too. At the December 1972 meeting of the board of directors, parents discussed "staff confusion as to exact guidelines for the celebration of Christmas holidays in the classrooms . . . in the light of the new 'no religious content in the program' policy." Twenty-three years later, the board is still discussing whether and how to integrate religious holidays into the classrooms.

One thing that *has* changed is the center's financial picture. Twenty-three years ago Red Caboose was — well, disorganized. Cheryl Heiman remembers having to sign up in a log if she "needed" a check on payday. "The teachers who signed up first got the checks," she recalls with a grin. "The rest waited until more money came in, till somebody paid a bill." It's hard to imagine a system like *that* surviving for long. When Wendy became the director in 1983, one of her first tasks was to take the financial management in hand.

"A lot of directors are quite lacking in business skills," points out Diane Adams, who for many years was the director of Madison's 4-C. "They may know how to supervise staff, but they don't have business sense. Wendy's very good with numbers. She knows how to make the budget balance. That's real rare among directors in this town." Over the years centers in Madison have come and gone like mayflies, often because of poor financial management. Right now, in January 1996, several local centers are in danger of closing. One bookkeeper "forgot" to pay payroll taxes, and now the center owes the IRS

$50,000. Another center had a long, slow enrollment crisis that just never got better; if the director had stayed on top of things, the center might have pulled through.

Upstairs now, Wendy stands in front of a row of metal cabinets, filing papers. The center has had eight withdrawals in the last two weeks, and all but one of the families were on public assistance. "One mom couldn't get child-care funding, so she's gone," says Wendy. "Somebody else didn't go to her job, so she lost her funding. Somebody else moved. We've lost Ayesha, Shaunté, Rayshaun, the twins, and Bruce and Tony will be leaving. It's wild." She looks up from her filing and shakes her head slightly, a Wendy sign of disgust. "I really feel for these families," she says. "They need the continuity so badly, more than anybody. These work programs put someone somewhere for 16 weeks and then it ends. That's what happened to Rayshaun. And then they say the family's on the waiting list for another program, so the kids *could* be back. Like maybe we'll still have an opening. It's infuriating. Luckily for us, it's a good time for filling slots."

The timing *is* lucky; having weathered months of low enrollment, Red Caboose is not in a position to lose slots now. For each slot that goes unfilled all year, the board of directors would have to raise fees at the center $2 a week—and that's *before* covering increases in utilities, insurance, food, and salaries.

In Madison, as elsewhere in the country, centers sometimes have trouble enrolling three-to-five-year-olds because of a surplus of preschool slots. Why are there too many slots for preschoolers but not nearly enough for one- and two-year-olds? In a word, money. Caring for five-year-olds can be profitable; caring for infants and toddlers is almost always a money-loser. One reason Wendy is careful to keep in touch with the other centers is so she can track the competition. This morning she's looking at an article in *Isthmus*, the weekly Madison paper, about a new 24-hour, for-profit center slated to open on the east side. The owners, a mother and son, told the reporter that they will provide high-quality care. They plan to stay open longer, serve hot meals to parents and children, and pay their teachers better to keep turnover down. They also plan to charge $145 a week for full-time preschoolers, compared with Red Caboose's top preschool rate of $141. According to the article, its owners are hoping to tap the market created by the huge influx of single mothers who will have to go to work under W-2, all of whom will be paying a percentage of the cost of care. Many of these women's children will wind up in provisional care because it's cheap. What in the world makes these owners think their center can compete?

This is one of the most bitter ironies of Wisconsin's welfare reform legislation: on one hand it creates an enormous need for child care; on the other it chops availability by depressing prices. If it's implemented as written — and now, in early 1996, there is every reason to believe it will be — W-2 will drive good providers and centers out of business just when it should be giving them more incentives to stay in the field.

To someone like advocate Pat Mapp, this just doesn't make sense. For years she's been working to make Wisconsin a national leader in the country on child-care issues. Now, she says, "all that work is down the tubes." For Mapp, W-2 represents a setback in terms of how people think about child care as well. "The whole idea was to fix in the public mind that child care is not just a welfare issue, that it cuts across income groups," she explains. In this she is battling a perception that is more than 160 years old.[28] "We wanted to make child care a majoritarian issue," continues Mapp. "*Then* you'd have something." But in the here and now it's clear that W-2 will strengthen the link between child care and welfare, not weaken it. Child care, at least in Governor Thompson's mind, is back where it's always been: a quick fix for an expensive, deep-rooted problem.

There's a full house in the Turtle Room, all eight kids actually healthy and here. More than a foot of snow fell on Madison last night, but it takes more than that to close schools and offices. The one-year-olds are in their chairs, waiting for Cheryl to dish up lunch: fish-and-veggie loaf, bread, salad, and beets. This last item is always a big hit with the one-year-olds, who often go through several bowlfuls. Cheryl's serving lunch because Ernie has taken a rare day off. After six weeks in the hospital and rehab, Ernie's daughter Maria is coming home at last. She hasn't had a seizure since December 11.

Cheryl spoons beets onto each child's paper plate, then races to the kitchen for a refill. By the time she gets back, the Turtles are clamoring for more beets. Only Tom refuses them, shaking his head and whining fretfully. He's still recovering from an ear infection, not feeling himself at all. Moser works his spoon, squeezing beets between his fingers. Anna H.-K. sucks her thumb and holds on to one ear, a sure sign that she's tired. Stephen scatters food across his part of the table, getting some into his mouth every once in a while. Forest, a girl with short brown hair and big eyes, deconstructs a beet and slowly eats it. Anna C. sits beside her, chewing methodically.

Cheryl lowers herself into Ernie's chair behind the table and cuddles Tom in her lap. Lora, who's subbing for Ernie, cuts beets for Stephen and serves

Breakfast with the Turtles: Cheryl gets a kick out of EmmaRose

Moser more fish. Moser rubs his eyes but keeps eating. Cheryl looks down; Tom's eyes are half-closed. He's going to sleep in her lap. She carries him into the bathroom to change his diaper before nap, and Lora takes her seat. Anna C. pauses in her methodical eating, looking up from her plate. "Pear, please?" she asks. "We aren't having pears yet," Lora tells her. "More bread, please?" asks Anna C., and receives it.

Lora's been subbing at Red Caboose for years, and she sounds and acts just like a regular teacher. Now, for example, she keeps up a running monologue, fueled by the occasional word or phrase from one of the Turtles. "Nice asking, Anna," she says after Anna C. requests pears yet again. Lora serves her a slice with the tongs. "Oh, Forest said more pear please. Jimmy said please.

Here's more pear for Stephen. More pear please? OK, Jimmy. What nice asking, Jimmy, and Anna, and Forest. Are you singing a song, Moser?" Moser wags his head and hums tunelessly, and Lora wags her head back, mirroring his movements. The Turtles eat pears for what feels like a very long time—10 minutes, which is about how long the Bumblebees take to eat an entire meal.

Downstairs, Tom is sound asleep in a crib, the covers pulled snugly up to his chin. Cheryl sets up the rest of the cots, then hurries to the kitchen for more pears. She deposits them on the table and starts the lullaby tape. Every day she sends up a little prayer that the continuous play function on the boom box won't choose this particular naptime to wear out.

By 11:30, when Sue comes in for her shift, only the two Annas are still at the table. Anna C. holds her cup out for more milk, then steadily eats pears. Moser—nukker in his mouth, blanket in his hand—heads downstairs toward his cot. On the floor by the table Roberto builds a tower of wooden blocks. Today's lunch was relatively neat, but still the table and the floor are a mess, milk spilled everywhere, dirty utensils strewn across the table. Cheryl kneels, mopping up milk with paper towels. She stacks dirty cups, bowls, and silverware on a tray to carry back to the kitchen. Sue starts collecting loveys, the special stuffed animals, pacifiers, and blankets the one-year-olds sleep with. She comes in from the hallway holding a small brown bear. "Ma bear!" says Anna C., breaking into a smile. "I'll put it on your cot, OK?" says Sue. "And nukkie too," says Anna anxiously. "You can have that when you're all cleaned up," Sue assures her.

There's a lot to do before the transition from play to sleep is finished. Every child gets her face and hands cleaned and her diaper changed. The table and floor must be cleaned, the chairs put away, food and dishes stacked and carried back to the kitchen. Cots must be set up, loveys fetched and arranged, lights dimmed, backs rubbed. The three teachers work together effortlessly, Lora fitting herself into the room's routines. Cheryl sprays a mixture of water and bleach onto the table and wipes it clean, except for the spot where Anna C. is still sitting, calmly chewing bread. "Mama," says Anna in her calm, breathy voice. She's not asking for her mother, only describing her, perhaps conjuring the beloved face for herself. "Daddy," she says, her face crinkling into a smile.

By 11:45 the transition is almost complete. The Turtles who sleep downstairs, which is most of them, are settled on their cots. A row of tiny sneakers, arranged neatly in pairs, is lined up at the foot of the stairs. Sue sits crosslegged on the floor between two cots, rubbing Moser's and Stephen's backs with either hand. Tom cries restlessly in his crib, and she gets up to soothe him, pulling up his blanket and patting his back a few times. He cries harder and she lifts him up, carrying him around the room as she settles other children. Jimmy, whose cot is next to the play kitchen, gets up and runs a toy car into the oven. Sue helps him back onto his cot, Tom whimpering in her arms. Upstairs, Cheryl finishes changing Anna C.'s diaper and turns off the light. The Turtle Room is warm and dark, the soft piano music hypnotic. That's part of the reason children sleep better and longer here than they do at home. Necessity helps, too, knowing that there is no real alternative to sleep. And some kids seem to check out at the center because it's not home, almost as if they can will themselves awake with their parents but don't bother at day care.

Sue helps Anna C. down the steps and over to her cot. Still holding Tom, she gives the girl her pacifier and bear and tucks her in. Anna H.-K. lies awake on her cot upstairs, sucking her thumb, a hand on one ear. "Jimmy came in late, so you might want to save him for last," Cheryl tells Sue softly. "I'll get these two down to sleep, and then I'll be down to help." Roberto and Anna H.-K. are both good sleepers, so their cots are upstairs. Light sleepers are placed downstairs, away from the door and any noise that might seep through it. Cheryl fixes a new bottle for Tom and passes it down to Sue, who deftly rearranges the boy with one arm and gives him the bottle. Calmer now, he lies in her arms, holding the bottle without drinking, watching the fan whir overhead.

Now Cheryl begins hunting for Roberto's pink pacifier. "Don't worry, Roberto, we'll find it," she says reassuringly as he sits on his cot. Tom starts to cry again, a fretful, misery-laden whine. Jimmy, on his knees on his cot, rattles the plastic dish drainer on the toy kitchen sink. Sue sits on the bottom step, rocking Tom in her arms. The pacifier found, Cheryl settles herself on the floor upstairs between the two cots. "I'll take Tom. I only have two up here," she says. Sue hands him over and then crosses the room to the toy kitchen, lifting anything that can be moved, shaken, or rattled out of Jimmy's reach. Then she lays him back down on his cot, covers him, and sits beside him, rubbing his back with one hand and Forest's with the other. Anna C., lying on her cot, sucks on one pacifier and fondles another. "Pillow," she says clearly, moving her tongue around the rubber nipple. At naptime she comes alive, naming objects and chatting to herself until the teachers have to shush her; they don't like to do that, since she's normally so quiet, but it's become something of a game.

The heat comes on with a drone of white noise. Forest is fast asleep on her cot, and so are Roberto and Anna H.-K. Cheryl rocks Tom gently back and forth, back and forth in her arms. His eyelids flutter and half-close. From downstairs come the sounds of Anna C.'s voice and Sue's murmuring answers, soothing her toward sleep. Cheryl carries Tom downstairs and lays him in his crib, asleep again. She pats his back for a minute, making sure, and covers him up. She adjusts the window shade, turns down the heat, and kneels on the floor beside Jimmy, who's almost asleep. Sue pats Anna C.'s back, firmly now, telling her without words that it's time to stop talking and go to sleep. The piano music sounds like rain, the notes spilling into the quiet, marked by Sue's percussive pats. The quiet between songs is filled by the low hum of the fan. Cheryl, patting Jimmy's back, yawns herself. Anna C. lifts her head up and looks around the room. She's the last one awake. "Go to sleep, Anna," whispers Cheryl, and finally she does. The whole process, from start to finish, has taken less than half an hour.

Naptime is one of the toughest times of day in any child-care program, but especially for the littlest kids, infants and toddlers. The one-year-olds in the Turtle Room are used to a variety of schedules. Some, like Tom, wake up every morning at five o'clock; others, like Roberto, sleep till eight or nine. It takes experience and patience to weather the prenap crankiness and exhaustion of eight children—and to put them all to sleep at the same time. The naptime routine is nothing short of amazing. Each child seems to get the individual attention he or she needs to get to sleep, whether it's a back rub, soothing conversation, or finding a lost toy or pacifier. To parents who have struggled to put one small child down for a nap, this seems nothing short of a miracle.

Giving kids personal attention is one of the things Cheryl, Ernie, and Sue do best. It's also one of the things that makes Red Caboose's toddler program exceptional. Child care in general is a labor-intensive business, and the younger the children, the more attention they need. This partly accounts for why, in this country, child care for younger kids is so controversial. Back in the mid-1960s, when Head Start was beginning to convince Americans that early childhood experiences might be important after all, infants and toddlers weren't part of the picture. The assumption was that parents or other family members would care for them at home. As a result of this and other assumptions, this country tends to ignore the needs of kids from birth to three. In 1993, 54 percent of American women with children under three were in the labor force, but programs for "under-threes"—both child care and social services—were and still are in very short supply nationwide.[29] By contrast, many European governments focus on supporting families with infants and toddlers.[30]

The Family Support Act of 1988, which was an early step toward addressing the problems of the welfare system, recognized this shortage by exempting welfare mothers with children under three from going to work or school. In their book *Starting Right*, Sheila B. Kamerman and Alfred J. Kahn write, "If, indeed, the exemption [from work] of welfare mothers with children under age three is changed to include them, federal concerns with the supply of infant/toddler care will be essential." [31] That exemption has been changed in Wisconsin and is on its way to being changed elsewhere, thanks to federal welfare reform. But infant care and toddler care are still quite scarce.

Some of the parents on the Red Caboose board would like to see the center do infant care. Cheryl is enthusiastic about the idea, despite the difficulties involved—the ratios, for instance. State licensing allows one teacher for four babies. Even Cheryl might have trouble lavishing personal attention on four babies at once. Wendy, who's raised two kids of her own and has worked with children for more than 25 years, thinks it's impossible.

Anyway, Red Caboose has been down that road before. In 1982 the center opened Purple Crayon, a program for kids under two, in the home of a teacher named Barb Hoffman. The idea was to provide Red Caboose–style care for infants in a homier setting. The setup was more like a center's, though; the three teachers had planning time built into their hours, and they worked overlapping shifts, just like the teachers at the center. Janet Grady, now the lead teacher in the Grasshopper Room, was one of the three infant teachers. She remembers Purple Crayon with great fondness. "It was fun to watch the babies interact with each other," she recalls, smiling. "Mealtimes were challenging. We had all these high chairs, and each of us would feed two kids at a time and sort of keep an eye on the ones who could feed themselves. We spent a lot of time on the floor. In fact, we hardly ever stood up!"

Because infant care is so labor-intensive, and therefore expensive, the teachers at Purple Crayon agreed to a lower hourly wage than that of those at the center. Janet didn't mind, since it was her first real job, but other teachers did. The board of directors hoped the program would break even, maybe even make a little money. But despite the lower wages, Purple Crayon lost money. Too much money. In June 1984, Purple Crayon officially separated from Red Caboose. For years afterward Barb Hoffman kept it going as a family child-care home by doing all the work herself.

Today what little infant care exists is mostly awful, a conclusion reached in a 1995 joint study done by researchers at the University of Colorado, UCLA, the University of North Carolina, and Yale University. *Cost, Quality, and Child*

Outcomes in Child Care Centers looked at centers in Colorado, California, North Carolina, and Connecticut, rating them 1, 3, 5, or 7, as described below.

1.   *Inadequate:* Children's needs for health and safety not met; no warmth or support from adults observed, no learning encouraged.
3.   *Minimal:* Children's basic health and safety needs met; a little warmth and support provided by adults; few learning experiences.
5.   *Good:* Health and safety needs fully met; warmth and support for all children; learning in many ways through interesting, fun activities.
7.   *Excellent:* Everything in "good," plus children encouraged to become independent; teacher plans for children's individual learning needs; adults have close, personal relationship with each child.[32]

The study found that care at most centers in this country is poor to mediocre, a conclusion that should horrify every family that uses child care. Almost half the infants and toddlers observed were in care rated 1 or 3—less than minimal quality. About 8 percent of the infant and toddler rooms rated a 5 or 7, good or excellent. "Babies in poor-quality rooms are vulnerable to more illness because basic sanitary conditions are not met for diapering and feeding," wrote the study's authors. "[Babies] are endangered because of safety problems that exist in the room; miss warm, supportive relationships with adults; and lose out on learning because they lack the books and toys required for physical and intellectual growth."[33]

Those losses can last a lifetime. In February 1997, *Time* magazine reported on a wave of new studies highlighting brain development. Most of the studies gave credence to what scientists had long suspected: that the human brain is literally and physically shaped by experiences (or the lack of them), especially in the first year of life. After birth, neurons in the brain go through a tremendous growth spurt; the axons and dendrites that send and receive signals explode with new synapses, many more than the brain will ultimately use. Over time, the synapses that are least used disappear. Rich, stimulating sensory experiences—plenty of things to look at and listen to and react to, plenty of warmth and physical interaction with others—trigger electrical activity in the brain, which in turn affects how many and which synapses become permanent. For instance, wrote J. Madeleine Nash in *Time*, rats living in toy-strewn cages had about 25 percent more synapses per neuron in their brains than rats kept in sterile, uninteresting boxes. And researchers at Baylor College of Medicine found that the brains of children who are rarely touched don't grow as big as they should. A baby who is deprived of experiences and love—by bad child care, parenting, or both—will feel the effects of that deprivation for the rest of her life.

Experts like pediatrician Penelope Leach make a convincing case for parental care. "However taxing an infant's care may be for his or her own family, few other caregivers are ever going to do it as well as most parents because nobody will ever do as much for money alone as they will do for that atavistic mystery we call parental love," she writes. "So why are Western societies so sure that the future lies with day care rather than with parent care?"[34] Maybe because so many American families have no choice. Without paid maternity and paternity leave, in a culture that puts few if any resources toward supporting families, many parents *have* to go back to work before their children turn three. Welfare reform only exacerbates the situation, forcing the youngest, poorest babies out of the home.

So often in the debate on child care, theory bumps up against reality, the *shoulds* knock against the *have-tos*. Parents *should* stay home with their young children—except for welfare moms, who *should* work at subminimum wages no matter how young their kids are. And theory is often used to change the nature of reality: If parents stayed home with their babies, they wouldn't *need* child care for infants. So there's no sense in making sure that what care there is is good enough; there's no sense in spending scarce government resources on identifying and regulating quality care.

High-quality child care costs money, but poor-quality child care costs, too. The High/Scope Perry Preschool Study found that for every $1 invested in its high-quality preschool program, society saves $7.16 over the lifetimes of the children in remedial education, welfare payments, and court and prison expenses.[35] And there's no way to measure the human costs. "Doing what is right and doing what is necessary to save our national skins are one and the same," says the final report of the National Commission on Children. "Our best instincts to nurture, protect, and guide the young, when translated into policies, programs, and voluntary action, benefit society as well. Some of these benefits are easily measured—healthier, better-educated children; decreased crime, violence, and their associated costs; increased tax revenues and lower welfare payments; improved productivity of American industry and labor. Others, while not as readily quantified, are equally significant—stronger families; more active, inclusive communities; a freer, fairer society; a more optimistic citizenry." [36]

It is probably harder to measure quality, to quantify it, when it comes to infant and toddler care. For older children, study after study has correlated the level of teachers' experience and education with the quality of care they provide. For younger children, other factors intervene. Back in 1973, Dr. Ronald Lally was the director of the Syracuse Children's Center, one of the few programs at the time for kids under three. He was quoted as saying that for those working with infants and toddlers, professional credentials are almost meaningless, because so much depends on the teacher's affect—how warm, nurturing, and loving she is. Or, as Cheryl Heiman puts it, the gush factor. All the courses in the world can't make up for a cold, unresponsive caregiver. The warmth of a teacher like Ernie is what babies need, and it's up to their parents to make sure they get it.

February

The Turtle Room has been laid low this week with some kind of virus. Half the kids are home with fevers. Wendy's got it, too. She's sticking around for the Monday lead teacher meeting, but then she's going home. At midday—naptime—the four teachers plus Wendy gather on the floor in the Sunshine Room. "All right," says Wendy, getting the ball rolling. "What's the good word?"

One by one, the teachers report on the past week's enrollment. "Eight," says Cheryl; that's full enrollment for the Turtles. "Eleven point six," says Gary; the decimals represent part-timers. The Bees are at 16.9, the Grasshoppers at 16.1. Wendy adds them up and gets 52.6—four-tenths of a slot down. Not bad, considering how low enrollment's been all year.

"So Bruce and Tony are leaving and the two new ones from Children's House are coming," she says, figuring on a pad of paper. Children's House, another nonprofit center on the east side, has just closed, and Red Caboose got a few of its kids. "That'll put us at 53.2."

Gary, eating onions, peas, and rice from a plastic container, says to Clark, "Geri brought up Nicholas's not being potty-trained. She's fine about moving him up, but she heard Crystal going through the roof about being real stressed out over your kids. So we were thinking about moving Emily up."

Decisions about when and how to move children from one room to another are not made lightly. The welfare of both the child and the new room must be taken into account. Nicholas's mom is concerned that her son would be one of the few Bumblebees still in diapers; what kinds of problems would that cause, for Nicholas and for the teachers? All these decisions are interconnected, which is why the lead teachers get together every week to go over changes. In order to move Nicholas or Emily from the Elephant Room to the Bumblebee Room, one of the Bees has to move upstairs to the Grasshopper Room. Clark, thinking about it, says, "I can move up Lateef. He's the guy we've primed for it for three weeks. I told him it means having group time, nap, going outside with the Grasshoppers." There is some concern, probably justified, about how well Lateef will do with the more structured schedule of the Grasshopper Room. He's been making short visits over the last few weeks, but moving up is a whole different ball game.

"It seems to me we should just tell Lateef he's moving," says Wendy.

"How do you think he'll do, Clark?" asks Janet. "Right now our kids are very into writing. We're doing these alphabet books. And when we sat down with him, he said 'No thank you' and went back to the Bumblebee Room."

"He might do fine," says Clark thoughtfully. "He was spelling his name for me the other day."

"He was also feeling left out," says Janet. "Does he have any friends in our room?"

"Teddy and him have been tight since the Elephant Room," says Clark, naming one of the Grasshoppers. "Skye and him."

"We feel bad because he just wanders around," says Janet.

Clark says, "Lateef's Lateef. He often plays by himself, but he also plays with other kids. I've seen him initiating kids in a game. 'We're gonna kill some Injuns, some Injuns, some Injuns . . .'" His voice trails off sardonically.

Wendy raises her eyebrows. "He really said that?"

"Yeah," says Clark, flipping his pencil into the air and catching it. "His strengths are that he's very good at verbal problem solving."

"We haven't seen any of that," says Janet.

"My sense is, let's give him a new locker and tell him — " begins Wendy, but Clark interrupts her.

"And love him. This is a kid who really enjoys physical cuddling."

"Patricia is for this?" asks Janet, referring to Lateef's mother.

"Yes," says Clark. "And it's my feeling he wants to be up there."

"Because after half an hour he wants to go back to the Bumblebee Room," says Janet. "He does want to be in the Grasshopper Room when it's free play time, but when it's organized play he doesn't want to do it. Our kids are getting ready for kindergarten next year, so we do a lot of that."

"Knowing Lateef," says Clark, "whether he comes now or next month, you'll have to encourage him."

The discussion moves on. "Our new business coordinator, Kathi Sullivan, starts her training tonight with Louise," announces Wendy. She looks down to see what's next on her list. "Does everyone have new sub lists?" She lists upcoming training courses being offered, and asks if anyone's interested. There's an April workshop in Lincoln, Nebraska, that costs only $65. "But how far is it?" asks Wendy, ever practical.

"About 10 hours," says Cheryl.

"That's OK," says Gary facetiously. "We get mileage reimbursement."

Wendy laughs. "Yeah, we could wipe it out with one fell swoop," she says, then gets serious again. "Someone from Meriter Hospital wants someone to give them a workshop on child's play, the teacher's role."

"They all have B.S.'s and B.A.'s," says Clark. "What do they want from us?" There is just a hint of defensiveness in his voice.

"Some of them aren't that well trained," says Wendy. "I think a lot of them are working on C.D.A.'s." The child development associate credential, or C.D.A., is the only credential specifically for child-care providers. It was developed in the 1970s as a way to recognize child-care workers with experience but no formal training or education. To get a C.D.A., a provider has to fulfill 120 hours of approved coursework and pass an "assessment," which includes monitoring. The assessment costs about $325, so many child-care workers don't bother with the degree.[37] A few years back, as part of the center's push to become nationally accredited, six teachers at Red Caboose—almost everyone who hadn't gone to college or had an associate's degree—got C.D.A.'s: Cheryl, Sue, Denice, Clark, Carolyn, Crystal. Of the other teachers, four have college degrees, one is just a few credits shy, and one has two associate's degrees.

The talk at the meeting turns to Children's House. The closing of another good nonprofit center sends a shiver around the room. The big question, as always, is why.

"All the teachers left, that's why," says Wendy.

"They only had eight families left," says Clark.

"Is Magic Penny stable?" asks Cheryl. Magic Penny, Big Oak, and Red Caboose are the only three nonprofit centers left on the east side.

"It's more stable," says Clark. "But they'll always have trouble, that tiny little center." Clark probably knows more about other centers than anyone in Madison. As a big wheel in the Wisconsin Childcare Union, he spends several nights a week meeting with child-care teachers all over the state, organizing nonunion centers, even stepping into other unions' negotiations when they break down. He's like a one-man clearinghouse on Wisconsin child care.

Wendy asks if anyone wants to add to the agenda of the upcoming all-staff meeting. Gary puts down his lunch and strokes his beard. "If there's any more money for supplies, we need more of these," he says, and holds up a little plastic baby dressed in mint green, the kind that fits into a Little Tikes dollhouse. Wendy writes it down.

"I have a question," says Clark. "If a library book is destroyed, do we have a slush fund for that?"

"It comes out of your room's educational supplies fund," Wendy tells him.

"Mumble mumble grumble grumble," says Clark cheerfully.

"If it's any consolation," says Gary, a sly smile lighting up his face, "we've paid for a few books out of our room's fund."

"So have we," says Janet.

"We don't use library books," says Cheryl. "It's cheaper for us to just buy books. We only buy edibles." She grins. The Turtles put *everything* into their mouths.

"Adds a little fiber to their diet," jokes Wendy.

After the meeting, the lead teachers linger for a few minutes, talking about W-2. "Things don't look promising," says Wendy. "We haven't made any headway on copays. In the 4-C newsletter today there was an example of a single parent making $20,000 with two kids in a licensed center, who'd be paying half her disposable income." Various advocates around the state are trying to persuade the assembly that the copays are way too high. The numbers that the Department of Health and Social Services come up with seem out of line to everyone except the department.

"The copays are an incentive to make less money," explains Clark. He and the other members of the ad hoc coalition are trying to use this fact to encourage the Republican leadership to change the copays. The whole idea of welfare reform is to structure things so that working people are better off than those on the dole, which would not be the case as things stand. "W-2 goes out of Joint Finance and into the House by March first," adds Clark. "Tommy wants it gone so he can run for vice-president. His ace in the hole is welfare reform, so he needs it passed and done so he can run."

Cheryl makes a wry face. Tommy Thompson as vice-president is not inconceivable; the *New York Times* has been hinting about the possibility, and the governor makes no secret of his political aspirations.

On that less than cheery note, the lead teachers disperse to their afternoon duties.

Valentine's Day is a Wednesday, the first day in more than a week with a full complement of Turtles. Illness is one of the major drawbacks of a child-care center, especially for working parents. The littlest kids seem to get everything. Now the kids are better but Ernie's out with strep and a sinus infection, so Lora's taking her place.

Valentine's Day is one of only two holidays officially celebrated at Red Caboose, the other being Halloween, because neither is a religious holiday (although there have been heated discussions about the religious significance of Halloween). This morning, as if in honor of the day, Anna H.-K. greeted Moser by crowing, "Hi, Precious!" She's been calling him Precious ever since, to the teachers' delight.

At 10:30 the Turtles are in the Sunshine Room. Cheryl is on the floor with Haley, a new Elephant, who's been like glue ever since she caught sight of Cheryl. Since Haley has been crying nonstop all morning, the Elephant teachers are only too happy to let her sit with Cheryl.

Roberto and Marina appear at the door at their usual time. Marina is elegant as always in a long-sleeved black sweater and slim plaid pants. Roberto shrugs off his coat and wanders over to a pile of cardboard blocks made to resemble bricks. His pacifier is in his mouth. "He calls that his *chucho*," explains Marina.

"Oh, OK," says Cheryl. "He used that word last week and I thought he meant a choo-choo train." It's hard enough to understand the Turtles as they begin the long process of acquiring language; when they're acquiring *two* languages, like Roberto, misunderstandings are inevitable.

Anna H.-K. waits patiently for a turn to hang from a wooden bar. She points to Moser and shrieks, "Precious! Precious!" Cheryl practically rolls on the floor laughing. Anna H.-K. knows a good parlor trick when she produces one. Over at the busy box, Tom cries briefly. "Tom, are you frustrated?" Cheryl calls to him. Anna H.-K. and Moser take turns lying down in a plastic tub. Jimmy, walking by Cheryl, shoves Forest out of his way. Forest sits down abruptly, her face crumpling. "Mama!" she wails. Cheryl reaches around Haley and pulls Forest onto her lap to comfort her. Lora stands beside her, observing the kids at play.

"Yesterday Wendy gave me a little project," Cheryl tells her. "There was a drawer full of files on all the kids and teachers who've ever been here. I had to clear out some of the files to make room for a new stack. And you know, some of them were from before Wendy and I were here." That would make them more than 20 years old; those kids are grown up now. Cheryl laughs. "We sat and read the names off and said, 'Wow, remember this one?'"

It's amazing that after such a long time and so many classes, Wendy can still name every single one of her kindergartners from 1974. Her longevity is one of the things that gives Red Caboose its strong sense of continuity, the fact that Wendy can and does remember back almost to the very beginning. Another factor in that continuity is the second-generation phenomenon: Emily Lyman, who teaches in the Grasshopper Room, was once a Red Caboose kid, and so was her twin sister, Alice, whose son is now at the center. Gillian was a Red Cabooser, too; now her daughter, Marley, is a Grasshopper, and she sits on the board of directors.

One of those now-grown children, Jeremy, will never forget a particular day he spent at Red Caboose more than 20 years ago, when the teachers let him and another boy take every single toy off the toy shelves and pile them in the middle of the floor. The teachers said they could do it as long as they promised to put them all away again afterward. The experience had a profound effect on Jeremy—and on his mother, Ann. "It made a big impression on me," recalls Ann, who now lives in New Jersey. "This is something not even very many parents would let their kids do. I can't *imagine* other settings where they would allow kids to do that."

Ann appreciated Red Caboose, especially after Jeremy's first day-care center, run in a church basement. "The teachers and people who ran it really acted like you were a charity case," she remembers. "You had to work, so they were helping you out. They basically thought you were on the fringes of society. They were very upper-middle-class people, running this necessary social evil."

Ann heard about Red Caboose from her friend Sue, whose son was at the center in 1973 and '74. A retired social worker in Ontario, Wisconsin, Sue remembers Red Caboose as an island of sanity in a time of social despair, a fundamentally nurturing place. For her, the symbol of it all was Wendy. "Wendy was always very special," recalls Sue. "She really stood out. She had that kind of charisma and groundedness. She was the reason I trusted the place. Somehow she *was* Red Caboose."

Twenty years later, the parents remember Red Caboose much more clearly than the kids. Which is only natural. Still, it's strange to watch the children spend their days here, moment by passionate moment, and to know that they will remember little or nothing of these years. Long before Roberto is grown, he will have forgotten marching merrily up and back in the Sunshine Room loft. Jimmy will never recall coming down the canvas slide and bumping his head. Haley will forget all about cuddling on Cheryl's lap, or Cheryl herself. These early experiences and relationships will be forgotten, but their impact will live on in the children themselves, their attitudes toward the world, their thoughts and feelings, the adults they become.

At five of eleven on this February morning Cheryl announces, "It's cleanup time, Turtles!" Few parents expect their one-year-olds to clean up, but here they really do, maybe because they're expected to and because everyone else is doing it. Stephen puts a book back on the shelf where it belongs, and Lora applauds. "Stephen is a helper, a helper, a helper," she chants. "Stephen is a helper, yes he is. Who else is a helper?" Tom pulls himself up and cruises over to a doll carriage, saying, "Da, da, da." At 12 months (his birthday was last week) he's the only Turtle who doesn't walk, though Roberto still occasionally reverts to crawling and Stephen has only recently become fluent in two-legged locomotion. Anna H.-K. stands watching in her habitual position, sucking her left thumb, stroking her right ear.

Back in the Turtle Room, Cheryl cleans hands with a damp paper towel while the children arrange themselves in chairs. They don't have assigned seats, although sometimes a teacher will sit beside a particular child to help with eating or to prevent the results of overexuberance. Sue sits on the lid of the sensory table, making holders for valentines out of paper plates and construction paper. She makes them every year, taping them onto the kids' lockers. The teachers bring in valentines for each Turtle, and sometimes a few efficient parents will bring in valentines for everyone, too.

Cheryl sits down behind the table and begins serving lasagna. The kids snatch their sippy cups, drinking greedily, as soon as Lora fills them with milk. Something about the weather—gray sky, wind, temperatures in the 20s—makes everyone enormously thirsty. "I told Stephen's dad we'd give him a lot to drink this afternoon," Cheryl tells Sue, who nods, acknowledging the implicit instruction. "He's been cranky when he gets home, and what seems to solve it is they give him a lot to drink." Roberto points to the lasagna, asking mutely for more. "Roberto likes lasagna," Cheryl says. "But then I think Roberto likes everything we serve him, even when it's overgarlicked." She's half talking to him and half to herself, the way parents and good teachers do with young children, narrating thoughts and actions, echoing the kids' words, reinforcing every tiny lingual leap they make. Roberto, with more lasagna on his plate, feeds himself with two hands, spooning up lasagna with his right hand, picking up pieces of bread with his left.

Sue sits quietly, eating from a paper plate. She's wiry-looking in blue jeans, canvas sneakers, a blue sweatshirt with three bears appliquéd on it and the logo "Beary Good Friends." The current high school volunteer, Andrea, is sleeping in the brown armchair. She's a large girl with doughy cheeks and fat braids in her hair. The high school volunteers are sometimes great, occasionally terrible. Most of them are crazy about kids, or at least like them. Cheryl doesn't want to call Andrea's school and tell them the girl is sleeping through the mornings; she tries to give Andrea as many chances as she can, encouraging her to come in and play with the kids. There's not much she can do beyond that. Falling asleep in a chair is not the lesson Andrea's supposed to be learning.

Lora sits on the floor, eating salad off a plate. "It's so yummy," she says to the Turtles. Jimmy matches her bite for bite, stopping when she does, swallowing when she does. Then he shakes his head wildly from side to side, chanting, "No no no no no," as if to rid himself of this outside influence. Tom picks up Roberto's spoon and puts it into his mouth. Cheryl gently removes it and gets Roberto a clean spoon. "Pretty soon we'll have to take down the snowflakes," she says to the Turtles when she returns. "What shall we put up? Some suns?" The paper snowflakes hang suspended on strings from the ceiling. Cheryl's being a bit optimistic; it's been known to snow in Madison in May.

At 11:20 Cheryl brings out a bowl of orange slices. She peels them one by one and hands them out. The kids don't have much appetite, maybe because of the special snack they had this morning: heart-shaped cookies brought in by Tom's mother, a combination Valentine's Day and birthday treat. Then "Mo!" says Stephen suddenly.

"Hey, a word!" says Lora.

"He's been saying a lot of words," says Cheryl. "He calls his dog Arf. Of course, that's really the dog's name." They crack up. "Listen to this," Cheryl says to Sue, and turns to Anna H.-K. "Anna, who's this?" She points to Moser. "Precious!" the girl answers promptly. The teachers crack up again.

At 11:30 Cheryl leans forward. "Andrea, yoo-hoo, it's time for school," she says, not unkindly. The girl slowly opens her eyes and heaves herself out of the chair. She pulls on her coat. "Bye-bye," chorus the Turtles. They love saying good-bye, as long as it's not to their parents.

After lunch, the Turtles migrate downstairs while Lora changes diapers and Cheryl cleans up. The cots are in place, the loveys given out. Moser, with his nukker and blanket, climbs up and down the steps of the play structure. Anna H.-K. tries closing herself into the dishwasher of the play kitchen. The fact that she doesn't fit doesn't faze her in the slightest. "Bye-bye, Precious!" she calls to Moser. Sue laughs. "We need a movie camera," she says. "People would never believe some of this stuff." Now Moser carefully opens the play microwave door, inserts his pacifier, closes the door, presses some pretend buttons, opens the door, removes the pacifier, and reinserts it in his mouth—a letter-perfect imitation of microwaving. Sue bursts out laughing. "He nuked his Nuk!" she says.

By noon all the Turtles are in clean diapers. Sue pulls down the thermal shade and turns on the heater. Cheryl lays Stephen on his cot beside the slide and covers him. "It's night-night time," she tells him. "Lora's done diapers, it's time for naps."

Upstairs, Roberto, Tom, and Anna H.-K. are hurling plastic baby dolls onto the floor. Cheryl kneels beside them, gathering up the dolls. "It's time to clean up the babies and go night-night," she says. "Ni-ni!" says Anna H.-K. cheerfully. She toddles over to a cot and lies down. Tom crawls over, peeks over the edge of the cot, and grins at her. The girl pops up to her knees. "Tom-as," she says, drawing the word out. Cheryl shakes her head. "Anna, Anna, Anna," she says fondly. The girl is lying on Tom's cot, or what the teachers hope will be Tom's cot; this will be his first day not sleeping in a crib. Cheryl lifts Anna H.-K. onto her own cot and puts Tom onto his. He promptly crawls off. Cheryl goes to the kitchen for Jimmy's medicine. "The refrigerator looks like a pharmacy," she comments when she comes back. Carolyn, the Bumblebee teacher, passes the Turtle Room on her way from the kitchen, shaking a bottle of pink medicine in either hand.

Tom, intoxicated by his new freedom, crawls over to Anna's cot and pulls her hair. "This is gonna be interesting," says Lora. Cheryl turns on the tape, soft piano music, and turns off the light. Tom crawls across the floor to the square of light made by the open bathroom door. Lora fixes his bottle and lays him on his cot. She covers him with a blanket and goes to Anna's cot to rub her back. She's picked up the unofficial Red Caboose style of rubbing backs: a firm circular motion, interspersed with equally firm pats.

Cheryl closes the bathroom door so just a thin strip of light shows under it. She sits down beside Tom, who's on his back with his bottle, and starts rubbing him, shoulder to chest, a comforting smooth motion. "Tom, one day we're going to figure out how to put you to sleep without a bottle," she murmurs. The three teachers are all rubbing backs, moving through the dim room from one cot to another, soothing, comforting, lulling the Turtles to sleep.

March

After a week of mild weather, the sudden cold snap is disorienting. It's frigid, so cold even the Grasshoppers won't play outside. Today is Friday, bagel day, and five toddlers are here for breakfast: Moser, Anna H.-K., Stephen, Tom, and Natasha, who's been coming two days a week since mid-January. Tasha's settling in nicely, especially when compared with Betty, another new part-time Turtle who cries on and off all day. As Cheryl puts it, "Betty's a challenge, but we'll get through it."

Cheryl and the other teachers tend to understate kids' distress, not out of insensitivity but because they know that parents need to be at work. If parents didn't have to work, their kids would be home with them, not spending their days in the Turtle Room. The last thing Cheryl would ever do is call a parent to come get an unhappy child. She doesn't even like to call when kids are sick. A parent who gets a call from Cheryl or Ernie or Sue *knows* there's something really wrong.

This morning Cheryl's working in the kitchen, subbing for Max, but she carries in the Turtles' breakfast tray herself: a red plastic basket filled with toast so buttery that it's soft, buttered bagel halves, and a pitcher of milk. "Tasha's mom's all worried," says Ernie as Cheryl sets the tray down. Ever since Natasha started here she's had one ear infection after another. "She says, 'Maybe I should take her out of day care,'" Ernie continues. "I told her, 'Don't worry, she'll have a few ear infections and it will get better.' She said, 'You think so?' I told her I *know* so."

Stephen tries to insert a sodden bagel piece around his pacifier. When this doesn't work, he starts to climb out of his chair. For the third time this morning, Ernie lifts him—all 20-some pounds of him—back into his chair and pushes it close to the table. Cheryl's sub arrives, Emily, a college student with straight brown hair and a calm manner. By 9 A.M. Emily's downstairs with the Turtles, playing and supervising as if she's known them for months. Ernie's in the bathroom, deep into diapers.

Andrea, the high school student, seems almost lively this morning. She slings her coat along the back of the brown chair and walks slowly downstairs, where she stands watching the children. The Turtles are playing with colored beach balls, each one almost as big as a child. Anna H.-K. carries a green ball up the steps of the play structure and sits on it in the window. Moser, watch-

On the playground, Tati and Stephen wait for their turns at the basektball hoop

ing and learning, carries his pink ball up the steps, over to the top of the slide, and sits on it, getting ready to roll down. "Let's put the ball away first," says the sub, hastily removing the ball.

Ernie, coming out of the bathroom, spots Tasha poised at the top of the stairs, ready to step down. She turns her around and helps her crawl down backward. "This is how to go down," Ernie explains, climbing down along-side the girl. "Don't get sick on me again, Tasha, or Mommy will take you out of here," she adds, patting Tasha on the back. Downstairs, Tasha promptly climbs up the play structure steps, joining the other Turtles in the window, where they're bouncing up and down and chanting, "Ma! Ma! Ma! Ma! Ma!" Stephen bumps into her and she starts to cry. "Tasha," says Ernie, hugging her. Stephen goes down the slide, banging his head at the bottom, and *he* starts to cry. Anna H.-K., balancing on her stomach on a ball, shrieks at Moser. Ernie, who's now hugging Stephen, says, "Anna, you don't have to use a whining voice. You can talk to Moser. You know how to talk very well."

Only minutes have passed since the end of breakfast, but it feels like hours. Every teacher and parent feels this sometimes, the drag of time; the remedy is to immerse yourself in the present, the here and now. So Ernie lifts a plastic tub full of bristle blocks—spiky plastic blocks that fit together to make shapes—from a shelf and sits down with it on the floor. Soon all the kids are gathered around her, jockeying for blocks.

Moser loses interest first, heading for the play kitchen. Ernie and Stephen build a shape together with bristle blocks. The sub sits on the floor with Anna H.-K., trying to get her to identify colors. "Red," she says, holding out a red block. "That's red. What color is this?" She holds up another block. She has no better luck with Moser, but that's OK; she's not really trying to test them or teach them the colors, just expose them to the idea and the words.

Ernie asks Andrea to make a bottle for Tasha. Tom, spotting Tasha on the floor with her bottle, starts to wail. "Andrea, you're gonna hate me by the end of the day, but could you go make Tom a bottle please?" asks Ernie. Moser comes over and squeezes Tom in a hug, trying to comfort him. Tom looks momentarily stunned, then scared, but he leaves off crying long enough for Andrea to bring him his bottle.

"OK, which of you children is wearing perfume?" asks Ernie as a familiar odor fills the room. She peers down the back of Moser's pants while Andrea checks Tom. It's Anna H.-K., and Ernie takes her by the hand and leads her upstairs to change her. Tasha, seeing Ernie leave, breaks into sobs. Andrea, who's showing more initiative this morning, brings Tasha her bottle, but the girl keeps crying, heading determinedly up the stairs toward Ernie. "Are you angry?" asks Ernie, reappearing with Anna H.-K. "What can I do for you? Should we go downstairs with a blankie and a baba? You got up early this morning."

Cheryl comes in from the kitchen with a cup of coffee for Ernie. It doesn't make economic sense for her to be working in the kitchen at her hourly wage, but Wendy has trouble finding subs for Max. The kitchen routine is tough; there are only two hours between breakfast and lunch, barely enough time to prepare 53 meals. But Cheryl likes the change of pace once in a while.

Downstairs, Stephen falls on his face while trying to climb into a doll crib and starts to cry. Ernie runs to fetch him, leaving Tasha upstairs in the armchair, crying for her. She carries Stephen upstairs, sets him on a blanket on the floor, and sits down herself. Moser promptly sits down in her lap. Two minutes later, when Roberto and his mom appear at the door, Moser leaps up to greet them. Marina is early today because she caught a ride downtown with her partner, Hakki, an astrophysicist at the university. Usually they walk, Marina pushing Roberto in the stroller, enjoying the fresh air and their time together.

Marina, 37, is also an astrophysicist, but unlike Hakki she does not have tenure at the University of Wisconsin. She took a leave from a tenured job in Italy in 1993 to visit him and got pregnant almost immediately. The couple agreed that she would stay in America for as long as possible, to make a family for the baby. And they are very much a family, despite the fact that Marina and Hakki have never married. But their time together is likely to be short; Marina will have to go back to Italy eventually, or lose her tenured job there.

She and Hakki are a study in contrasts. She's petite, with sharp features, everything about her clean and precise. Hakki is 18 years older, a large, genial Turk who grew up in Istanbul and lived for years in Germany. He's a handsome man with sandy hair and eyebrows, an engaging manner that complements Marina's sharper focus. He's relaxed and affectionate around Roberto, in some ways more like a grandfather than a father, maybe because this is his second family. He has two grown sons in Texas.

"When my other children were growing up," he explains with a smile, "I was too concerned about my own life. With Roberto, I know what I am. I feel like I can spend more time. It's a different feeling."

Still, the lion's share of the childrearing is done by Marina. On a typical day the three of them get up around eight and have an hour or so before Hakki leaves for work. Their small frame house has a commanding view of Lake Monona. Inside, the rooms are light, with a European elegance: Oriental rugs, a comfortable red couch facing the fireplace, a cactus in one corner of the living room. After breakfast Marina spends what she describes as "relaxed" time with Roberto; they read some books, maybe watch "Sesame Street," and then get ready to leave. She bundles him into the stroller and they walk to Red Caboose.

The very first day Marina left Roberto at Red Caboose, he cried. She waved good-bye and walked out of the room, around the corner into the hallway, and stood there listening until he stopped crying a few minutes later. Then, only then, could she walk out of the center. Now he hardly ever cries when she leaves. Marina thinks it's because he was used to having her leave him with a nanny, but who knows? There aren't any hard and fast rules for this kind of thing. So much depends on how the child is feeling that day, where he is in the ongoing struggle for autonomy, what's happening at home. Some kids pass through phases, cheerfully waving good-bye for several months, then clinging to their parents' legs every morning, begging them not to go. It's so hard for a parent to know what to think or do.

At least with the nanny Marina was home some of the time, so she knew what was going on. But on the whole she, like Tom's parents, didn't like the at-home arrangement. Over the space of a few months Roberto had two nannies, and Marina wasn't crazy about either one. Most of the young women she interviewed didn't have much experience, so Marina wound up hiring two older women. Both nannies were bossy, always telling her how she should be doing things. And they didn't provide enough stimulation for Roberto. "It's a sort of dull environment at home," says Hakki. "You can go to the park. For one year it's OK. But then—" He gestures widely.

When the second nanny quit, Marina and Hakki thought of Red Caboose. Hakki had glimpsed the center on his way to work every day, and Marina had heard about it from other mothers at the park. She went to a few other centers and didn't like what she saw. "I visited a place where they had a child who couldn't go down the stairs yet," she remembers. "They forgot him once at the top of the outside stairs, and there was ice on the stairs." Her one worry about Red Caboose was that Roberto would get sick a lot—a fact of life in any kind of group care. When a slot opened up in December 1995, Marina and Hakki enrolled.

Three months later, things are going well. "The teachers are very commonsensical," says Marina, sipping a cup of thyme tea. "They're very open to the requests of the mothers. They are clever; they have a way of making parents feel relaxed. And then they make an effort to try to remember what happened to the child during the day, especially Sue." Cheryl is probably good at that, too, she says, but Cheryl's shift ends at two o'clock, so she's never there when Marina picks up Roberto.

"Who's Cheryl?" asks Hakki. Roberto is nestled in his lap, looking at a book. Marina gives him a look, the tiniest of reproaches, and then reminds him who Cheryl is.

Like so many parents of young children, Marina is always aware of time passing, ticking off the minutes she's away from her son. She had to go back to work to keep her American visa when Roberto was four months old, but she's struggled to be with him as much as possible. This year she set up her schedule so that Roberto never spends more than six hours a day at Red Caboose. This gives Marina about four and a half hours of work time; she does the rest of her full-time job at night after Roberto goes to sleep. If she were back in her old job in Italy, she'd be putting in at least eight hours a day in her office, so she considers herself lucky. "My women colleagues in Italy have had no choice," she explains. "They feel like I have found an easy way out. It is true."

Now, in the Turtle Room, Roberto hovers near the door, gathering the inner resources to join the other children. He's wearing his favorite outfit, a pale blue sweatsuit featuring a picture of a smiling cat and the word *spacecat*. Tasha crawls over to Ernie's lap and starts to cry. "Are you tired?" Ernie asks her. "Do you want to go ni-ni?" Tom and Anna H.-K., standing at the table, begin to scuffle; Tom, who isn't quite walking yet, grabs hold of Anna to steady himself. "Let go Anna!" she says distinctly.

Marina puts a bottle of Tylenol into the plastic tub marked with Roberto's name in the bathroom. Each Turtle has a tub for diapers and other supplies. Roberto's recovering from another ear infection, and he might need Tylenol at naptime. It's not quite 10 o'clock yet, but the Turtles have been so fractious that Ernie decides to bring out a snack a little early this morning. She gets up to fetch a box of graham crackers. First Tasha, then Tom, then Stephen break down in tears. "You guys all have PMS today!" Ernie says in mock exasperation. "Oh Ernie, Ernie, what did you do?" scolds Marina facetiously. "You've been a very bad Ernie!" She's one of the few parents capable of meeting Ernie on her own sardonic level.

Tears spill out of Tasha's big blue eyes. "How's Betty today?" asks Marina, mistaking Tasha for the newest Turtle. Poor Betty. She's been here only a few days and already she has a reputation. Each child adjusts at his or her own rate to the strange new world of Red Caboose. Part of Betty's problem may be that she comes only two days a week, which gives her too much time in between to forget. Three days a week seems to be the magic number that makes it easier for kids to adjust.

Now Tasha, staring at Marina, bursts out crying again, as if being called by the wrong name is deeply disturbing. And maybe it is. When Ernie explains the mistake, Marina slaps herself on the cheek. "No wonder you're crying," she says, trying to cheer the girl up. "That's really terrible to make a mistake like that. Bad, bad, bad!" Tasha, fascinated by this display, stops crying at once and stares at Marina.

The advent of the crackers calms things down. Roberto sits in his mother's lap, sucking on his *chucho* and fingering a graham cracker. Tom alternately takes bites from a cracker and sucks a bottle. At one point he grins and reaches for Roberto's pacifier. "Tom, that's not yours, sweetie," chides Ernie. "Ah Tom, you're learning some tricks!" says Marina. Foiled, Tom wanders over to the toy piano in one corner and presses some keys. Moser sits down again in Ernie's lap.

At 10 A.M., as if by prearranged signal, the Turtles begin clustering at the door to the Turtle Room. They know it's almost time to go to the Sunshine Room. The Turtles, Elephants, and Bumblebees schedule their time in the Sunshine Room so they don't overlap. Sometimes the two- and three-year-olds spend time there together, but the one-year-olds need the room to themselves so they don't get hurt and so they can explore at their own speed. "It's not time yet, you guys," says Ernie. "We still have 15 minutes." The sub goes down the hall to find Tasha, who's wandered into the Elephant Room. Ernie sends Moser to the kitchen with instructions to ask for more crackers, please. "You have to take your nukker out of your mouth to talk," she reminds him.

Marina, meanwhile, is getting ready to take her leave. "Roberto, shall I go bye-bye?" she asks. She's careful to keep her tone light, her apprehension hidden. With Roberto still recovering from an ear infection, there's no telling how he'll react. He stares at his mother as if considering, and after a long minute he says, "Bye-bye!" "OK," says Marina with relief, putting on her coat. "Bye-bye, Roberto!" Stephen, upset by any departure, buries his face in Ernie's breasts. She hugs him fiercely, then shows him her shirt, covered with snot. "You did this to me!" she says, leaning forward and touching her forehead to his. "But I love you anyway." He giggles, and a new snot bubble forms under his nose.

By 10:25 the Turtles are in the Sunshine Room at last. Tom stands before the busy boxes, holding himself up and twirling the knobs and levers. Moser and Stephen come over to join him. Roberto thrusts a brown and yellow dinosaur at Anna H.-K. and makes a gargling sound low in his throat, a big smile on his face. Anna fondles her own dinosaur reflectively. The two of them move across the room to a green plastic mountain, made for toy cars, where Roberto gathers an alpine menagerie of plastic animals — several dinosaurs, a gorilla, a pig, a sheep, and a cow. He moves the gorilla in and out of the tunnel in the mountain. "Whoo, whoo!" he says, aping the sound of a train. He has to interrupt his game to defend his turf when Moser, sidling up behind him, makes off with a plastic sheep. Roberto shrieks and grabs Moser's shirt sleeve. From across the room Ernie says, "Moser, Roberto was playing with that. I bet you two can play together." Moser drops the sheep and escapes. Next Stephen toddles over and tries to take an animal. Roberto protests loudly and wordlessly, using his voice as a kind of weapon to keep the other boy away. Stephen gives back the animal, and a minute later the two boys are sitting together, trading plastic animals and toy cars back and forth.

Peace reigns fleetingly, but then the boys get into trouble, both of them howling and grabbing at the same toy. Some child development experts would say that expecting one-year-olds to share is like expecting snow in July — it could happen but it rarely does. Cheryl, with 15 years of experience with one-year-olds, pays little attention to experts. "My goals for the Turtles are to learn to get along with other kids, how to be in the same space, to share the space, learning how to take turns," she explains. "They do at this age, even though people tell you they don't." Last year Cheryl, Ernie, and Sue took an infant-toddler class at MATC together, hoping to learn some new things. "The teacher had never worked with one-year-olds," says Cheryl with exasperation. "She had never worked with anybody under the age of three. And they had hired her from the university to teach this course at MATC. We went and did our time and laughed all the way home at night." She smiles, but it's really not funny. Sometimes Cheryl thinks she and some of the other Red Caboose teachers should get together and teach a course. They certainly have a unique perspective. Few teachers in Madison — in the *country* — have been doing child care for as long as Cheryl.

The Turtle teachers are remarkably effective in teaching the toddlers the rudiments of social negotiation — sharing, empathy, compassion — but there's only so much a one-year-old can manage. Especially a tired one-year-old. Emily, the sub, deftly separates Stephen and Roberto, distracting each with his own toy. Anna H.-K. stands in the middle of the room, sucking her thumb, holding onto one ear. Tasha is in Ernie's lap, looking at a book, barely holding herself together. Whenever Ernie has to put her down for a second, Tasha bursts into tears. By 11 o'clock, as the toddlers clean up the Sunshine Room, she's openly sobbing. Even Moser, the powerhouse, looks exhausted, crying as he puts away plastic dinosaurs.

Back in the Turtle Room, the children sit in their little wooden chairs. As Ernie comes around with wet cloths, washing faces and hands, Emily entertains them with a stuffed duck. From down the hall comes the sound of Kenny's crying, and then a second later Carolyn's voice, saying, "Kenny, sit down and take a time-out. You don't hit me." Roberto rubs his eyes and lays his head down on the table. He revives a bit when Cheryl carries in lunch—cheese, cottage cheese, bread, spinach, salad, and milk. He pinches up cheese and salad, holding a piece of bread carefully in his left hand. When he drops his spoon, he says, "Uh-oh," and leans over to see where it fell. Sue, who arrives during lunch, puts down her paper plate and goes to the kitchen to get another spoon.

By 11:40 Tasha's out cold on her cot, lying on her back, arms up over her head in surrender to sleep. Emily cleans the table while Sue changes diapers. One by one, the Turtles make their way to their cots. Moser lays himself down, nukker in his mouth. Sue carries Tom downstairs and settles him in the crib, where he lies on his back, staring at the ceiling and fretting. He often sleeps on a cot now, but naptime is easier on him—and on everyone—when he's in the crib, especially when he's not feeling well. Stephen, on his cot, clutches one of his sneakers, doing and undoing its Velcro closure. Sue finishes the last two diapers and settles the toddlers on their cots. She hands Roberto his *chucho* and goes down the hall to the kitchen to make Tom a new bottle, which she hands him in his crib, covering him up once more. Emily puts on a lullaby tape and sits down on the floor between Moser and Stephen, rubbing a back with each hand.

But the naptime peace doesn't last long. At noon, while the other kids are still going down, Tasha wakes up, frets for a minute, then starts to cry in earnest. She's wide awake, but she still looks exhausted. Emily tries to lay Tasha down, but she immediately cries again, so Sue picks her up and holds her, rocking her on the floor, then stands up—no mean feat, scrambling up from the floor with a 25-pound kicking weight in your arms—and, still holding Tasha, fixes her a bottle. At last they sit down in the armchair together, Tasha in Sue's arms, sucking at her bottle, taking in the sights of the dim quiet room. The process is repeated again and again—Tasha falls asleep, Sue lays her down, she startles awake a few minutes later and howls. By 1:30, Tasha is awake for the fourth time, this time in a stroller in the hall, sucking on yet another bottle. "She's fighting it," says Sue, pushing her wearily up and back, up and back in the hall. "She's really tired, she's rubbing her eyes, but she won't go to sleep."

By now Moser and Anna H.-K. are up from their naps, sitting on the couch in the hall. The first thing Moser said when he woke up today was, "Anna! Anna!" When Sue carried him out into the hallway and he caught sight of his friend, his eyes lit up. "Precious!" Anna crowed, greeting him. Now they sit on the couch together, eating crackers. When they start getting restless, Sue brings them down the hall to the Sunshine Room, leaving Tasha, asleep in the stroller, with the sub, who's watching the nap room. Sue sits down on the floor in one corner, and Moser plops into her lap to hear a book. Anna H.-K. toddles over and stands listening, one hand holding a cracker, the other down her pants.

Clark puts his head and then the rest of his body into the room. He's full of ginger today, having just made what he considers yet another outrageous discovery about W-2. This one concerns the provisionally certified caregivers. "It turns out that the Department of Health and Social Services discovered that it will need a waiver from the feds to charge less for a lower level of quality," he says. "And it turns out it's not in the capabilities of the feds to grant a waiver on that particular item. So now if we get provisional level 2 certification, those caregivers would be reimbursed at the same level as level 1 certification." In other words, the state would pay the neighbor next door who's never done child care before the same amount of money that it would pay Red Caboose to care for a low-income child. "It gets worse and worse," continues Clark. "Now not only will you not have any training, but you can be reimbursed at exactly the same level as somebody with training. So what they're gonna do is change the regulations so you don't need training to do child care." It's hard to believe that would actually happen in Wisconsin, with its relatively strict licensing regulations. Maybe Clark is being melodramatic. Maybe this is all part of the legislative process, this push and pull, scare and retreat, part of coming to a compromise. Or maybe it's reality.

"The union will not tolerate level 2 care in our community," Clark goes on. "We would be out there encouraging provisional providers to get training or certification. Failing that, we would aggressively picket, telling parents that this provider has no training and you can buy something just as good for the same money, and at least the provider is trained and has annual visits." He pauses, surveying the room, the toddlers happily engaged with Sue, a few Elephants clambering up and down the ladder into the play structure. "We got to throw the bums out," says Clark suddenly. "We have to tell them, 'Don't destroy the children.' More and more I'm talking to providers, directors at group centers, teachers at centers, who are saying, 'What we must do is make W-2 fail instead of trying to fix it in a way that'll make it work.' And the way to make it fail is to hold the line on tuition. If you hold the line on tuition instead of dropping it, thereby dropping your quality, poor folks who are participating in W-2 will not be able to afford child care, period. It seems very cruel that they would be forced to put their kids in who knows what kind of care, but it would shine a spotlight on the fact that we should not compromise quality in order to fit kids into slots. It's the old story about those folks who would like to go across and get the rain, but who don't want to break the earth and who don't want the thunder. It can't rain without thunder."

At three o'clock Tasha wakes up again and starts screaming. The rest of the Turtles are in the Sunshine Room, beginning the process of cleanup. Olga, a volunteer in the Elephant Room, wheels in a big TV in a wooden case and turns its face to the wall. Moser and Anna H.-K. promptly sit down in front of it, ready for Friday afternoon movies, which won't actually begin for another hour. By the time Olga's finished arranging the room for movies Tasha is asleep yet again, this time on the couch in the hallway. Olga sits down beside her to keep an eye on her.

Snack is served at 3:30, apples and graham crackers, and the Turtles devour it. At four o'clock, as the kids from the other rooms are heading toward the Sunshine Room for movies, Marina shows up to claim Roberto. He's on the changing table, and she takes over, finishing up. Tom, in a great mood after his long nap, uses a toddler-size chair as a walker, pushing it in front of him all around the room. After Roberto leaves, only four Turtles are left; Ernie, back for the second half of her shift, walks Moser and Anna H.-K. down the hall for movies. Tom and Stephen are too young to sit still for movies, so Sue takes them into the Elephant Room to play, a rare treat. Stephen stands mesmerized in front of a wire cage, watching Harry the guinea pig chew a cardboard tube. Then he and Tom follow Sue to the play kitchen area. Sue sits down in a small plastic chair at a table and pretends to make toast in a wooden toaster. She sets out plates and cups, and the three of them cook and serve an imaginary meal, Sue just as absorbed in the play as the children.

The back door bangs open, and a minute later Ernie's daughter Maria appears. She's wearing a crash helmet, walking slowly down the hall with a cane. But she's walking! Sue and Wendy and other teachers come out into the hallway to greet her and exclaim over her progress. Maria sits down on the couch.

She often comes and waits for Ernie to get off work so the two of them can walk home together down Willy Street.

At 4:30 there is a small influx of two-year-olds, those who have reached the end of their attentiveness. Moser's mother comes to pick him up, leaving only three Turtles. Sue puts a Raffi tape into the tape recorder, and the noise level begins to rise to its usual Friday afternoon level. Ernie brings Anna H.-K. in from the Sunshine Room. She walks up the three steps into the small Elephant Room loft and looks down over the children, those in her care and the rest. On the tape Raffi sings, "Tingalayo, run little donkey run," and Ernie begins dancing, standing in the pillow loft, shaking her body from side to side gracefully. Moving to the music, snapping her fingers, singing along, still there's a kind of elemental sadness to her. Behind the wisecracks, the jokes and sarcasm, lies an enormous grief.

On a Wednesday morning the Turtles are eating oatmeal with raisins, honeydew melon, and milk. Outside, March is a lion, bringing driving snow and freezing air, the last of a long, cold winter. Every child in Madison has cabin fever. On Willy Street a woman has rammed her car into a telephone pole, and a police car and ambulance have just arrived at the scene of the accident. Ernie goes out to see the action, and Cheryl slips into her place. Stephen watches Ernie disappear and then breaks into huge, gulping sobs, trying to climb out of his chair. "Just till Ernie gets back," says Cheryl, sitting him down again firmly.

Moser, at the table, opens his mouth as widely as possible and roars like an enraged lion, much to the dismay of Jimmy, sitting beside him. Moser ignores Jimmy's wordless protests and roars again. "Moser, are you listening to Jimmy?" asks Cheryl. "Daddy," says Jimmy, apropos of nothing. "Your daddy went to work," says Cheryl with a smile. "He probably said, 'Bye, Jim, have a good day!' " Jimmy's father owns a chain of Mexican restaurants in town. He's one of the few dads who regularly drops his child off in the morning. Soon the rest of the Turtles at the table—Anna C., Forest, Anna H.-K., plus Stephen and Moser—are babbling "Mama!" and "Daddy!" with varying degrees of linguistic facility. Cheryl talks to each of them in turn, telling them that their mother and father went to work. When she gets to Moser, she notices that he's spilled his oatmeal. "Moser, look at that," she tells him. "You're dripping oatmeal all over your nukker." Moser lifts his nukker, examines it contemplatively, and shakes it. Globs of oatmeal fly in all directions, which Cheryl tactfully ignores.

Oatmeal is one of the messier meals, and the toddlers need a good washing before they can go downstairs and play. Anna C. is the last child at the table, as usual, eating in her slow, methodical way, her jaws working silently, her lips pursed into a rosebud, a blue pacifier upended beside her bowl. Ernie wipes down the table and sweeps around Anna C. as Forest emerges from the bathroom, sobbing pitifully, holding out her hands in supplication. "You *have* a new diaper," says Ernie, who has just changed her. But she knows very well what Forest wants. Sighing, Ernie puts down the broom, goes into the bathroom, and comes out with a clean plastic diaper—Forest's current lovey. The girl carries it reverently downstairs, her tears drying on her cheeks. Next it's Moser's turn to cry; he's lost his nukker downstairs. "Did you leave it in the window?" asks Cheryl. "Why don't you go look for it?" From outside comes the sound of a train whistle, long and low. "What do I hear?" says Cheryl. "I hear a choo-choo! I do!" The Turtles clamber all over one another, trying to get to the big window downstairs. If Tasha were here she'd be the first one at the window, dying to see the train. But she's gone for good. Two weeks ago, after yet another ear infection, her mother took her out of the center. Did she quit work? Is she going to try and work at home around Tasha's naps? No one knows for sure.

After the excitement, Moser goes back to puttering in the play kitchen. Stephen and Jimmy play companionably with a toy high chair until Stephen suddenly starts crying. Cheryl, coming in from the Sunshine Room, says, "Stephen, what happened? Jimmy, Stephen's crying. That tells me he probably has an owee. Where does he have an owee?" Jimmy obligingly indicates Stephen's face, where moments ago he poked him, entirely without malice. "Did you hurt Stephen?" asks Cheryl. "Yup," says Jimmy placidly. "We don't hurt our friends," says Cheryl. "That's not OK. Stephen, do you need a hug?" She folds Stephen into her arms. Anna C., meanwhile, climbs the steps to the play structure and slides down, grinning shyly. "Bookie," she says at the bottom. She picks up a book of zoo animals and begins naming the ones she knows: parrot, elephant, tiger, lion, bear. The ones she doesn't know—owl, camel—she calls *ducky.*

Outside the window, tiny snowflakes fall steadily. Cheryl folds up the crib and puts it away; Tom's out with the flu for the third day in a row. Anna C. and Forest sit together on the floor, playing with a tub of bristle blocks. Anna C. piles several brightly colored blocks on top of one another. "On," she says, adding one to the pile. "Off," she says, taking one away. She makes a tower with a handful of blocks, gets up, comes back with a stuffed dinosaur, and puts it on top of the tower. "Likes it," she says, and grins. Anna H.-K. starts to cry, tussling with another child over a toy turtle. Cheryl pulls another turtle off the shelf. There are at least two of every well-loved toy in the room: two pull-along turtles, two sets of blocks, two teapots, two dolly high chairs. Much of the room's toy budget goes toward making sure the Turtles don't *always* have to share.

Now five of the children—the two Annas, Jimmy, Stephen, and Forest—are making precarious bristle-block structures. Jimmy piles three green blocks together and points the whole construction at Moser, making shooting sounds. There was a time when the teachers would have instantly put a stop to any kind of gun play. But they've found over the years that the more they try to restrain kids from violent toys, the more doggedly the kids pursue them, resorting in the end to the old standard, the thumb and index finger. You can't very well take *those* away. So now the teachers' unspoken policy is to ignore weapon play unless it's causing a specific problem.

By the slide, Ernie is playing with Stephen, the two of them handing plastic plates back and forth. "Do you like dishes?" she asks him. "You can come home and wash mine." Bored now with the blocks, the Turtles begin heading upstairs, climbing or crawling up the steps. Jimmy throws his head back and looks up at the ceiling over the table, pointing. "What are you looking at, Jimmy, the fan?" calls Cheryl, releasing Anna H.-K. from the bathroom. "The fan is going round and round. What are you looking at? The snowflakes? I hope pretty soon we can take those snowflakes down and put up something more like spring. Some sunshine?" She looks around the room, sniffing. "Well, who needs a diaper change?" she says. Ernie, still sitting downstairs with Stephen, calls up, "Smells like an Anna H.-K." Cheryl peeks down the back of Anna H.-K.'s pants. Ernie's right. Ernie's almost always right about poop. Not a talent that would be worth much on the job market, but it sure comes in handy in the Turtle Room.

Moser clambers back down the stairs, bored by the lack of action upstairs, maybe getting away from the dreaded changing table. He pulls a huge green ball from one corner and starts rolling it around the room. Anna C., following his lead, tries to lift a pink ball out of the corner, but it's stuck. She spends several minutes patiently unwedging it, but when she finally does, Jimmy grabs it away. Undaunted, she goes back for a purple ball. This time Anna H.-K. grabs it. So Anna C. goes back again to the corner, wrestling out a pink ball. She manages to play with it for a minute until Stephen appropriates it. Now all the balls are taken, so she picks up a stuffed rabbit instead. Any other child would have been howling long ago, but Anna C. is unusually calm, not nearly

A watchful Anna C. on the playground

as proprietorial as the other one-year-olds. Cheryl, who has been watching this scene unfold, spots an abandoned ball and passes it over to the girl. "Anna, you can have the green ball," she says.

This is exactly the kind of thing Anna's mother, Rachel, was most afraid of when she enrolled her daughter at Red Caboose. In child care as in life, the squeaky wheel gets the grease, and quiet kids like Anna C. are sometimes ignored. "I was worried about it, and I didn't tell the teachers I was worried about it for a long time," says Rachel. Her voice is low, her words rapid, spilling out with a kind of restrained urgency that makes her seem wise beyond her 31 years. "I didn't say a lot of things I wish I had said. And the main one was, 'Anna's such a good, *easy* child, I'm afraid she's gonna be left to her own devices and not get enough attention.' Those words were in my head for weeks and I never said them to anyone."

In many ways Rachel and her husband, David, are typical members of the well-educated middle class. David recently finished a Ph.D. in astronomy at the university, and Rachel is a writer. Like many women, she finds herself caught between generational expectations. "I heard a lot from my mother about how much she disapproves of full-time child care," she says. "I also heard a lot from my mother about how miserable she was when she was at home with her kids, and how important it is to have work and to find a balance." The couple lives frugally on David's postdoctoral salary and on family gifts, but Rachel never really considered staying home full time with Anna. She knew that she had to keep writing for her own sake if for no other reason. She also knew that she wanted to be home with her daughter at least some of the time.

For a while Rachel and David hired a young woman to come to the apartment for three hours a day while Rachel wrote in the other room. But as Anna got older, Rachel found it harder to work at home. "The decision to send her out of the house for care was not because I felt it was important for her to have more social life, or because I thought a center was good for her, although it turned out that it was good for her," she says guiltily. "I needed to get her out of the house because I worked at home. And I definitely felt weird about that. I still feel weird about that."

Guilt and need make a potent mixture, for Rachel as for so many working mothers. It helps in a way if the need to work is financial, because money and numbers are undeniable, black and white, factual. When the need to work is emotional or psychological, many women find it harder to defend their choice, to themselves and to the world. In the needs sweepstakes, kids always win; their needs come first. But it's impossible to give up all of yourself, all of what's important to you, and still be a good parent. Our own mothers learned that back in the 1950s.

Rachel's ambivalence about sending Anna to Red Caboose is not unusual. What is unusual is how aware she is of her own feelings and all that contributes to them. That awareness sometimes leaves her feeling paralyzed. For almost two months she kept her worries about her daughter to herself.

Only when she was thoroughly miserable did she schedule a conference with Cheryl. "I just didn't know," says Rachel. She has short curly brown hair and expressive hands that move as she talks. "I felt it was hard to get information out of the Turtle Room teachers at the end of the day. I would ask how things went, and they would say, 'She's fine, she had a lovely day.'" David went to the conference, too, though he was less concerned than Rachel was. "I always felt good about the teachers," he explains with his usual insouciance. "I completely trusted them. I had that anxiety that's kind of abstract, about leaving Anna alone, but I was never worried that something bad was happening to her, or the teachers weren't paying attention to her."

Rachel came away from the conference feeling better. "Cheryl reassured us that she was noticing what was going on with Anna, and that Anna was fine after we left," Rachel says. "And I could see when I picked her up in the afternoon that she was fine, and she often didn't want to leave. And I felt a lot better just having talked to Cheryl about it." But she still worries about her daughter, still wonders if she's doing the right thing. Her ambivalence has not been put to rest.

At least she knows that Cheryl and the other teachers take her concerns to heart. Now, as the children lose interest in the colored balls, Anna C. and Forest open the doors of the oven and dishwasher in the play kitchen and sit together. Anna H.-K. wanders over and pushes Anna C. out of her treasured spot. "You can tell people no, Anna," says Cheryl from the floor. She leans over and hands Anna C. a doll. "Here's a cuddly baby," she tells her. "If someone tries to take it, you tell them no."

Cheryl moves off, negotiating several other exchanges, bringing out another tub full of toys. A few minutes later she's discussing one of the other children with Ernie when she hears Anna C. cry, "My baby!" "What happened to your baby?" asks Cheryl, breaking off her conversation. Moser, standing nearby with a guilty look on his face, clutches the doll. At this point, Cheryl *could* just take the doll from Moser and hand it back to Anna C. with a brief lecture. Instead she says to the girl, "Tell Moser that's *your* baby." She wants Anna to learn to stand up for herself, to be assertive. "Moser," she continues, turning to the boy, "I gave that baby to Anna to play with. You can get a baby over here in the box."

The telephone intercom buzzes, and Cheryl hurries upstairs to take the call. Wendy's at a conference today, and as usual Cheryl is filling in, fielding calls about enrollment. This one is a mother desperately looking for full-time care for an 18-month-old. If Cheryl knew there was going to be an opening in the Turtle Room soon she could work something out, maybe move someone up to the Elephant Room a little early. But none of these kids will be ready to move for months. Cheryl suggests that the woman call Big Oak, the only other center nearby that takes toddlers.

By 10:30 the Turtles are in the Sunshine Room, enjoying the larger space, the freedom, the new and different toys. Outside the sky is steely, the air alive with snowflakes, the kind of day that makes you want to stay home in bed. Ernie, gazing out the window while the children play, says, "I just want a newborn baby right here." She pats herself high on the chest, under her chin. Cheryl sighs. "Yeah, it's that kind of day," she agrees, "when you just want to cuddle a baby all day." Then she laughs. "But I sure don't want to go through those two to teen years again!" Even Ernie has to grin, recognizing the truth when she hears it. She doesn't want to go through those years again either. But she sure does love snuggling her babies when she gets the chance.

The March board meeting feels curiously rudderless. Wendy's absent, off backpacking out west with her husband. She usually arranges her vacations so she doesn't miss the board meeting, but this time she couldn't. She's been such a leader for so long that at first everyone who speaks at the meeting keeps looking around, as if to find her. But the board president, Sarah, keeps things running smoothly.

Besides the usual reports—enrollment is pretty stable; Kathi Sullivan, the new business coordinator, is working her way up to speed—there's a special report from the education committee. Rachel and another parent have come to tell the board about the proposed new diversity policy, which they and the rest of the committee have been arguing over for months. Up until now, the center's strict no-holiday policy has led to a virtual ban on discussing or even mentioning anything that might be construed as a religious celebration—Christmas, Hanukkah, Kwanzaa, and so on. This has caused strain in the classrooms. A three- or four-year-old doesn't understand why she's not allowed to stand up and tell everyone what her family did at Passover, or why a donation of a favorite Christmas book is rejected. And the teachers are so open with the children on every other subject that this distinction often feels arbitrary. Yet the struggle to revise the policy has been controversial, because the issues at stake go to the heart of Red Caboose's nonpartisan, egalitarian philosophy. After months of discussion, the committee has finally come up with a draft.

Rachel begins by giving background on some of the committee's discussions, talking smoothly and quickly. "What was interesting to me," she says, "is that the main things that came up were from the teachers. The issues for them were not wanting to squash children who said, 'There's a book I brought from home, can we read it?' It's been really awful for them and for the kids to have to say, 'No, it's really nice that you brought this book, but let's just put it aside.' Another big issue was consistency. We talk about Native American religion with spirit gods, and talk about African religions, and if you're going to have to get rid of one kind of religion you should get rid of all kinds of religion. And we talked about how even if you try to exclude religion from the classroom, it seeps in."

All of which is to explain why the new diversity policy—if the board approves it—opens the door for teachers to talk about religion with the kids. "We strive to help every child feel proud of his or her own family and culture and to appreciate the rich variety of families in the center and community," reads the new policy. "We respect family cultures and invite parents to share traditions with us. . . . Religious holidays are not celebrated at Red Caboose, and the teaching of religious doctrine is specifically excluded. Staff respond to children's questions about religious holidays factually and non-judgmentally, perhaps beginning, 'Some people believe or observe. . . .'"

Julie, the other parent from the education committee, takes over. "It was never our intent to say, for example, 'Easter's coming up, let's all draw pictures of Easter baskets,'" she explains, leaning forward uncomfortably in the little chair. "But if someone comes in and says something about how they're going to color Easter eggs, you certainly don't want to shut them up or invalidate who they are. So a teacher might say, 'Isn't that nice, this person does that. What do *you* do this time of year?' And let everybody share what's special about them." Or parents might visit their child's class and do a special project or presentation with everyone.

What nobody wants is a policy that would let teachers stand up and teach religious doctrine—whatever that means. "There's this continuum," says Rachel. "And at one end is, 'We eat latkes at my house 'cause I'm Jewish,' and at the other end is, 'You must believe Jesus Christ is the son of God,' right? And then there's a huge gray area. I guess the hope is that if parents come into the classrooms they will discuss with staff the way the presentations will be made, that that will be a safeguard to deal with the issue of what is doctrine." The board members are impressed with the amount of thought and consideration the committee has given to the new policy, which passes easily. The old-timers know they'll be hearing about this issue again, though. It's been discussed off and on at Red Caboose for the last 25 years, and will undoubt-edly be discussed again. But now it's time to move on.

Sarah, who works at the state capitol as a legislative aide, has agreed to give an update on what's happening with W-2. After the initial flurry of media cov-erage last fall and early winter, the bill has dropped out of the public eye. But behind the scenes it's been making its way through the legislative process.

"As everyone knows," she begins, "the bill was passed by the assembly and a week later passed by the senate, party line vote." She pauses, then amends, "Actually, not a party line vote. What am I saying? A lot of Democrats voted for it. It's considered the AFDC replacement program, and they had to pass something because two years ago the Democrats passed a law to repeal AFDC as of December 1st, 1998."

She recaps for the board the main elements of W-2—no more entitlement, copays based on cost of care, provisionally certified caregivers—and moves on to recent developments. "The point is to create more slots," she explains. "There's a demand for some 40,000 child-care slots just in Milwaukee. These people were really smart. They thought, 'Well, hell, there's a lot of grand-mothers and neighbors and others who could provide child care, let's give them jobs as child-care providers and not require them to get any certification or training or anything.'

"Low-income families are essentially going to be forced to go to those kinds of care providers. We're just not going to see those sorts of families here any-more, because the copay they'd have to pay to come to a place like this is going to be too high. Way too high. That's how it affects Red Caboose. Under W-2, if you earn $5 an hour you're going to be better off than if you earn $15 an hour because of the way the copays hit you."

The board has been listening attentively, in the same rapt, fascinated way people view the scene of a car crash. The real question about W-2 is no longer *whether* but *when* it will take effect. The plan is so radical and violates so many federal laws that the state has to get 40 or 50 waivers from the federal gov-ernment to implement it, which will take time. Sarah thinks W-2 could go into full effect as early as June, and she wants the board and the center to be prepared for the fallout. "I think we're going to see less diversity here, racially and economically," she tells the directors. "And the fear that I have and that Wendy has is that Red Caboose will end up catering to middle-class families to survive."

Not only would that violate the center's long-standing philosophical commitment and mission, it would have practical ramifications as well. Income from the food program would drop, and other sources might dry up, too. Last year, for instance, Red Caboose got a $22,000 grant from Community Development Block Grant, or CDBG, to redo the playground. To qualify for the grant, at least 51 percent of the center's families had to be low- or moderate-income. Under W-2, who knows if the center would qualify again?

Sarah paints a grim picture, and the board is suitably depressed. It is a sad and thoughtful group of parents and teachers who head for the darkened parking lot and home.

SPRING
THE ELEPHANT ROOM

April

It's Good Friday, and the Elephants are jumping. On trampolines, that is—little round bouncers about a foot off the ground, scattered around the Elephant Room. Spring this year is an unwilling visitor; it's sunny outside but still chilly, a damp, grinding cold that keeps the kids inside all morning. The two-year-olds are even more restless than usual. Gary Dosemagen, the lead teacher, says he doesn't know *what* they would do without the trampolines to burn off frustration and anger and plain old rambunctious rowdiness.

In this midwestern state, Good Friday is a holiday for lots of parents, so there aren't many kids at the center. There are a couple of days like this throughout the year: the day before or after the Fourth of July, the Friday after Thanksgiving, the days between Christmas and New Year's. On low-attendance days, as they're known, one or two teachers in each room take the day off, depending on the numbers. There are 8 Elephants out of 12 scheduled to come today, and since one teacher is needed for every 6 Elephants, both Gary and Mary Pusateri, the other morning teacher, are here. Bad luck for the center, but good luck for the kids, who will get that much more attention than usual.

Four trampolines are set up, a child bouncing away on each. Kylen, an elfin boy with a devastatingly sweet smile, claims one immediately. Ulric climbs on another, wearing a turquoise Red Caboose T-shirt and pants with a design of multicolored rabbits; his big brother, Mirko, is outside with the other Grasshoppers. Erica and Jimmy have the other two trampolines. Jimmy, only recently moved up from the Turtle Room, is still feeling unsure of himself here. He hovers, one leg up on a trampoline, the other keeping contact with the floor, his favorite blue blanket clutched in his hands. It takes several weeks for a two-year-old to settle into new routines, into the customs and traditions of the Elephant Room.

Gary crosses the room, past the play kitchen area, past the carpeted ramp leading to a small, pillow-filled loft, past the cage holding Harry, a black-and-white guinea pig, and puts a tape in the boom box. Raffi's voice pours out of the loudspeaker. "Oh, my favorite song," says Gary, and cranks up the volume. Mary sings along with Raffi: "Tingalayo, run little donkey, run." She has neat dark hair streaked with gray, an expressive voice. She's been here eight years, and she also works in the after-school program. Kylen climbs off his trampoline and tries to climb onto Erica's. Erica naturally begins shrieking. "Erica, do you want to tell him, 'That's mine!'?" asks Gary encouragingly. "Mine!" she says. Kylen gets down and climbs onto Jimmy's trampoline, now abandoned. Instantly Jimmy climbs onto Kylen's old trampoline. Maybe in his mind this makes up for any perceived violation of territory.

And territory's what it's all about here in the Elephant Room, how to establish it and protect it from any and all invaders. In that sense maybe the two-year-olds should be called Lions or Wolves instead of Elephants, for their sense of what belongs to them and the way they defend it ferociously. It is the teachers' work to watch this process unfold, to guide it, to begin to open the two-year-olds to the possibilities of empathy and compassion. It's exhausting, draining work. It's also exhilarating. Gary survives by keeping his sense of humor intact. Now, for instance, Clark comes in from the hall. Putting his palms together in a *namaste*, bowing solemnly, Clark asks, "You guys have any bubble wands?" Gary opens a cupboard, pulls out one tiny bubble wand, and hands it to Clark. "You return that," he says warningly. Clark stares at the wand aggrievedly, his disbelief dramatized only slightly, and departs. Gary grins. "You give them all you have, all you have," he says, holding his hands out, palms up, "and it's not enough." Gary has an unsettling ability to speak in metaphors. He's clearly referring not just to Clark but to two-year-olds, the field of child care, the lot of child-care teachers in general.

By 9:15 there are six Elephants jumping on trampolines, bouncing to the music. Mary brings out a tubful of gauzy, translucent scarves, and some of the kids wave them as they jump. Kylen wears a turquoise scarf on his head and bounces, giggling. Mary puts a scarf over her face, too, mirroring what Kylen's done, and hops up and down on the floor. Only Haley stands aloof, a chunky girl with blond ringlets and round pale eyes. Haley's been coming to the center two days a week for almost two months, but she's still unhappy here much of the time. As Mary says, Haley's very "female-identified," meaning that she attaches herself to any and every woman who comes within reach, clutching them, calling them all "Mama," and refusing to have anything whatsoever to do with Gary.

So while the others jump, Haley sits on the couch, drinking from a bottle, twirling a strand of hair with one hand as she sucks. She doesn't see Gary step playfully onto one of the low trampolines and jump, a big grin on his face, his head coming perilously close to the ceiling. But the other Elephants do, staring as if hypnotized. Jimmy's mouth hangs open as he watches his teacher jump—loose-limbed, bigger than life, twisting his knees from side to side in time to the music.

There's a tangible pause when Gary steps off the trampoline at last, a collective drawing in of breath, and then the Elephants are at it again. Ulric gets off his trampoline and throws himself provocatively across Kylen's, getting in his way. Gary lifts Ulric off and puts him back onto his own trampoline, holding his hands. "Should I help you jump?" he asks. "No!" says Ulric, pulling away sharply. If he can't do it by himself, he won't do it at all. Halfway across the room he veers toward one of the meal tables, drawn irresistibly toward a puzzle lying half done. So Gary holds Kylen's hands instead while he jumps. "This is a lot of work!" he jokes, bouncing on the floor, holding the boy's tiny hands in his big paws. Kylen is open-mouthed with delight.

Haley, tired of her bottle, slides off the couch, picks up a book, and begins wandering the room, looking for someone to read to her. "Shall I read to you, Haley?" asks Gary, holding out one hand, but Haley walks away without even making eye contact. She spots Mary, who's now sitting at the table with Jimmy doing puzzles, and bulls her way across the room, inserting herself into Mary's lap and thrusting two books into her face. Not to be outdone, a cheerful boy named Andres pushes another book at Mary. Claire climbs off her trampoline, clearly thinking about joining the group at the table. Instantly Ulric climbs onto Claire's trampoline and begins bouncing, waving a scarf in the air. Claire sits down on the floor and sobs luxuriously. "I want it!" she wails. "No, no, it's mine!"

"Claire, you got up," says Gary reasonably. "There's another one." He points to an unoccupied trampoline, but it won't do. Nothing will do except the one Ulric has laid claim to, and since that's not forthcoming there is no consolation possible. Raffi finishes singing "Day-O," and "Tingalayo" comes on again, to much applause. Ulric, Claire, and Erica jump, side by side, on three trampolines. Then Erica lies down on hers, and Claire follows her. Ulric looks at the girls and leaps even higher on his trampoline, then scampers off and begins picking up scarves from the floor.

In a few minutes the Elephants will split into two smaller groups, as they do each morning and afternoon. Mary's group—Haley, Jimmy, Ulric, and Erica—goes to the Sunshine Room. Gary's group stays behind. While Gary clears away the trampolines—you've got to keep moving in the world of two-year-olds—Claire tucks a plastic bottle under each arm and climbs a couple of steps to a wooden structure built underneath the long windowsill. This is the Elephant Room's good-bye window, looking straight out onto the playground, where at the moment the Grasshoppers are cavorting with their coats on. The windows are decorated with various art projects—white bear shapes, colored hearts, paper towels stained pink. Each project has a child's name carefully written on it, so it can eventually go home with its maker. If parents were to keep every single one of the projects brought home by their two-year-olds, their houses would overflow. Most parents follow the advice of Denice Watson, an afternoon Elephant teacher: "Admire 'em, hang 'em on the refrigerator, then throw 'em away when your kid's not looking."

Claire goes back to the shelf for two more bottles. Each bottle is filled with a mixture of oil and colored water; the oil makes interesting bubbles and waves inside the water when the bottle is shaken. Claire, working hard at her task, lines up 19 bottles on the wide windowsill, yellow and clear and blue, green and pink, swirling and still. Inside one bottle tiny champagne glasses and palm trees made from glittery paper float in a yellow sea, like messages in a bottle from a far-off land. The bottles are very beautiful, and Claire steps back to admire them for a minute. Then she walks away. To a two-year-old, the *process* is the fun part, arranging the bottles on the shelf; now that it's done, Claire feels quite sensibly that it's time to move on. She goes to a round basket on the floor near the sensory table and picks out a plastic smock, pulling it on over her head.

Meanwhile, Andres and Kylen, also fascinated by the bottles, begin a different kind of process. Each boy lifts a bottle from the windowsill and drops it onto the floor below, a fall of about two feet. "Oh, no," says Gary, catching a bottle in midair and setting it gently down. "I don't want them falling down here. I'm afraid they might crack. I don't want them to crack."

Now Gary pulls a thick stack of construction paper from a shelf and fans the rainbow-colored pieces out onto the table. He fills a plastic cup with water and brings it to the table, then opens another cabinet and brings out a couple of flat, thin boxes of watercolors. Claire, sitting at the table with a pacifier in her mouth, reaches for one as Gary puts it down. "I want this one! I want this one!" she says around the rubber nipple. Gary hands it to her. Under his breath he sings, "Tingalayo, paint my little donkeys, paint." He grins as Andres pulls on a smock. "Are you guys my little donkeys today?" he asks. "No!" says Claire. "No?" asks Gary, amused. "How about Tingalayo, paint my little piglets, paint? You like that one? No? Well, what should I sing?"

"Cats!" answers Claire firmly, and Gary obliges, singing, "Paint my little kitties, paint." "We need brushes," says Claire, and Gary goes to get them. As he moves he keeps up a running monologue that occasionally swerves into dialogue. "I saw a movie about a pig," he says. "*Babe.* That was kind of a different movie. Somebody want bumpy paper?" "No, smooth paper," says Kylen, seated now at the table. Gary pulls out a sheaf of old-fashioned computer paper, the kind with perforated strips of little holes on either side—obviously a donation from someone who has upgraded a printer—and sets it on the table. Andres dips his brush into the cup of water, then into a brand-new set of watercolors, and begins to paint.

All the kids in Gary's group now have brand-new sets of watercolors. In the thin plastic boxes the squares are intensely colored, fresh and untouched and saturated with promise. And the very first thing each two-year-old does is dip a brush into the water and then carefully, obsessively, dip that brush into each square of color, one at a time, until every single square in every single box is black. Claire, her pacifier put away in her locker, paints big black swatches on a sheet of pink paper. Kylen's paper sits in a puddle of water, a wash of black paint swirling across its surface as he moves his brush. Andres brushes layer after layer of black paint onto his paper. After some minutes he sits back, satisfied. "Look at this!" he crows, and Gary does. "Wow," says Gary. "I call that very black."

A good teacher lets two-year-olds do things their way whenever possible, and Gary is a very good teacher. He watches, bemused, as Claire neatly makes each of her colors black, hardly spilling a drop of water or paint. "Studies in black," says Gary fondly. "We've done it before, haven't we, guys?" Claire isn't even supposed to be in the Elephant Room today. Just turned three, she's in the process of transitioning to the Bumblebee Room. But Claire needs the comfort of familiar routines right now; she and Lydia have been staying with their grandparents all week while their parents are away. So this morning, when Claire arrived at the center in tears, Gary said she could stay in the Elephant Room. She's cheered up some but she's still rocky, still prone to falling apart suddenly and sobbing over things that usually don't faze her.

From the Sunshine Room comes the sound of crying, Haley's crying. Mary's group is taking turns balancing on a short wooden plank. The plank has one end on the floor and the other propped up on the red mat, eight inches or so off the ground. The two-year-olds slowly, carefully, using their arms for balance, walk up the plank and jump off onto the mat. Haley finishes her turn and tries to butt back into the middle of the line, but another child blocks her, and she starts to cry.

Soon the allure of the board fades, and Mary's group looks for other games. One corner of the Sunshine Room houses a kind of junkyard office, with several old computer keyboards—not hooked up to anything—and a real but nonworking telephone. Haley sits in front of a keyboard, not touching it, looking at a book in her lap. Jimmy sits down next to her and touches the keyboard. "No, Jimmy," says Haley. When he doesn't stop, she shouts, "No!" and slaps his hand. "Haley, gentle," warns Mary from across the room. Jimmy stands up, turning a block over and over in his hands, his lower lip stuck out. He's not used to this kind of treatment, either at home or in the Turtle Room, and it stings. He looks down at Haley, who is instantly alert to danger and wags a finger in his face, warning him off.

At 10:15, Mary disappears into the hallway. She comes back a minute later with an armful of coats, which she lays on the floor, face up. Ulric steps up to the hood of his coat, deftly inserts his arms into his sleeves, and flips the coat over his head to settle on his back—the so-called day-care flip. "Good, Ulric, you flipped your coat," says Mary. She arranges Jimmy's coat on the floor and leads him over. "Put your arms in there and flip it up," she explains. He gets his arms partly into the sleeves and stops. Mary ties his hat on. "Let's try again," she says patiently. "Let's put your arms in here, put them way down." Erica, meanwhile, flips her coat on, but since she started at the wrong end she's wearing it upside down, the hood sticking out over her bottom. Mary helps her take it off and holds it correctly while the girl flips it on. "Yes!" says Mary, laughing, and Erica laughs too, her pride in herself almost palpable. "You did that all by yourself. Wow!" Next Mary starts all their zippers, encouraging them at least to finish zipping their coats by themselves.

Getting the kids to dress themselves as much as possible definitely helps the teachers, struggling to deal with several children at once. But it's more than a convenience for grown-ups; it's a big step toward independence for the children. Each room works on empowering children in its own way, with its own set of expectations. For the Turtles, that includes learning to say no and to be gentle with one another. For the Elephants, physical self-care—zipping, tying, brushing, wiping—is a priority, though there are always grown-up hands ready to help.

Transitions like this, from inside to outside, are hard enough in the summer, when there aren't any coats or hats or boots to keep track of. On a day like today, the energy and strength and wit required to move half a dozen kids from the Elephant Room to the playground seem overwhelming. As Mary's group waits by the back door with their coats on, Gary tries to round up his kids and move them outside. Kylen, Andres, and Claire are at the sensory table, which is filled with runny mud. Claire scoops mud on top of plastic animals, then packs a handful into a plastic tub. Her arms are slick and brown all the way up to the elbows. Gary shepherds her into the bathroom to wash, and tells the other two that it's time to go outside. "I want to read!" says Kylen. "How about if we read outside?" asks Gary, sweeping bits of dirt out from under the sensory table. He's not really cleaning up, just containing the chaos. "No, I have to read inside," insists Kylen.

Meanwhile Claire, her hands "washed," muddy streaks still striping her arms, charges out of the bathroom yelling, "I want my Nuk!" "When is your Nuk for?" asks Gary calmly, lifting the wooden cover onto the sensory table. "Nap," admits Claire. Cornered by Gary's logic, she picks up a green plastic dish and throws it into the rack holding dress-up clothes. "No, Claire, that's not what we do with dishes," says Gary patiently. "Please get the dish down." Claire looks at the dish, looks at Gary, and then, as he begins to approach her, climbs into the dress-up rack and gets the dish. Gary retreats, satisfied, and begins cleaning the table, spraying germicide and water and wiping it off. Kylen sits stubbornly on the couch, holding a book with a deathlike grip.

Happy screams come from the play kitchen, where Claire and Andres are now putting round blocks into empty macaroni and cheese boxes. "Cookies for a picnic!" says Claire. "Can't get out!" says Andres, holding up a box with pieces of wooden toast wedged inside. He turns the box upside down and shakes, and the toast slides out. "Whee!" he calls, a smile on his face. He puts an empty box over each hand and roars at Claire, who giggles. He pretends to wash his boxed hands off under the toy faucet. Claire stands on a piece of toast, then picks it off the floor and serves it on the table. "One more minute, Elephants, we're gonna go outside," calls Gary. "Telephone!" calls Andres. "Telephone?" asks Gary, grinning. "Well, I'm going to go put *my* coat on." "It's

Mama!" calls Andres. Claire holds up another phone. "I'm going to go get your coats," says Gary. "No!" says Claire, falling to the floor and beginning to kick and flail. "I want to be by myself a while!" "You can be by yourself by your locker for a little while," says Gary. "Thank you!" yells Claire, heading out the door. "Stay here, Claire," begs Andres. Gary heads for Claire's locker to get her coat. "I'll do it by myself," says Claire, suddenly cooperative. She lays her pink and purple coat on the hallway floor and flips it on, then shrugs it off and runs into the empty Sunshine Room. By his locker, Andres flips his coat on correctly. Kylen gets one arm into a sleeve and stops, and Gary comes over to help. Then he pokes his head into the Sunshine Room and says, "I don't see a teacher in there, Claire." The kids aren't ever allowed to be unsupervised, and they know it. Gary adds, "I'm getting a coat so Ulric can go outside." "No!" screams Claire, collapsing at the door in a tantrum. "I'm going to take the kids out, and I'll come back for you if I need to," says Gary calmly.

Claire stands up. She walks determinedly into the Sunshine Room. A minute later she comes out, rebellion accomplished. She spots her coat on the floor, picks it up, and thrusts it at Gary, who's striding toward the back door. "You can put this on me," she says regally. Kylen trails behind, still clutching his book. And with that the Elephants finally get out the door.

On a Wednesday morning in late April, the two-year-olds are finishing a lunch of shepherd's pie ("And there's a good, fresh shepherd in it," deadpans Clark), bread, beets, and oranges as Denice comes through the door. In each of the other three rooms, one teacher works a split shift—early morning and late afternoon, with a few hours off at midday—so the same teacher might be there for both drop-off and pickup. The split shifts are draining but much appreciated by parents, who get to hear about their child's morning and afternoon. But there are four Elephant Room teachers—two in the morning, two in the afternoon—and their shifts barely overlap. Parents who want to know about their two-year-old's morning or nap usually have to wait until the next day, and hope they remember their question.

Mary, sitting at the table with the children, eats homemade spaghetti from a plastic container. She leads the conversation around to the events of the morning. "What did you do with the bean bags this morning?" she asks the two-year-olds. "Shake them," says Kylen. "Put them on our foot," says a small girl named Georgina, lifting her legs and feet, opening her arms wide. "We did that a week ago," says Mary. "You still remember that?" "Uh-huh!" says Georgina cheerfully. "My favorite!"

Gary and the Elephants play ring-around-a-rosy in the wood chips

Haley is the first one done with lunch. She lifts her paper plate, which still has food on it, carries it carefully over to the garbage can, and drops it in, then settles herself on the couch with a book. She's made progress over the last few weeks, but naptime is still the hardest part of the day for her. Gary approaches her. "Come and wash your hands in the bathroom," he says gently. "You can bring your book." Obediently she follows him, standing in front of the sink with her hands in running water. "And while you're doing that," he says, pulling down her pants, "I'm going to check your diaper." Haley begins to cry. "You know me, I do this every day, check your diaper," he says reassuringly, pulling apart the adhesive on either side of the plastic diaper. He removes the old diaper, slipping it out from between her legs, and asks Haley if she wants to sit on the potty. She doesn't, so Gary brings over a new diaper. "My diaper!" she cries in greeting, and the two of them take a minute to examine the animals decorating the edge of the plastic diaper. Haley stands in front of the sink, her pants puddled around her feet; Gary squats beside her, his long legs nearly touching his chin. He points to each animal as he names it. "There's a butterfly, a mouse, there's a—oh, that's supposed to be an aardvark," he says. "I never did do too well in zoology. There's a zebra, you got a hippo on there too, and look, you wore your bears shirt today, your three bears." He touches one finger to the pink and white bears on her sweatshirt, and finally she smiles.

Dressed again, Haley runs out into the Elephant Room and lifts a toy farm off a toy shelf. "Amma," she says, meaning *animal*, and begins piling plastic animals into the barn. Jimmy carries his paper plate to the garbage can. The floor under the lunch tables is littered with spoons, orange wedges and peels, bits of beets, a blue plastic checker. Ulric has spilled his milk, and Mary mops it up with a paper towel. She stops Akeem just as he's about to throw his metal spoon into the garbage along with his paper plate. Denice, on medicine duty, uncaps a bottle of white goop, struggling briefly with the childproof cap. She measures some carefully into a cup and watches Akeem swallow it.

The minute Haley spots Denice, her sangfroid dissolves. "Mama, Mama," she cries, clinging to Denice's jeans-clad leg. Through the bathroom window, Jimmy's feet can be seen waving in the air; Gary's got him on the changing table, cleaning a poop. The bathroom window is a relatively recent improvement. Before the window was put in, a teacher changing diapers or wiping bottoms had no way of keeping track of what was going on in the bigger room. And that same teacher, alone in the bathroom with children in various stages of nudity, was vulnerable to suspicions or even accusations of wrongdoing.

Gary, being a man, is particularly aware of such uncomfortable and even dangerous situations. For him the bathroom window is a relief on many levels.

Denice administers pink goop and Tylenol to Erica, who swigs them without protest, and Haley watches closely, peering over Denice's shoulder the whole time. The other kids are beginning to get settled, climbing onto—and off—their cots themselves. That's another change from the Turtle Room, where the teachers spend a lot more time helping the one-year-olds in various ways. If a Turtle has trouble going to sleep, or wakes up after 20 minutes, there's a teacher to push her in the stroller, give her a bottle, cuddle and sing to her. But the two-year-olds are expected to be more self-sufficient. Such independence is good for them, and it's a necessity: with 12 kids instead of 8, the Elephant teachers have no choice.

Haley rifles the bookshelves, looking for just the right book, then climbs onto the couch. The Grasshoppers stream by on their way out to the playground, and two of them, Mirko and Meghan, peer into the room, looking for their younger brothers. Haley starts to cry. "Mama!" she sobs, sitting alone on the couch. If Denice stops to comfort her now, the crying will escalate, so she keeps doing what she's doing, setting up cots, helping kids off with their shoes, washing down the lunch tables. Haley calms down, at least until Erica climbs onto the couch and tries to take her book away. At that point Denice intervenes, redirecting Haley to another book. "Usually it's nonstop tears by this point with Haley," she comments to Gary, who's finishing up diapers. "She and Mom overslept today, so enjoy the peace and quiet while it lasts," he replies.

Denice sends Georgina to her locker to find her blankie, and sends Kylen, who wants Haley's book, for another book. Haley catches sight of Denice and leaps up to follow her, like a paper clip drawn irresistibly to a magnet. "You can go to your locker and get your blankie, too," Denice says to Haley, but the girl doesn't move. When Denice goes into the hall to collect blankies and pacifiers, Haley toddles after her, tears streaming down her face. Denice comes back into the room with her arms full of blankets, trailed by Haley. "Georgina," she says, dropping a blue one onto Georgina's cot. Georgina looks at it with distaste and bursts into tears. "That's not my blanket!" she cries. It's a horrifying moment for her—this alien lovey dropped from above, unknown and unwanted. Denice scoops up the blue one, trying to figure out what happened. "Oh, look at that," she says, and drops a white blanket onto the girl's cot. The blue one goes to Jimmy. Erica gets her green blanket, Wesley his butterfly-shaped pacifier. Haley jumps up and down behind Denice, crying. "Haley,

Haley, slow down," says Denice in a voice that is forceful but kind. "I need to go to your locker and get your blanket." "Where's my baby, please?" says Erica politely, but Denice doesn't hear.

Gary closes the window shades as Denice comes back into the room. "I'm going to get you a bottle of milk," she says, leading Haley by the hand to her cot near the window. "Mommy!" cries Haley, tears streaming messily down her cheeks. All the other children are settled on their cots, stroking blankets, sucking on pacifiers, looking at books. Haley's white blankie is nowhere to be found; her mom must have forgotten to bring it today. When Haley realizes she's not going to get her blanket, she becomes hysterical. "Mommy!" she screams, jumping off her cot to follow Denice. "Gary's going to get you your bottle of milk, and I'm going to read you a book," says Denice, obviously struggling to stay calm. "Why don't you sit down?" She opens a high cabinet near the Elephant Room door. "Uh-oh," she says to the room at large. "Gary went to the library, and you know what he got? Spot books!" She brings out a pile of white books with brightly colored illustrations, instantly recognizable to the kids as books about Spot, a brown and white puppy who gets into all kinds of trouble.

"How about if we read one?" continues Denice loudly. "Ulric needs to sit on his cot, because I'm afraid he's going to fall if he stands on it. Should we read this one together? It's called Spot—Goes—to a—Party." She pauses dramatically between each word, making her eyes wide with pretended delight. Denice is a consummate showperson, which may be one reason why the children adore her. As she begins reading, holding the book up so the Elephants can see the pictures, reading the words upside down, Gary comes in with a bottle of milk. Haley zooms off her cot. "It's a costume party!" enthuses Denice as Haley grabs the bottle from Gary's hands. He grins. "You don't have to say thanks or anything," he says. Haley lies down on her cot, holding her bottle to her mouth with one hand, twirling a strand of hair with the other. "Look, there's a kitty," booms Denice, pointing to a picture of a cat in the book.

Gary gathers cushions from the pillow loft and positions them strategically between cots so that later, when he's rubbing backs, he doesn't have to sit or lie on the hard floor. It might not have bothered him 10 years ago, but now, in his 40s, a little padding goes a long way, especially for someone as bony as Gary. He grabs a handful of tissues from a box and walks around the room wiping noses. The children listen intently to Spot's latest adventure, all except Haley, lost in her own world.

Finally Spot is unmasked in his alligator costume, to everyone's delight.

"After nap, we're going to read all of these," says Denice. She has a way of emphasizing certain words so that they are absolutely compelling. "These are some of our *favorite* ones. We are *so* glad Gary went to the library. You know what, though? It's time for nap. We'll read another one *after* nap." Haley screams, sitting bolt upright on her cot. "Mommy!" she shrieks. "Haley, here I come!" calls Denice loudly, making her way over. "I'm going to help Andres lay down and cover him up." She suits her actions to her words while Haley screams for her. Gary works the other end of the room, covering Georgina and Kylen. Denice hands Haley her paperback book, the one she reads while rubbing backs in the darkened room. When Haley starts to cry again, Denice says quickly, "Where's my book? Do you have my book?" And it works, briefly, the book a talisman, a magic piece of Denice in Haley's hands.

Gary sits down on a pillow between Erica and Akeem. Jimmy cries furiously on his cot, and Denice covers him. "All right, Jimmy, we're going ni-ni," she says soothingly. He rubs his eyes. Denice sits down near the windows between Haley and Wesley. With one hand she holds on to Haley, patting her head, stroking the girl's messy curls; with the other she holds open her book. Classical music plays quietly in the background. Gary, trying to get Caetano to lie down, starts counting, which works. "Ni-ni, Jimmy," says Denice firmly as Jimmy rears up off his cot again. She puts her book down and holds Wesley's hand while continuing to pat Haley's hair. "Mommy," cries Haley, though more quietly. Jimmy sucks on one finger, soothing himself. Georgina's asleep, Andres is asleep. Haley breaks out crying again. "Haley," says Denice, "I can see you need to cry for a while. Should we go into the bathroom and cry for a while and be sad?" "Yes," sobs Haley. "Then when you're ready to settle down, you can come back out on your cot," says Denice, leading her into the bathroom. It's a gift she's giving Haley, not a punishment. By *not* telling her to cheer up, to be quiet, to lie still—however much Denice might wish she would—she's giving Haley the opportunity to express her feelings.

And Haley has a lot of feelings to express. While Haley often sees her father, Jeff, she spends most of her time with her mother, Kirsten. The two of them live in a small, clean apartment in the YMCA off the square in downtown Madison, on a floor with other single mothers and their children. The Center for Women and Children referred Kirsten here, and it's one of the few places she could afford—$250 a month, including utilities. This Y, unlike more urban ones, is clean and cheerful. The elevators work, the walls are bright with painted murals. On this floor a baby gate keeps kids from wandering near the elevators.

The apartment has two small bedrooms, a tiny living room, a kitchenette, a bathroom. The white walls have been recently painted and are hung with photographs of a younger, balder Haley. Haley's bedroom has its own large-screen TV and a low child's bed. A needlepoint cat hangs on one wall. Haley and her mom have been living here for just over a year, ever since they moved out of the west side apartment they shared with Jeff.

Kirsten is a strong-featured 31-year-old with shoulder-length reddish hair, an earring high in the cartilage of one ear, an ironic smile. When she smiles, deep lines crease the sides of her mouth, laugh lines that add to her frank appeal. Before Haley was born, she worked as a clerk at a local hospital, taking a few college courses at night. She met Haley's dad in a drug and alcohol program three years ago. "It was one of those relationships where everybody was sure it was doomed to fail," she says. "We've had our ups and downs, certainly. The fact that we're both working on recovery and have had to deal with one or the other having a relapse has made it difficult."

Kirsten is afraid that she and Jeff, no matter how much they love each other, want different lives. "I have this dream of being a mom and dad, with a kid or two, having a home," she says wistfully. "Going to the beach on Saturday and having a picnic, you know? And he's still really caught up in putting on his leathers and getting on the highway on his motorcycle and looking cool. Though I like to do that once in a while with him." She grins. "It's kinda fun."

At first, Jeff, who's 38, was excited about being a father. He held Kirsten's hand in the labor room and doted on their newborn. Since then he's struggled with his role as Haley's father. For a while he was jealous of Haley because she came between him and Kirsten. And he had a really hard time when Haley cried. Now, says Kirsten, "he loves Haley to death. She looks exactly like him. But he forgets that she's a two-year-old and she doesn't know better. She's developing her own personality and she's figuring out just what her boundaries are and how much she can get away with. If she's gonna defy anyone, it's gonna be me or him. I'm still trying to get him to understand that. He's working on it."

Kirsten is reluctant to attribute Haley's avoidance of men to Jeff, but clearly there is a connection. "Jeff is in the process of starting an anger management group," says Kirsten, crossing her legs, jiggling one foot nervously. "We went through some times that were pretty rough, you know? There was some violence. Haley was a witness to it. Whether that has anything to do with it, I don't know. But now if Jeff and I are having an argument and I start to cry, she'll come over to me and say, 'That's OK, Mommy, that's OK.' She's only two years old. So she—she's been affected." Her voice trails off to a whisper on the last sentence, as if she would like to take back the words she knows are true.

Kirsten applied to the county for child-care funding, so she could have some time away from Haley to put her own life back together. In January she got a six-month grant that might or might not be renewed. Those first few weeks, the morning drop-offs were rough, very rough. Haley would cry and cling to Kirsten. Sometimes she cried so hard she threw up. Through it all Kirsten would smile and wave good-bye as if everything were fine, then walk out the door and feel her heart squeeze with sorrow. But she stuck it out so that she could, as she puts it, "do some things to take care of myself, like go to see my therapist, or get to some recovery meetings, or just be *alone* for a little while." For Kirsten, enrolling Haley was an opportunity for herself, and it took her by surprise to discover that it was good for Haley, too. More than good, in fact—transformational.

"I've seen so many changes in her as far as how she plays with other kids," explains Kirsten. Haley used to be something of a bully, especially with littler kids, but she's made real progress in the last two months. "She's much gentler," continues Kirsten. "She's talking a lot more. Sings songs, you know? She can count up to 20. If she's really thinking about it, she can do the ABCs. She's starting to pick up after herself. At nighttime, when we're trying to pick up her toys, she'll sing, 'Clean up, clean up, everybody clean up.' I don't know if they sing that here, but I know she didn't get it from me!"

She pauses, searching for words. "I think Red Caboose is responsible for a lot of Haley's growth as far as interacting with other people and learning things," she says slowly. "I don't know where she would be right now if she had never gone there. I know she's a smart child and she catches on to things, but I think they've really helped her as far as learning skills. *People* skills."

If the Elephant Room teachers could hear that, it would make their day. Because that's the whole point of what they do, what *all* the teachers here do: give kids the social and emotional skills they need, now and for the rest of their lives. "I went into this business because I felt there were children that people didn't realize needed love," says Denice with her rapid-fire, straight-from-the-hip bluntness. "I want children to realize they're really important in this world, that somebody thought they were important enough that they love their purple shoes, they love the barrette in their hair, they love the way they wipe the paint on their hands or on their pants. No matter what they do, it's important. Then those children will realize that they're important, and that can only make them better. And that makes them want to do more important things."

Denice is a zealot, the best kind. Her intense commitment to her work comes out of her own childhood, her own experience of growing up neglected and unloved. "As a child, nobody ever hugged me," she says. "I had the feeling that I was not worth anything. I didn't feel good about myself." These are statements of fact, not complaints; Denice is not a whiner. She just wants to make sure that other kids don't have the same experience she did. When she started kindergarten, for instance, she had never spent time with groups of other children. She was completely ignorant about the strange new world she was forced into, even the little things like using a public bathroom. "I peed in the line waiting for the bus every day on the way home from kindergarten," she remembers.

That kind of thing will never happen to Denice's kids — not her biological children, because she's chosen not to have any, but her kids at Red Caboose. "Kids like me are the ones who get lost in the shuffle, or they overreact because they don't know how to deal with things," she says matter-of-factly. "*Our* children are totally adept at everything. Their social skills are so good, they know how to deal with everything. They're ready for the world."

For a child like Haley, what she learns at Red Caboose can make the difference between success and failure. For the rest of her life.

May

The first of May dawns clear and sunny, with temperatures in the 50s after two days of snow — yes, snow. The teachers are particularly glad it's not snowing because they'll be spending part of the day on the steps of the state capitol, at a rally for Worthy Wage Day.

Worthy Wage Day is a national campaign run by the National Center for the Early Childhood Work Force in Washington, D.C. For almost 20 years the NCECWF has been *the* organization supporting child-care workers. Its 1988 report, the *National Child Care Staffing Study*,[1] confirmed what people in the field had long suspected: low pay and high staff turnover lead to poor-quality child care. In 1991 the NCECWF organized the first Worthy Wage Day, asking centers and family providers to shut down for a day to highlight both how crucial child care is for families and the dilemmas faced by child-care workers. Parents will tell their employers they're staying home because they have no child care

—at least that's the hope. "When enough folks complain to their employer, the employer will get the idea," explains Clark. "And when the employer gets the idea, then the stockholders and the board of directors of the employer will get the idea." The point is to put the notion of "worthy wages" on the national agenda, one family—and one workplace—at a time. In time, and with enough publicity, the message will travel outward from the traditionally self-sufficient family into the workplace and so into the national consciousness.

But here's the catch: many caregivers and centers *don't* close for Worthy Wage Day. Some don't want to strand parents without care. Some are too shy or too intimidated to explain why they're charging parents on a day when they're not providing care. At Red Caboose, as at other unionized centers, closing for Worthy Wage Day is high on the priority list at negotiations each year. There is at least the beginning of solidarity.

And so, on this bright cloudless day, more than a hundred child-care teachers are sitting in workshops in the First United Methodist Church. This year there are in-services and workshops on all kinds of subjects: how to talk to your legislator, how to be a successful advocate, how a bill becomes law, W-2. One of the goals of Worthy Wage Day is to transform the way child-care workers and teachers see themselves, a task that may be almost as challenging as transforming the way the rest of the world sees them. Like secretaries and nurses and those in other traditionally female jobs, child-care workers have been slow to assert themselves and their needs—and the needs of their charges. "You may feel that advocacy is not an issue that applies to you," wrote researchers Brenda Eheart and Robin Leavitt in 1985, describing the "average" child-care worker. "You are not interested in politics. You simply want to work directly with children and their families. . . . You must realize that child care is political, and that public policy directly and indirectly affects what happens to the children in your care, to the children without programs who need them, and to you, the professional."[2] Or, as one union member put it, "The hand that rocks the cradle needs to rock the boat."[3]

Social change comes hard. The last five years have seen more assertiveness on the part of caregivers, the beginnings of radicalization. Late in the morning, after the workshops are done, the Madison caregivers gather in the sanctuary of the church to hear the keynote speaker, a federal district court judge. Denice, Ernie, Cheryl, Sue, and Janet sit together in the back row. Amy and Gary sit together, as do Crystal and Carolyn. Wendy sits right up front, listening attentively, looking solemn. She's still recovering from the news of the death of her good friend Allen Everhart, who was the director of Red Caboose before her. Allen had been sick, so his death wasn't a huge surprise, but it's hitting Wendy hard. In the years after he left Red Caboose and Madison they stayed in touch. Now she feels as though she's lost both a colleague and a friend.

Allen would have supported Worthy Wage Day a hundred percent. Back in 1982, when he was director of Red Caboose, he told a local newspaper that parents choosing a center should look hardest at the people who work there. "The physical appearance of the building and the amount of toys and supplies are the elements some chain-type day-care centers promote," he said. "But these things are supplementary. The real capital is the staff."

When Allen was the director, staff wages were raised more or less by fiat; he and the board agreed on what the center could afford, and that's what teachers got. "Being in day care then involved a certain ideological commitment," Allen told me last year. "It was even more poorly paid then than now." In 1975, when Allen was hired, he made $2.91 an hour; teachers were hired at $2.15 an hour. "The union was inevitable," he added, "the only way wages and health conditions were going to rise overall." Clark, who spearheaded the drive to unionize, agrees. The way he remembers it, the impetus for the union came in 1984, the year after Wendy became director. Owing to a change in the tax laws, employees at nonprofits suddenly had a big bite taken out of their paychecks—26 cents an hour, on average. This was at a time when teachers were earning something like $4 an hour, so 26 cents was a lot.

Clark went to the board to ask if anything could be done to help, if maybe tuition could be raised to give the teachers a raise. "What a naive son of a gun I was," he remembers. "Six months later they said no. They said, 'Isn't that a selfish perspective to have, to ask parents for more money when they're hurting, just because you need it.' Or, 'Hey, in this profession, you know it's not gonna pay; why are you in it if you're not expecting to make crummy wages?' And 'Isn't the love of the children more important than making a decent rate?' All those things occurred. It was a bloody mess. My blood, mostly. I went to countless finance meetings and board of director meetings. I actually got thrown out of a meeting by the president of the board of directors."

Shortly thereafter, Clark and his wife, Belindah, were watching "The Bob Newhart Show" on television one night, an episode about lumbermen's insurance. "The motto for lumbermen's insurance was, 'Hey, somebody's got to insure these guys,'" recalls Clark. "And I turned to Belindah and said, 'Hey, somebody's got to organize these guys.'" A year later, the nascent union asked five centers to formally recognize bargaining units. Four said yes; the board at Red Caboose asked for an election. The ensuing struggle was difficult for everyone. Says Clark now, "At one point the president of the board said, 'We know you want to be recognized as a union. Just because my daughter wants some candy doesn't mean I'll give it to her.' That made it very clear how we were perceived."

The board minutes from that year, 1985, reflect little of the conflict Clark describes. The subject was raised at the board for the first time in February. In May the first parent subcommittee meeting was held to discuss parent reactions to the idea of a union. In August a memo went to Wendy and the board, asking for voluntary recognition of the Madison Childcare Workers Union, "which has demonstrated majority support among the Red Caboose teaching staff," wrote the two board members who sent the memo. "We feel strongly that the unionization of childcare workers in Madison is an important step toward providing higher quality day care throughout the city." On October 16, 1985, the board voted to recognize the union officially.

Ten years down the line, the union is an accepted presence at a number of Madison centers, most of them nonprofits. Many of the teachers at this Worthy Wage Day celebration are staunch union supporters. Clark is one of the few men here, buzzing the periphery, clapping people on the back, his long hair flying loose around his head. Two-year-old Erica, here with her mother, holds out her arms to Denice, who lifts the girl into her lap. Ernie sits beside them, cracking gum, one knee jittering nervously. The speaker is telling the audience how she recently asked her kids what they want to be when they grow up. The oldest son said a lawyer, the middle son said a vet, and her daughter said a travel agent. "And I said to her, 'Well maybe you might want to be President?' " says the speaker. "And she said, 'Mom, why would I want to be President? I'm a girl. I'd be First Lady.' " A chorus of ooo's and indrawn breath ripples across the room, the women in the audience registering shock and disbelief. This kind of self-effacement has afflicted child-care workers as a group for years.

"So what I would say to you," continues the judge, "is what you already know in your hearts, that the services you provide to small kids are probably more important than anything we do in society. And you can take that knowledge and transfer it to political action. The best experience I had for the job when I took office in the state assembly was not practicing law, not having been a teacher's assistant, but parenting children. You can learn something from everything you do with children." Denice nods in vigorous agreement. "So take those lessons you learn in this job and mobilize them into action, because as you do that the world will change. The world will no longer be a place where women are sent home because the boys have come back. The world will no longer be a place where five-year-olds can aspire to be First Lady and not President. The world will be a place where in the long run child-care providers will be recognized not just in this room but throughout society for the important job you all do."

The applause when she steps down is long and loud, as if the wishes and dreams of the people in this room could by themselves change reality. But it will take more than that. In our society, those who work with small children tend to be devalued. "From nursery nurses to pediatricians, from schoolteachers to juvenile court judges, all . . . who work with children are paid less and given less prestige than . . . colleagues who work with adults," writes Sandra Scarr, who has studied child care. "And the younger the child, the greater the 'taint'—elementary school teachers make less than high school teachers, and so on up the line."[4]

Scarr attributes this devaluation to the fact that taking care of children is seen as women's work. "In my view it is the low status of women that has tainted work with children," she writes.[5] There are other explanations as well. In our society, respect and power come from money, and the one thing nobody here is talking about is where the money for worthy wages will come from. There are only so many sources available: parents, business, government, private philanthropies. All four groups consider themselves stretched to the financial breaking point already. All four are busy protecting their own areas of righteousness, their own turf, which piece of the problem belongs to them and which they can hand off to someone else.

People within the child-care community have varying ideas of how to generate more money. Clark, for instance, has been heard to suggest that parents take out loans to pay for higher-cost care—unlikely, given that families already spend between 10 and 32 percent of their income on child care, making it the fourth-highest expense for most families.[6] He sees rising fees at centers like Red Caboose as a lever for social change. "Those who can afford it continue to pay them and continue to groan about them," he explains with a grin. "That's a very positive thing. For one teacher that's 8 children, 16 parents, and a whole bunch of grandparents and whoever else is gonna get groaned to by these people who say they're paying too much money for child care and they can't afford it and geez that's awful. We *hope* they're gonna complain to their employers. We hope they're gonna complain to their policy makers. And we hope they're gonna complain on the TV and the radio and the "Oprah" show and in a letter to the editor. We hope they're gonna complain and groan so it becomes an issue that folks *cannot* disregard."

In Clark's scenario, child care would become a labor issue. "An employer who wants somebody to go to work, and they say, 'Sorry, I can't find child care at your wages,' that's a message to that employer," he explains. But how many Americans would go to a prospective employer and say something like that? "The family myth of today prevents parents from asserting their common interests to assure good care for their children," writes Sandra Scarr. "Each of us believes that we should be able to cope independently."[7] The pioneer ethos of self-sufficiency still informs our self-image.

If by some miracle corporations were forced to bear some of the burden for child care, says Clark, they would find a way to pass some of that cost to government. "Look at how Social Security came about," he says. "Corporations like GM and Ford were paying pension plans that their workers demanded through sit-down strikes. Those corporations said, 'Gee, this is breaking our backs; let's have the taxpayers pay for all these retirement benefits.' And the idea for Social Security was born." In the end, he says, the only group who could and should pay for care is taxpayers. "A dollar a year per taxpayer would double the quality of care in the United States," he says.

Opponents might argue that child care, like other industries, exists in a self-correcting free-market economy. But child care isn't like other industries. In an article called "Current Price versus Full Cost: An Economic Perspective," two economists and an early childhood administrator explain that child care is an example of "market failure," a situation where market forces *don't* produce the best quantity and quality of services. This market failure, they write, exists for several reasons.[8]

First, early childhood services are a *social good,* meaning that while they are paid for by parents, society as a whole has a stake in the quality of care. Second, these same services are also *merit goods,* which means that they provide more good to the consumer than the consumer realizes. If parents *understood* the true benefits of high-quality child care and the dangers of poor care, they would be more willing to spend money on good care. Third is what economists call the *income effect,* a fancy way of saying that the cost of child care is high in relation to parents' incomes.[9]

To compensate for these problems, the industry has developed different kinds of subsidies. *Supply subsidies*—defined as "any gift, discount, or other contribution that lowers the apparent cost of a particular service from what it would be if market costs were paid for all of its components"[10]—include teachers' forgone wages, in-kind services, and tax credits that help establish or expand child-care services. *Demand subsidies*—those that allow families to demand more or higher-quality care than they can afford—include scholarships, government subsidies, and tax credits. *Redistributional subsidies* redistribute costs for services among clients—for example, the sliding fee scale at Red Caboose, where richer families essentially subsidize poorer ones.

The result of this market failure is the current child-care crisis. "The present system allows pockets of quality care to develop, but does not provide systematic provision of quality services for all children," write the authors.[11] How can the industry be brought into economic balance? More subsidies—that is, more money brought into the system from outside. "The bottom line here is that child care in this country *can't* rely exclusively on parent fees to support it," says Barbara Reisman, executive director of the Child Care Action Campaign in New York City.[12] "We need to look at a more shared system of paying for child care." Which is exactly what Worthy Wage Day is all about.

Clark knows perfectly well that Governor Thompson isn't going to appear on the capitol steps, checkbook in hand, just because of this rally. But that's not the point. "It's not our problem to figure out how realistic it is," shouts Mary Babula, program director for the Wisconsin Early Childhood Association, over the sound of the crowd. "It's our job to say what we want. If we're not speaking up, then absolutely there *won't* be any more money. If everybody puts in a little piece, I think there will be more money. But only if we scream and yell about it, and if parents scream and yell about it to their employers and to the people they vote for. We don't have a solution yet. It's just that everybody has to help look at different priorities."

"Worthy Wage Day is billed as community education," Clark told me later. "The only effective component of it is raising the consciousness of people in the field. And that's the *only* thing that's gonna help us toward the day when we have reasonable, adequate compensation." Barbara Reisman agrees. "We could get a system in place here if we decided it was important enough, if parents and community leaders speak up," she insists.

By those standards, the day is a success. After a short march through downtown Madison, the group reconvenes on the steps of the state capitol, where speaker after speaker gets up to instruct, energize, enrage the crowd. The Red Caboose contingent grows. Seth, a Grasshopper, walks by with his father. Wendy bends down to greet Todd, who's here with his father. At the microphone a short fireball of a woman named Shag is leading chants. "What do ya want?" she shouts. "Worthy wages!" shouts back the crowd. "When do ya want 'em?" booms Shag. "NOW!" screams the crowd.

State Representative Tammy Baldwin stands up to talk about W-2. "The policies we've seen emerging from the building behind me are overtly hostile to the needs of young children," she announces, and the crowd erupts into cheers. "W-2 is the centerpiece of the antichild agenda. That program is going to dump tens of thousands of infants under the age of one year into the overburdened, overtaxed child-care system in this state next year. W-2 will establish a new, barely regulated level of child care, and along with that even lower wages for the individuals providing that care. Our hope is through empowerment. Empowerment of women, empowerment of underpaid child-care workers, and empowerment of children, who don't even get to vote."

Earlier today, Wendy attended a workshop on W-2, where she learned that some of its provisions are due to take effect this July. The copays, as she feared, will be steep. The lowest would be 7.5 percent of the cost of care—$35 or $40 a month *per child* in Red Caboose's lowest tier. Wendy also learned that provisional caregivers will be able to care for three children besides their own, and charge $57 a week per child. "At 45 or 50 hours of care a week," says Wendy, checking her math on a little calculator, "that's $3.45 per hour, before taxes." Far less than minimum wage. "And this is before expenses," she adds. "Even if you give them bologna on white bread, it still costs money to feed kids."

Of the families on county funding who are now at Red Caboose, most will probably get the minimum copay of 7.5 percent. That's good news for them and for the center, because it means there probably won't be a major exodus. The families who will suffer most are those a few steps up from the bottom, the so-called working poor. Right now Red Caboose has two such families, both of whom will probably lose their funding. "I don't know what they're going to do," says Wendy, shaking her head. "These are people who are totally struggling, especially the ones with more than one kid. They're really gonna get screwed."

Maybe things will change before W-2 actually takes effect. Maybe the negative comments and criticisms made at public hearings and rallies and on newspaper editorial pages will have some positive effect. Wendy does her best to be optimistic, but it's an uphill battle. "To have a good child-care system, our society, our culture, and our values would have to change so much," she explains. "Realistically, do I think that's going to happen?" She shakes her head. "Am I still gonna try my damn best to make it happen? You betcha. 'Cause otherwise I might as well go work in a shoe store."

At the rally, longtime Madison politician Spencer Black steps up to the microphone. He draws wild cheers and boos by mentioning several of the governor's pet projects that have recently gotten big subsidies. "What does it say about our priorities when some millionaire playing a game in the new baseball stadium is going to make more in nine innings than you make in nine months taking care of our children?" he thunders. Then feisty Shag is back at the microphone, exhorting the crowd. "We're gonna take that ball and, baby, we're gonna kick it!" she hollers. Wendy laughs. Mary, the Elephant Room teacher, strolls by with a sign that reads, "I care for 38 children so 56 people can work and go to school. I am not a babysitter."

One by one, teachers and parents step up to the mike and tell their stories. A young woman tells the crowd that her friend Holly, who used to teach at a center called Children's House, is now on her way to a new job. "Holly could no longer afford to do child care on what she is paid, so she had to leave the field that she has loved very dearly," she says. "She's been in this field for eight years, and now she's working as a children's librarian because it pays her a living wage. We've told her that the books we give to people are far more important than the people themselves."

The high point of the rally, at least for Wendy and some other Red Caboosers, is when Crystal Betterley, one of the Bumblebee teachers, gets up to speak. Crystal is a shy, grandmotherly woman, with short hair permed into curls and a perpetually worried look. She takes hold of the microphone with determination, as if she's steeling herself. "Hi," she begins. "I've been a teacher at Red Caboose Day Care Center for 13 years. I'm proud of that place." Her voice grows louder and more confident as she tells a story about a three-year-old whose life was transformed by his time at Red Caboose. "He looked very disheveled and rough," she says, "and I thought, This kid's gonna be trouble. But you know, I have never seen a child snap up knowledge the way he did. Every story hour he would sit with a light in his eyes. And one day he was gone. His funding was dropped. And when I think of it, it just breaks my heart." She raises her voice. "I believe there's a time in a child's life when they're open, like a little flower, and they are ready to accept encouragement and knowledge, and they're ready to learn. I know that child didn't go to any other day care. And I also know that the parents were almost unable to read, had a very limited vocabulary. The child did not go to a stimulating background. His chance was gone. I hope he gets another one."

Wendy listens in amazement, her mouth practically hanging open, her eyes shining. She is proud of this Crystal who is forceful and articulate in a new way, who can stand up in front of several hundred people and make her point. "We want poor children, we want all children to have equal opportunity to have a love for learning," Crystal is saying. "And I know one thing. I'm gonna be watching every single person I vote for from now on. I want to know where they stand in regard to families and children!" It's an incredible speech, the longest Wendy or any of the other Red Caboosers have ever heard Crystal give, and when she's done they clap long and loud for her.

On a sunny afternoon in mid-May, spring has come at last to Madison. Today is the day after Mother's Day, the day Madisonians traditionally put in their gardens, the day when all danger of frost is supposed to be over. There was a light frost last night, but by this morning all hints of winter are gone. The sunshine is brilliant, the magnolias in bloom, the trees covered with lacy green leaf blossoms. At 2:45 Gary raises the shades in the Elephant Room; nap-time is over. A number of kids are already out on the playground. Kenny and Andres pedal trikes, with Kylen riding along in back of Andres. Ernie walks with Stephen in her arms.

Denice is on her knees in the sandbox with Claire, Elena, and a few other children. Claire, in a little white dress with flowers on it, green tights, blue shoes with big bows and buckles, is pouring sand with her hands into a big bucket. She's in the fairy-princess stage, when only frilly clothes will do. The other kids are helping Denice pour handfuls of sand onto a slowly rising mountain in the middle of the sandbox. Denice, in blue jeans and a white T-shirt, is completely intent on her task. "Gettin' tall," she says. "A big moun-tain." Caetano pats the top with his shovel. Claire dumps a pink bucket full of sand on top. "Pat it with your hands. Be gentle," Denice reminds her. The mound grows and grows. "I like how Claire used her bucket," says Denice. "Does anyone else want to try a bucket?" One knee of Denice's jeans is ripped. Her bare feet are dug into the sand, her blue clogs paired neatly on the sand-box railing. The sand pile bears the imprints of many small hands. As the chil-dren add more sand, the shapes are half-erased, blurred, and then made again.

Anna C. appears at the open doorway of the center, standing sleepy-eyed and uncertain in tiny blue jeans, sneakers, a grown-up-style cardigan. She picks up a little yellow shovel and wanders down the playground. Crystal, wearing a gray sweatshirt and dark sunglasses, steps over the sandbox railing and sits down with Kenny in her lap. She begins digging, making a new sand pile with Kenny and Caetano. Kenny stands up to look at the top, a yellow scoop in one hand. Elena, wearing a purple long-sleeved top and terry pants, rolls in the sandbox for a moment. Then she stands up, covered from head to toe with sand, toddles carefully out of the sandbox, sits down on a tricycle, and pedals off.

Let's make a volcano: Denice dishes dirt with Kenny and other kids in the sandbox

Crystal pours sand onto the mountain from one side while Kenny pours sand onto it from the other. "Kenny's making a cake," she says conversationally. "The volcano's getting very big." Andres fills a bucket with sand and turns it upside down, lifting it with a flourish. The sand spills into a flat mound—it's too dry to hold a shape. "Do you play in the sandbox at home?" Crystal asks Kenny. "I don't have a sandbox at home," he answers. "I have a big house at home, though." "Oh, you're lucky if you have a big house at home," says Crystal. Kenny's words are much clearer, much more understandable, than they were when he started at Red Caboose last fall. "Do you go to the park to play with sand?" asks Crystal, continuing the conversation. "The park doesn't have sand," says Kenny, standing up to consider his volcano. The top is losing its point, the result of enthusiastic patting by a number of small hands.

As the afternoon wears on, more kids emerge from the cool darkness of the center, blinking in the bright sunlight—Adam, Emily, Roberto, Tom. Roberto's hair is parted on one side and cut short, making him look like a miniature man. Tom, too, looks different; his face is losing its baby sweetness, getting longer and more fully formed, acquiring a veneer of knowledge and experience. He's just starting to walk, still reverting to a crawl whenever possible.

Marina arrives, and Roberto runs to her for a hug. A freight train sounds its horn, passing through on a nearby track. When Marina disappears into the building to get Roberto's things, he panics, thinking she's leaving again. He races down the playground after her, sobbing. Marina, hearing him, turns back just as Sue scoops the boy up and lifts him into his mother's arms.

Kenny pushes a dump truck through the sandbox, rolling it accidentally over one of Tom's feet. Tom looks after Kenny, his face slack, not quite registering the pain. On the way back, Kenny rolls the truck over Tom's leg, and this time Tom shrieks. "Tom," says Denice, "that's Kenny's." Even the best teachers don't see everything that happens. Denice assumes that Tom's shriek is territorial—a reasonable assumption—and distracts him by lifting him away from the edge of the sandbox and handing him a yellow plastic shovel. "Look, Tom, let's put the sand up here," she says. Distraction works on minor injuries as well as on turf wars, so all is well again. Tom gets a scoop full of sand up over his head and flings it gleefully into the air and all over himself.

Kenny, meanwhile, is wandering away from the sandbox. "If you go away, your castle might get broken," Denice warns him, trying to prepare him for the inevitable. "I don't want it to get broken," he wails. "I'm going to get a drink of water," says Denice, getting to her feet. "If you want it you're going to have to stay here and tell people to be gentle with your castle. Akeem, will you be gentle with Kenny's castle? Caetano?"

Tom is still pouring handfuls of sand over his own head. Anna C. toddles up and down the ramp next to the sandbox. She pauses at the bottom of the ramp, looking meaningfully at the empty backseat of the tricycle pedaled by Kylen. Kylen shakes his head violently, and she obediently goes off. Theirs has been a very successful communication, even without the benefit of a single word.

At snacktime, Rachel comes to get Anna. She lifts the girl into her arms, and Anna lays her head down and smiles. "Mommy," she says. Snack today is hard-boiled eggs and crackers, eaten in the shady coolness of the Elephant Room. Denice gives Anna C. a snack to go—juice in a paper cup and crackers on a paper plate—because Rachel is taking her to a doctor's appointment. There's a faint but distinct smell in the room—fish going bad? a polluted lake?—which turns out to be the food for the room's newest pets, the hermit crabs. They eat something called trout chow, a combination of trout pieces and insects made into pellets. Wendy comes in to see how things are going, and stops to chat with Rachel about her own recent trip to New York City. "It was major women," Wendy says with a laugh, referring to herself, her two sisters, and her sister's twin daughters.

Snacktime today is very mellow. In fact, the whole day—the whole week— has been mellow. Haley and Andres, the newest Elephants, are finally begin- ning to settle in; it's not unusual for kids who come in from outside the center, either from another center or provider or from home, to have a tougher adjust- ment. As Denice says, things are starting to fit together again. She's enjoying the relative calm because she knows it won't last; summer is a time of change for kids and teachers both. "I'm having my beginning-of-summer depression," she explains. "There are new kids coming in and you think, Can I do it again? Old kids leaving that you're so attached to. And they're not even gonna ac- knowledge you on top of it. When they hit the Bumblebee Room, they don't want anything to do with you, because then they might have to stay in here." Almost despite herself, she grins; Denice may get depressed, but she doesn't stay that way. "Beginning of summer, beginning of fall," she muses. "Losing and renewing."

A gorgeous sunny morning in late May, the first clear day in a week of rain, rain, rain. The Elephants have been cooped up inside along with everyone else, and they're squirrelly as can be. What's worse, Wendy got a letter from the center's insurance company saying that she has to get rid of the trampolines because they're too dangerous. Gary is furious. "A couple of years ago it was wading pools," he says, referring to the last plaything outlawed by the insurers. "Now it's trampolines. Next it'll be walking. You know, we walk right along the street when we go out with the kids." Despite his irritation he grins at the thought of how the insurance company would phrase *that* letter, then frowns again. "We've never had an accident with the trampolines," he says. "If they had their way, they would sell you a policy that says you can't do anything."

So the kids are more than ready to hit the playground. Three-year-old Onawa grabs Anna C.'s hand and leads her to the swings. She settles herself on a swing and tries to get Anna to sit on her lap, but Anna, who until now has gone along willingly, begins to resist. To Joseph, who is pumping his legs on the next swing, Onawa says, "I'm taking care of her. I like to take care of her." She jumps off the swing and leads Anna away again. Anna walks placidly beside Onawa in her green and purple overalls, apparently not minding the attention. "You're taking such good care of Anna," says Carolyn, walking by.

Then Anna spots an unoccupied trike and pulls her hand out of Onawa's, set on her own course. "Anna, come on!" shouts Onawa impatiently. "I'm leading you!" Anna obediently swerves back to the older girl, who leads her up the long wooden ramp that looks out onto the parking lot. Cheryl, who's sitting on the edge of the sandbox with some of the Turtles, watches this interaction and laughs. Anna C. is the most obliging child she's ever seen. Luckily Anna's also getting better at standing up for herself when she has to.

Marina arrives with Roberto in tow. They're later than usual because Marina's mother has been visiting from Italy, and Roberto has been enjoying the time with his faraway grandmother. Marina leans over and hugs her son, kissing the top of his head. "OK, Roberto, *ciao*," she says. To Cheryl, she says, "I come around a quarter to five, I think." "Do you want a bucket?" Cheryl asks Roberto, drawing him into the play. Anna C., watching from the ramp, decides she wants a bucket too, and Cheryl gives her one. She carries it carefully, stepping up and over the wooden edge of the sandbox, and begins to dig fistfuls of sand. But Onawa reasserts her control, pulling Anna firmly out of the sandbox. Caetano grabs Onawa's other hand, Andres grabs Anna's other hand, and the four children promenade down the playground in a line, the two dark-haired boys bracketing the two blond girls like parentheses. Anna, the shortest, stumbles a little, keeping up with the older kids. Cheryl watches the procession with a grin. "Isn't that just too cute?" she says. "I wonder if Anna's that placid outside of Red Caboose."

The answer, of course, is no. Kids rarely act here the way they do at home, saving their worst behavior for their parents and families. This can drive parents to despair, but it's actually a good sign. Secure children can act up at home because they know their parents will love them no matter what. With other people, even the teachers at Red Caboose, there's always room for doubt. Like any healthy two-year-old, Anna C. throws tantrums at home, refusing to share and use words and listen and all the other things children learn to do as they become socialized. But she does it all in her own rather low-key way.

Now Haley trundles through the sandbox toward Cheryl, mumbling something unintelligible, clearly a complaint of some kind. "Wait a minute, Haley," says Cheryl. "Tell me again." Haley turns and points down the sandbox. "Do you need help?" asks Cheryl, getting up to follow her. "Do you need a bucket?" "Yeah!" says Haley, and Cheryl points her toward an unclaimed bucket. Haley and her mother have been on vacation for the last two weeks, and the break seems to have done the girl good. She seems bigger and more self-assured, and she hasn't cried all morning.

The line of four breaks up for a minute, the children squatting in the wood chips and scooping them up in their hands. Then Onawa gets up and once again takes Anna's hand. Caetano, on the other side, follows suit. The two bigger children step easily off the wood chips, over a low black rubber divider, but Anna C. has to sit down and slide off. Next Onawa tries to lift Anna onto the backseat of a tricycle. Anna seems willing but Onawa's not strong enough to lift her, so Anna steps up by herself. Onawa sits down beside her and Caetano squeezes in on the other side, squishing Anna in the process. Her sunny face registers distress, though she doesn't cry or complain.

But Onawa doesn't like the competition. She pulls Anna up and off the trike. Caetano leaps off and runs around to grab at Anna's other hand. Near the fence, the two would-be caretakers begin squabbling. Onawa tries to get Caetano to let go by yanking at Anna's arm. Anna looks confused. Onawa puts one arm around Anna's shoulders in a proprietary way and pushes Caetano's hand off her.

Nearby, Kenny is sweeping sand off the playground paths with a broom. Joseph, beside him, sings "Davey Crockett" in his high, sweet voice. Onawa and Caetano, with Anna C. sandwiched between them, do a kind of stumbling dance. Then Onawa lets go of Anna and beckons imperiously to Caetano. The two of them go into a little playhouse, abandoning Anna C., who looks grateful for the respite.

"Bumblebees, one minute to lunch," calls Carolyn. Cheryl begins gathering the Turtles. There's a sub in for Ernie today, a young woman who carries Tom in her arms while Cheryl takes Stephen and Dylilah, a new Turtle, by the hand. Mary comes out of the building to help the Elephants line up to go in for lunch. Children from three different rooms mingle on the playground. There is no sense of rigid boundaries among the different ages and teachers, no strict assignments of affection and affiliation. Haley is just as likely to sit in Cheryl's lap as she is to take Mary's hand. Carolyn has been pushing Turtles and Elephants on the swings right along with Bumblebees. The playground is everyone's turf, and so, too, are the children.

In the Elephant Room, the two-year-olds file into the bathroom to wash their hands while Jayne, subbing for Gary, wheels in the lunch cart. Hands washed, the children sit down at the tables by the windows, which today are decorated with crayoned hearts. Pink and purple and blue umbrella shapes hang from the ceiling. "It looks like soup," says Mary, spying a big bowl brim-

Heaven's angels: Andres tows Ulric and Kylen on a three-wheeler

ming with tomato broth. "I usually put the cheese in the bottom, for a surprise," she tells Jayne, who is ladling out portions. Turning to the kids, she
says, "My hands are a little wet. I'm going to shake my wings off. How about
a song?" "ABC!" calls Andres excitedly. While they sing, Jayne sets a bowl in
front of each Elephant, filled with broth, noodles, cheese, meat, and crackers.
Mary serves each child a piece of raw broccoli and cauliflower with a pair of
metal tongs.

The children dig in. Steam rises from the serving bowls, and Mary, eyeing
the small portions Jayne has distributed, says, "You think these guys don't eat
much, huh?" "Here come the noodles!" says Anna C., patiently waiting for a
bowl to reach her. From the hallway comes the sound of Kenny, shouting and

crying outside the Bumblebee Room door. "Milky, milky," chant Haley, Erica, and Forest, banging their hands on the table. "I'll get your milk as soon as I can," says Mary. "Banging on the table is not helpful. Eat your noodles if you're hungry."

Haley drops her spoon under the table. "Why don't you pick it up and rinse it off?" says Jayne, noticing her dismay. "It's right under the table." Haley kneels in a puddle of spilled water to retrieve her spoon. She waddles all the way around the table, getting down on her hands and knees and peering, but she doesn't see the spoon, sitting upside down in a pile of accumulating detritus. She begins to cry, for the first time this morning, but she stops quickly when Mary hands her another spoon. Erica sifts through the unwanted noodles and soup in her bowl, looking for oyster crackers. When she finds one she pokes it out with her fingers and eats it. Haley rubs her eyes. "Haley, are you tired?" asks Mary. This meal keeps the teachers busy dishing out more of everything—crackers, cheese, milk, noodles. Mary sprinkles oyster crackers on Wesley's bowl of noodles. "I don't want the yucky ones!" says Wesley, pointing to where a bit of tomato broth is touching a cracker. "This is cow milk," says Georgina primly. Andres holds up a big slice of cheese. "You found some cheese in your bowl," says Jayne. Mary, mopping up yet another spill, says, "This is one of those gravity days, when everybody spills their milk."

Caetano, accidentally on purpose, hurls his empty cup onto the floor. "Pick that up please," says Mary, deliberately not responding to this lukewarm provocation. Haley laughs, acknowledging reckless misbehavior with glee. She lifts her glass and takes a big gulp, and milk drips down her chin. She half-rises out of her chair, and Mary intercepts her. "Haley, will you bring the fruit over from the cart, please?" she asks. Delighted to be of use, Haley carefully carries a bowl full of green honeydew chunks to Mary, and is rewarded with a smile.

One by one, the Elephants finish their melon and cheese and crackers and soup and get up to throw away their plates. Mary sends Ulric to the bathroom to wash his hands, and then lets him put some broccoli and cauliflower in Harry's cage. "Put it where he can see it," she directs him. "That's right. Did he see it?" Ulric grins. Harry the guinea pig is a silent but important presence in the Elephant Room. He's furry, cute, and doesn't require much attention.

By 11:30 Mary has started changing diapers, and the two-year-olds are beginning their transition to naptime. "My mommy!" cries Wesley. "Mama come," says Haley longingly, then goes back to her melon. Wesley cries when Caetano leans over and deliberately shakes his hair into Wesley's face. "Talk to Caetano about it," suggests Jayne, who has been watching. "Don't do it," says Wesley with unusual fierceness. Caetano does it again and grins. "I guess I better help you sit up in your chair," says Jayne, scooting Caetano's chair away from Wesley's and straightening him. The minute she turns her back, he moves over and does it again.

In the bathroom, Mary has Ulric up on the changing table, cleaning a poop. Andres and Forest sit side by side on little potties. Haley gallops into the bathroom and spins clumsily around and around. "Whee!" she cries. She spins so hard that she falls to the tile floor. Mary lifts her up, pulls down her pants, and asks her to sit on the potty. "Is Andres going pee?" asks Mary, describing what she hopes is happening. Andres giggles. Soon Andres, Forest, and Haley are all shuffling around the bathroom, their pants down around their ankles, their bottoms naked. "Did you go pee-pee?" Mary asks Andres. "You went pee-pee. Haley went pee-pee, too!" She lifts Ulric off the table and pulls up his pants, then fits a plastic diaper onto Forest. "Did you eat a big lunch, and now you've got a big belly?" Mary says affectionately to the girl.

In the hall just outside the Elephant Room, Denice shifts restlessly from foot to foot, reading through a stack of papers. Once a year the Education Committee asks parents to fill out detailed evaluations of the center, rating various aspects of their child's care and adding comments if they want. Every year the evaluations are mainly positive, but there are always a few criticisms, justified or otherwise, and Denice is obviously wrestling with those at the moment.

"Parents want more feedback," she says, turning pages slowly. "It always shocks me when parents feel like they're not getting enough interaction verbally." Her voice turns bitter, unusually so. "I guess *maybe* they'd rather me just *leave* the children and stand for an hour and talk to them about what their child has done, *if* I have a chance to remember after all the time I spend with other parents telling them what *their* child has done." She shakes her head as if shaking off her anger. "I have to sit down and really look these over," she says in a tired voice. "I always try and give as much information as I can. It seems like these parents are all talking about communication in the morning, and that's the hardest time. With all the drop-offs you can only do so much. Sometimes I wonder how much of a wonder person parents expect us to be." She laughs. "It amazes me that they can't deal with the fact that we're just as fallible as they are. Not only that, we're *just* like they are."

Denice is right; parents *don't* want to acknowledge teachers' shortcomings. Which makes sense, given how guilty and conflicted they may feel about putting their children into someone else's care in the first place. This guilt has various repercussions—for example, a diminished ability to judge the quality of care. The University of Colorado study showed a distressing discrepancy between how good programs were and how good parents *thought* they were, with most parents overrating them significantly. The study speculated on why this is true and came up with several possibilities, one of which is related to parents' mixed feelings about child care. "The more [parents] value an aspect of care, the greater the disparity between their evaluation and that of the trained observer," wrote the study's authors.[13] And they're likely to value most highly those aspects of care they believe *they* should be providing: warmth, compassion, personal attention. The elements of love.

The flip side of this willed blindness is a kind of hypercriticism, where parents have little tolerance for a caregiver's lapses. Parents *don't* want to believe that teachers, as Denice says, are just like they are; they want teachers to be better than parents, do a better job than parents would do. Because if a parent really, truly believes that she would do a better job than her child's teacher, that her care would be better for her child, how can she emotionally justify leaving her child in someone else's care? How can she say good-bye and go off to work without tearing herself up inside in the process?

One Elephant is left at the table—Anna C., still methodically consuming chunks of honeydew. Forest, Andres, and Haley are standing at the good-bye window, each with a plastic dinosaur in hand, making them roar. The room echoes with their voices. In the bathroom, the next batch of Elephants is being diapered. Elena, Caetano, and Erica sit on potties. Denice and Mary bustle around, helping kids wipe, slipping on diapers, pulling up pants. Erica stands at one of the child-size sinks, scrubbing at the porcelain with a very soggy paper towel, the water running full blast. "Would you like to try to go potty?" Denice asks Anna C., who has finished lunch at last. She leads her gently to a small blue and white potty seat. "Look at these nice overall straps, they just come right down," she says, undressing her. Anna sits on the seat. "Look at that girl go," says Denice encouragingly. In her years at Red Caboose she has helped toilet-train hundreds of children.

Haley gallops into the bathroom and catches sight of Denice. "Hi, Denice!" she sings out, jumping up and down. A month ago she would have been crying, clutching Denice's leg, sobbing hysterically for her mama and her bottle. Denice hands Anna C. a wad of toilet paper. The girl applies it to the appropriate spot and stands up, revealing a pool of bright yellow urine in the potty. She's not quite sure what to do with the toilet paper, so she holds onto it for a minute before tossing it into the potty. "You did a good job," says Denice approvingly. "You made a lot of pee in that potty. Want to wash your hands?"

By the time Anna C. comes out of the bathroom, most of the Elephants are settled on their cots. Lora, who's taking over the last few hours of Gary's shift, reads a book about birthdays. Anna C. walks slowly to her cot, drags the blanket off it, and carefully tips the cot over onto its side, brushing off dirt invisible to anyone but her. Denice hands out pacifiers and blankets while Lora starts the nap tape, cheerful violin music, then sits down to read another book.

The Elephants twitch their way toward sleep. Haley lies on her cot, sucking on a bottle of water, twirling her hair. Erica sucks the green satin edge of her blanket. Elena wads her blanket into a ball, then lays her head down on it, clutching it with both arms. When the book is done, Lora pulls down the heavy shades, leaving an inch or so of light at the bottom, enough for the teachers to be able to see what they're doing—and enough so that someone outside could see into the room. Gary pioneered this arrangement so that he would never be totally alone with a room full of sleeping or resting children. Male teachers are especially vulnerable to accusations of child abuse, despite the fact that those fears are largely unfounded. One study found that out of 8,000 reported cases of physical and sexual abuse, only 2 involved child-care programs.[14]

"As Gary says, we have to turn on the curtains and close the music," quips Denice, making a last sweep around the room, pulling up quilts, tucking kids in. Haley follows Denice with her eyes but doesn't move from her cot, doesn't cry. Denice sits between Haley and Andres, holding her paperback book in one hand, rubbing Haley's belly with the other. The music washes over the two-year-olds, neatening up the atmosphere the way snow neatens a landscape, covering the bumps and irregularities, making time flow smoothly and melodiously through another midday interlude.

June

Early June, and Denice is still fuming about the parent evaluations. When she went back and examined them closely, she realized that most of the current Elephants had moved up from the Turtle Room, which probably affects their parents' expectations. It's easy for the Turtle teachers to talk with parents at the morning drop-off. "In the morning in the Turtle Room, you only have like four kids sitting in the Sunshine Room with Ernie," Denice explains. There are *always* more than four kids in the Elephant Room in the morning. And they're older, more mobile, and generally more rambunctious than the one-year-olds, which to Denice's mind makes life that much more interesting.

The Education Committee is one of the few committees Denice is willing to sit on. When it comes to children themselves and the issues that affect them directly, Denice can be very patient. But she has little tolerance for bureaucratic business and politicking. She grew up in Madison in a large family. At 15 she left home and dropped out of school. She spent a few months working with the Neighborhood Youth Corps, taking care of children at UW Hospital. "I was working with children who were having seizures, they were having cancer, and they were still loving, you could still make a difference in their lives," she explains. Among her other jobs was being a maid for a sorority house. At 18 she got her G.E.D.

She started working in day care soon after. Her first interview was at what she describes as a Christian center. "All the women were wearing dresses and high heels, makeup, fingernails, and at the time I was wearing a blue jean skirt I had made out of a pair of pants, a halter top, and a backpack," she remembers with a grin. "They told me they would hire me, I was a really nice person, but I needed to wear better clothes. And I thought, Anybody who would judge me on the way I look, I don't want to work for them." Then she remembered that two of her nieces had gone to Red Caboose. The center had a summer opening in the Bumblebee Room, and she was hired. That was the summer of 1979. She was 20 years old.

When the summer job ran out, Denice got some hours through an adult neighborhood program, and when that ran out she was hired as a long-term sub for the Bumblebees, and when the person she was subbing for quit, she got the job. After four years in the Bumblebee Room she switched to the Turtle Room, where she worked with Cheryl and Ernie for another four years. Then she moved to California for two years with her boyfriend. She came back to Madison a few times to visit, and she always subbed at Red Caboose to earn her bus fare back to the West Coast.

When Denice moved back to Madison for good, she started subbing again and eventually was hired in the Elephant Room. Working with two-year-olds wasn't her first choice, but she was lucky to get hired at all; teachers stay forever at Red Caboose, and the center rarely has to do a hiring. She could easily have gotten another child-care job—most centers are constantly looking—but for Denice, as for almost everyone else here, Red Caboose is home.

"The staff is really close," she explains. "They have one common cause: they actually believe in making life good for children. Plus, they're all a little bit off the wall." She laughs, a kind of throaty *heh-heh-heh*, the trademark Denice laugh. "I always joke that none of us would make it in the real world," she goes on. "We'd have to dress different, we'd have to learn different attitudes. We're all a little bit strange, a little immature, still like to put stars on our heads and dance around with dolls. People in three-piece suits with their little ties and their little oxford browns, doin' what we do? Unh-unh!" She laughs again. "We've been around each other a long time, and we've gotten our aggressions out on each other. Everybody's seen everybody else at their worst and at their best, and they're accepting. You can say to someone, 'I don't like what you're doing,' and then you can still work with that person. Or you can go to Wendy and say, 'I am sick of this shit and Wendy you're part of the problem,' and the next day she's coming up to you and saying, 'So, can I help you get a sub?' You don't find that in a lot of workplaces."

Maybe it's this closeness, this familial relationship, that makes Red Caboose different from other centers. The staff is hardly homogeneous; there are teachers in their 20s and teachers in their 40s, those with kids—from infants to grown children—and those who will never be parents. There are teachers like Amy and Janet, with college degrees, and those like Denice who, if they weren't required to by state licensing, would never set foot in a classroom again. And yet, as Denice says, they pull together in some essential way. The children can tell, and so can the parents. Long after their children have gone on to elementary school and high school they stop by to visit, they call Wendy to reminisce, they bring in toys and paints and clothes, they send money. When Red Caboose threw a 20th anniversary bash three years ago, several hundred people, many of them alumni, showed up.

Denice might not fit in at other workplaces, but she's right at home at Red Caboose. She didn't go to college, she hasn't studied early childhood education, she has little interest in theories. In a field struggling to become more professional in order to gain more respect, Denice is an odd duck. Her lack of formal education makes her less professional, but her years of experience, her warmth, and her basic connection with children make her a superior teacher. She herself is ambivalent about where she fits in. "I think they should make the qualifications for day-care teachers really high, so that no scum off the street comes in and wants to work," she says, "but out of maybe 50 scum there's going to be one that's me. Who never had any money. Never had anything, and nobody gave 'em a chance, and they were good. And somebody like me might never have the chance. So that sometimes bothers me. Because I feel there are people who are naturally born with a love for children, to make their lives better."

To many parents, Denice *is* the Elephant Room. She's not the lead teacher, but she's there at pick-up time, when there's more time to chat about how things are going. Her frank manner and high energy appeal to grown-ups as well as to kids. And despite the fact that Denice landed in the Elephant Room by chance rather than by design, she has come to love the two-year-olds. "This is the age group that shows me that you *can* make a difference," she explains. "In the Elephant Room, you take a plant and rip it out of the pot and point to it and say, 'Roots,' and the kids are like, 'Thank you, we love you forever.' And then you say, 'And you can pull the roots off,' and they're like, 'Ahh! You're our god! We will love you all day. All day we will say, Hi Denice! Hi Denice! And hug you. And when we leave, we will find you and say, Bye Denice! Bye Denice!' You've made a difference. You've given them the sight of the plant, to be able to look at it, feel it, destroy it, taste it, smell it, hold it. One little thing like that can make their day. You ask them what did they do and they say, 'Denice pulled a plant out of a pot and we got to pull the roots off.' That's the coolest thing we could do.

"You don't see as drastic a change in any other group as you do in this one," she continues. "They walk into our room basically with no social skills, no verbal skills, no potty skills, no art skills, no nothing skills, and they walk out of our room being little kids." She laughs. "In our room we can make or break a child. If they're a biter, we can break that forever. If they come in with a personality like, I am just ready for the world, we can promote that. We can have fun with that."

One of the ways Denice has fun with the kids is through art. Most afternoons at four o'clock, after snack, Denice can be found setting up an art project in the Elephant Room or outside. Usually the projects are simple and messy and without a lot of adult subtext. Back when she was working in the Turtle Room, before High/Scope came into vogue, Denice and the other teachers used to painstakingly prepare projects for the one-year-olds. One time, for example, they made number boards. Denice spent hours cutting numbers out of paper, from 1 to 12 for each Turtle. "Then we sat there and tried to get them to glue on these things," she remembers. "You know"—her voice goes high and super-cheerful, a parody of a nursery-school teacher's chipper tone— " 'We're going to glue, and you can cover this with glue, and here's your two little shapes for number 12.' What did they get out of it? A lot of glue is what they got out of it. Which is exactly what it should have been. Totally physical, totally glue. The parents were thrilled. I could have given the kids a bunch of ripped-up scrap paper and they could have had even more fun with more paper and less pressure. Instead I worked my butt off to do something because parents expected it."

So Denice's art projects now are exactly what the kids need and want: hands-on activities they can really dig into. One warm afternoon in mid-June, for instance, while the Elephants are out on the playground at wake-up time, she pulls out a big bag of noodles, some empty glass jars, bottles of rubbing alcohol and food coloring. After snack the kids will color noodles, and later in the week they'll glue those noodles onto cardboard or string them onto necklaces or use them however else they want.

Before the art project, though, the Elephant teachers—Denice and Lauren, who's been hired to replace Belindah—have another activity scheduled, one they're not looking forward to. Harry the guinea pig has been sick for several weeks. The vet prescribed antibiotics, and for a while Harry looked better, but then he started refusing the medicine. No one knows exactly what's wrong with Harry, but he's getting worse; yesterday when Lauren picked him up, a big clump of fur came off in her hands. The vet thinks it's time to put Harry out of his misery. So Lauren went to a bookstore during naptime and found a book to help the two-year-olds deal with the fact of Harry's death. This afternoon, after snack, she's getting ready to read it, and other books, to the Elephants.

Lauren settles herself on a pillow on the floor of the loft. Andres, Haley, and Evan sit on the couch, listening intently to *Chicken Soup with Rice*.[15] "In April I will go away to far-off Spain or old Bombay," she reads. Denice carries Peter, a small dumpling of a boy with a tear-stained face, up the ramp into the loft, sits down on the floor, and settles him in her lap. Today is Peter's third day at Red Caboose. The morning went well, but he woke up crying from nap and has been miserable ever since.

"Mix it once, mix it twice," reads Lauren, holding up the appropriate number of fingers, "mix that chicken soup with rice." Evan, who recently moved up from the Turtle Room, tries to buckle a strap on a dress-up purse. As Lauren reads, the Elephants pick up on the words, repeating them like a Greek chorus. "In July, I'll take a peek into the cool and fishy deep," reads Lauren. "Where chicken soup is selling cheap. Selling once, selling twice, selling chicken soup with—." She pauses, and half a dozen two-year-olds yell out, "Rice!" Haley nods approvingly, yelling with the rest of them.

Now Lauren is ready to tackle the problem of Harry. "Who's been really really sick in our room and getting lots of medicine?" she asks the two-year-olds. "Me!" says Andres with enthusiasm. "You? No, you're OK," says Lauren, "but Harry's been really sick. And we took him to the doctor, and we got medicine, but he's not getting better." A sudden hush falls over the children; Lauren's words or her tone of voice or both have clued them in. Bad news is

Project time: Denice tells Kaya and Kylen what they can do with a balloon and some paint

coming. "So I brought a special book to read about someone's animal," she continues. "This animal is a dog, our animal is a guinea pig."

"But dogs get sick too," puts in Denice. Peter is now sitting beside her, raptly watching Lauren, who opens the book and begins to read. "Ben went to pat his dog good morning," she reads. "She was an old dog." She gives special emphasis to the words *old* and *dog*, maybe because that's the title of the book, *The Old Dog*.[16] In the distance one of the many freight trains passing through Madison sounds its horn, a long, drawn-out wail. "He patted her, but she didn't wag her tail," reads Lauren. "Uh-oh," says Denice sympathetically, getting them ready.

"Ben got his father," continues Lauren. "He shook his head and put his arm around Ben. 'She's dead,' he said softly." "Ohhh," says Denice, modeling a dawning comprehension. Lauren goes on reading. "Ben looked at his dog, but she didn't look back. She just lay still. Ben didn't understand." The children are silent, taking in this idea. "Is she sleeping?" asks Andres hopefully. "It looks like she's sleeping," says Lauren, showing him the picture, "but she's not." She starts reading again: "He walked to school slowly, and when he came home, old dog wasn't at the door to meet him. Ben drank his milk, but old dog was not there watching him." "Where *is* old dog?" asks Denice. Silence. No one can answer that question.

"Death means someone isn't there, he thought," reads Lauren. "He was very lonely. It would never be the same. He closed his eyes. He almost saw his dog. 'I miss you,' he said into the air, and he began to cry."

"Uh-oh," says Denice. "Ben is crying. Why is he crying, Haley?" But Haley is fighting quietly with Andres over a stuffed badger. Denice takes it away from both of them. Andres's mother arrives to pick him up, and he jumps up to greet her. "No old brown and white dog was there to comfort him," reads Lauren. "She's up in heaven!" calls out one of the Elephants. Lauren holds the book up so the kids can see an illustration of Ben. "Is he laughing or crying?" she asks. "Laughing," says Evan happily. "I think he's crying," says Lauren. "Laughing!" insists Evan. Elena, who's been snuggling with her mother on the floor of the pillow loft, suddenly bursts into tears. Peter starts crying, too.

"Maybe we want to talk about this book," says Denice, putting the stuffed badger down. "Do we know that Harry is sick, too? Harry's an animal, just like that dog, huh? Is Harry an animal?" Several two-year-olds nod. "Is Harry getting sick, too?" asks Denice, pressing on. "Do you know that Harry has an owee? Do you think maybe Harry should go to sleep and not come back anymore?" "Yeah," says Haley uncertainly. "You know what?" continues Denice.

"We're gonna take Harry to a doctor and we're gonna have that doctor help Harry go to sleep so he doesn't have an owee anymore, and then we're not gonna see Harry anymore." "Doctor? Harry?" asks Haley. "We're not going to see Harry anymore," says Denice again. "So tomorrow when you come, Harry's cage is gonna be gone. We're gonna be looking for Harry's cage, aren't we?" "It closes!" says Haley. "It closes just right," says Denice. "We're gonna close it and put it in the basement. So maybe you want to say bye to Harry?" Peter bursts into tears again, burying his face in Denice's lap. Moira, Elena, Erica, and Caetano run down the ramp and over to Harry's cage on the floor. Denice lifts Peter, still sobbing, and carries him over to the cage too. "I'm ready to cry," she says.

On the floor in his cage, Harry stands, shivering. "He's an old guinea pig," says Denice to the children, clustered around the cage on their knees. "Harry's having some special seeds today." "Poopy," observes Haley. "Is he pooping again?" asks Denice. "That's part of his problem. Harry's our friend. Maybe someday we'll get another Harry. In like 10 years. Yeah." Lauren catches her eye. "Gary *does* want to get another guinea pig," she whispers. Denice shakes her head in disbelief. Harry's medicines and vet bills have not been cheap, and the money to pay for them has come out of the Elephant Room's budget for supplies. And Lauren and Gary have been coming in late at night to give Harry his medicine; Denice, who lives out in the country, didn't volunteer.

Now Denice deliberately shifts gears with the Elephants. "But you know what?" she says in a loud voice to the drooping children. "We still have our birdies on the playground. We can feed them anytime we want, huh?" She suddenly notices that Haley has a bottle in her hand. "Haley, can you go put that in your locker?" she says. "This is not a time for a Haley bottle. You know what we're going to do today for our project?" She crosses the room to show the two-year-olds the noodles and jars. The children follow her across the room, and the atmosphere lightens palpably. There's only so much sadness that two-year-olds, or any of us, can take.

Since there are only seven Elephants today, Denice decides that instead of splitting into groups, everyone will do the project together. She clears the table while Lauren sweeps the floor. Elena hops from foot to foot in front of her mother and her baby brother, Justin, who's strapped into his car seat. Denice steps out of the room, carrying the snack tray back to the kitchen, and Peter starts howling. "Peter, come and help me!" calls Denice, waiting for him. He runs after her, clutching his stuffed monkey.

While they're waiting for Denice to come back, Lauren asks, "What are we going to do for our project? Are we going to color our noodles?" She sounds a little like a cheerleader, but her repetitions help the Elephants through the tedious but necessary transition between reading and doing the art project. As Lauren begins shepherding the children toward the basket near the bathroom, helping them put blue vinyl smocks on over their clothes, Erica lays her stuffed animal on top of Harry's cage, to comfort him. "That's not a good place to put your bunny," says Lauren, not catching the intent behind the gesture. "You may go and put it in the loft on the couch." Erica does, but she still looks sad.

At 4:15 Peter's mother arrives. "Mommy!" he cries, coming undone at last, running over to her. "We were a little anxious but we still had—" begins Denice. She stops herself before she can say "We still had a good day," and says instead, "He really liked the crabs." Peter's mom kneels, rocking him in her arms, while he sobs and sobs. She lifts him up and carries him up into the loft, where she sits down and lifts the edge of her shirt. Breastfeeding is the one sure comfort after a stressful day.

Meanwhile, the rest of the Elephants are sitting on the silver line, the metal strip that divides the carpet and the linoleum, watching Denice open the windows. Elena's mother, Mary, sits next to her in a chair. Denice pours a little rubbing alcohol into each empty glass jar. "Each kid gets a jar to shake," she tells Lauren, and Lauren distributes them carefully. "Can you smell it? Can you smell the yuck?" asks Denice. She wants to make sure no one decides to take a drink. "Ooo, it smells strong, doesn't it?" says Mary. "Mary, we can just start sending you a paycheck," jokes Denice. "I should pay you guys for teaching me all these things," says Mary, smiling.

"OK, I'm gonna put some color in. Haley needs to sit down," calls Denice. Haley, at one end of the line, pushes Erica out of the way, so that Erica is now on the end. Denice pours a different color dye into each jar, yellow and blue and green and red. She mixes red and blue to make purple, and yellow and blue to make a different shade of green. The kids watch her attentively. At the back of the room, where the kids can't see them, Haley's parents, Kirsten and Jeff, stand in the doorway. Some centers have one-way windows where parents can watch their kids, but Red Caboose is so open that it's hard for parents to catch a glimpse of their children without being seen themselves. Kirsten and Jeff are making the most of an unexpected opportunity. Jeff is tall, with a mustache and goatee, wearing a black T-shirt with a black leather vest over it. His muscular arms are covered with elaborate tattoos—a skull, a bird—and he seems fascinated by what Denice is doing.

What she's doing is adding a handful of noodles to each jar, screwing the lid on very tightly, and handing each jar to a child to shake. Haley gets a green jar, Evan has orange, Moira has purple, Caetano and Elena have green. When the pale noodles are bright with color, Denice unscrews the lid of each jar and pours them out onto a paper towel, making lurid little mountains. Soon her hands are covered with dye, orange and turquoise and purple and yellow and green and red, a rainbow of color on her fingers. Peter, done nursing, hops off the couch and runs over. "Do more! Do more!" clamor the Elephants, so Denice pours more alcohol and dye into the jars for another round.

Kirsten and Jeff have moved closer and closer to the line of children. Now they kneel, side by side, behind a toy shelf, a few feet away from their daughter, who for a while is completely engrossed in the task at hand. Finally Haley spots them. She climbs to her feet, points to the pile of blue noodles in front of her, and says proudly, "Look, look!" Then she walks sturdily to the basket and pulls off her smock. "Do you need to wash your hands, Haley?" suggests Kirsten. Haley disappears obediently into the bathroom. When she emerges, her father holds out his hand. She tries to run past him, but he grabs her and gives her a kiss. Haley wriggles free, looking for her mother. Kirsten hands her daughter a bottle of juice and the three of them leave the center, the two grown-ups first, Haley a step or two behind, sucking on the bottle, twirling a strand of hair. They walk that way through the parking lot, warm in the late spring sun. After a minute, Kirsten half-turns, reaches back, and takes Haley's hand. Going home.

All through the spring, W-2 has been gaining momentum, a specter taking on flesh and bones. In early May the New York Times ran an editorial praising Governor Thompson's "bold, risky welfare plan." The editorial mentioned the governor's "generous health and child-care subsidies to all working-poor families," but said nothing about copays or provisional care. President Clinton went on the record to praise W-2 as well. But now, in mid-June, the President is backpedaling, saying he's not sure about granting the federal waivers needed to implement W-2—good news for W-2's opponents. The consensus is that Clinton is waiting for Congress to pass its own version of welfare reform. That way a Democratic President, rather than a Republican governor, could take the credit for "ending welfare as we know it."

One of those opponents is Dorothy Conniff, who oversees the child-care unit for the city of Madison. Conniff, a longtime children's advocate, is deeply worried about how W-2 will affect children and families. In an article she wrote for the WisKids Journal, she quoted Governor Thompson as having said,

"Every parent participating in W-2 can rest assured that their children will have quality care while they work." Conniff went on to ask, "What are the realities of child care in Wisconsin? . . . How good is the quality of care that is available to parents? The more we know, the more the Governor's statement resembles a wish rather than a fact."[17]

Conniff is also worried about how W-2 will affect child-care providers in Madison. In late June she calls a meeting of providers, and about 40 people show up, crowding into a small room on the second floor of the Madison Senior Center. Most of them are caregivers, teachers, and administrators. Most of them are women. Wendy and Kathi are here from Red Caboose, along with John, Todd's father. Rachel was supposed to be here, but her daughter, Anna C., is home sick, so she's not coming.

The problem for caregivers and centers is the copay. The state wants to re-quire low-income families to pay part of the cost of care, but it can't and won't enforce that requirement. Collecting the copayments will be up to providers, who have no real way of making families pay. They can threaten to disenroll children, but most centers are loath to do that because they worry that those kids will wind up in a bad care situation or even home alone. Anyway, by the time a child is disenrolled the family already owes a lot of money—money that will *never* be paid once the child leaves the center.

Mary Ann Cook, the administrator for the county's Economic Assistance and Work Programs, got one of the first copies of the copayment schedule yesterday, and she spells out the dilemma for the crowd of anxious caregivers. W-2 will have four tiers. Families on Tier 1 will be placed in private employ-ment, regular jobs, and will get the earned income tax credit—the same credit all working families get. These are the families Wendy and Clark and Pat Mapp are most worried about, the ones who make too much to qualify for W-2 but not enough to pay for decent child care or otherwise support their children. Families on Tier 2 will get subsidized jobs, where the state chips in money so an employer can hire someone inexperienced for a while. Eventu-ally, the hope is, those workers will be brought up to speed and will be hired in the usual way. Tier 3 is community service jobs, which will pay $550 a month, period, no matter how many children are in the family. "The rationale," says Cook in a neutral tone, "is to replicate the labor market, the argument being you don't get a raise when you have a baby, and it shouldn't be different for people on assistance." Tier 4 is a sheltered work and/or treatment program designed to get people who are now unemployable into the labor market, pay-ing $515 a month.

"The bottom line," says Cook, "is if you are a family of one mom and two kids making $1,785 a month—the cutoff for W-2—you're paying all of your child-care bill." If those two kids were preschoolers who went to Red Caboose full time, their monthly bill would be about $900. And, of course, taxes, rent, and food also have to come out of that $1,785. And health care. Under W-2 families will also have to pay at least $20 a month toward health coverage. Add that to the child-care copays and, says Cook dryly, "you see where the issue's gonna come." And it's coming soon: the child-care copays will start to kick in on August 1st. "Our staff have looked at some of the changes," says Cook, "and for some families, particularly those with several children, it's going to be dramatic. A lot of people are going to have a shock."

Now Dorothy Conniff addresses the effect W-2 will have on child-care providers. "What we've learned over the past few years is that the loss of a few enrollments can cause financial ruin to a day-care center," she says, acknowledging what everyone in the room knows. "Day care is a very marginal business. It requires a stable enrollment to keep it functioning." She passes out worksheets, talking as she goes. "What we hope," she says, "is that you will do an estimate of the financial hit you're gonna take, and that we can use that as a basis for looking for solutions. We want to have a sense of what the size of the problem's gonna be."

Conniff and her staff already have a good idea of the size of the problem. They've calculated that an "average" center in Madison serving 20 families would be trying to collect $3,900 a month from parents. More expensive centers will have to collect more—on average, an extra $1,960 a month. A center like Red Caboose could easily be trying to collect $5,860 a month in parent copays—about 34 percent of the center's total revenue. Wendy shakes her head. No way is any center going to collect that much money from poor parents, not even close.

Isn't it disingenuous for the state to impose copays without at least *trying* to enforce them? Isn't the state enacting welfare reform without bearing the true cost? Isn't this just another way to make child-care providers bear the economic brunt of social policy? Later in the meeting David Edie, director of the state office for child care, sidesteps these questions carefully, trying instead to put a positive spin on W-2. And it *does* have some good elements. Under W-2 there will be just one funding stream instead of the many convoluted funding sources that exist now. That's very good news. And the state is putting another $100 million toward child-care funding for poor families. This isn't as good as it sounds, because that money is going to have to cover many more families. More families will get something, but many families will get much less than they need.

"I think the assumption is that every family is gonna get a worse deal under this program," says Edie at last. "What I'm saying to you is that there are a whole lot of folks out there who are trying to pay for child care now with *no* subsidy from *anybody*. A lot of people are going to be getting a *better* deal under this program. The change on families is not a one-way street. Some families are gonna get less of a benefit, but a whole lot of families are gonna get more of a benefit. It's hard to say what choices they're gonna make, given the financial arrangements of this program."

Edie makes some good points, but he's still evading the underlying issue of quality care versus cheap care. It may be hard to say what choices poor families are going to make under W-2, but it seems clear what choices they *won't* be making: they won't be buying high-quality, high-cost care. They simply won't be able to afford it. The state is putting financial pressure on poor families to go for the cheapest and lowest-quality child care available. That pressure will inevitably have repercussions on the families and children who succumb to it.

Dorothy Conniff, who has been listening intently, now asks, "Is there room at some level in the state to consider the quality of the child-care system, and what the effect will be on the quality of care available? We struggle very hard to support quality in programs. And it's a real struggle."

"We live in a political system," says Edie flatly. "The vote for W-2 was overwhelming, 100 to 31 in the combined houses. People voted on what they thought was right. If someone can make a case to them that this isn't good for families and children and programs and business, they may rethink it. There was a lot of concern about the copayment system by the legislative leadership as it went through. And it got better. They added $25 million in the last couple of weeks."

"I think David has made a very important point that we should never forget, despite the fact that half of us never vote," says a woman sitting in the crowd. "This is a democracy, and it takes active participation. Call your legislators, let them know what is happening. There is goodwill in the legislature toward making this work. W-2 is not uniformly a bad program. But there has to be knowledge, and all of you know that the child-care industry was not talked to while this whole thing was drafted. In January the legislature comes back into session, and we can talk with them again."

Perhaps the most incisive comment of the whole meeting comes from Judith Wilcox, a member of the county board. After listening to almost an

Story time: Lauren reads to a small group of Elephants

hour of horror stories and despairing comments, she speaks up. "I think you should focus on the fact that you folks are business," she says firmly. "And God knows if there's anything our legislature is looking at, it's business. I mean, *way* far and above what the impact is on families is what is the impact on business. So forget your social role and focus on the message you want to get across: Are they really trying to put you out of business? We're subsidizing many, many businesses in the state. Seems to me that day care is a business that keeps other businesses in business, because they provide employees at a time when it's very difficult to get employees. So make the arguments they're gonna hear. Not 'Do this because it's a good thing,' because they're not gonna hear that."

The two arguments are not, of course, mutually exclusive. In its 1991 report, the National Commission on Children pointed out, "Doing what is right and doing what is necessary to save our national skins are one and the same. Our best instincts to nurture, protect, and guide the young, when translated into policies, programs, and voluntary action, benefit society as well. Some of these benefits are easily measured—healthier, better-educated children; decreased crime, violence, and their associated costs; increased tax revenues and lower welfare payments; improved productivity of American industry and labor. Others, while not as readily quantified, are equally significant—stronger families; more active, inclusive communities; a freer, fairer society; a more optimistic citizenry."[18]

The commission's words fell on deaf ears in 1991, and they go equally unheard now. Wilcox's suggestion is more to the point, politic advice for a group that hasn't had much of a role in shaping policy. It's tempting to argue the case against W-2 as a good versus evil kind of thing, because moral issues *are* at stake. Child-care teachers and administrators know they're right to draw a distinction between good child care and care that is mediocre or damaging. They know it's not just a question of turf wars but a real concern, one that is backed up by the research.

But, as Edie points out, the legislators have voted overwhelmingly against the moral high ground. Their votes say either they don't care what happens to children or they can't politically afford to care. Judith Wilcox is right: the only useful strategy is for caregivers to emphasize their role in keeping other businesses afloat, to position themselves *within* the business community rather than standing outside like some kind of poor relation.

It's a sad commentary on our society that money takes precedence over the health and well-being of children, but it's not a new one. It's time for the childcare community to acknowledge reality, to become politically savvy. To grasp the nettle and go on.

SUMMER
THE GRASSHOPPER ROOM

July

Eight children are lined up in the Grasshopper Room hallway, sweating and fidgeting. Children come and go in a room all year long, and different kids attend on different days; still, each year a group personality seems to develop that lasts the whole year. This year's Grasshoppers have had little interest in sit-down projects—making alphabet books, for example, a traditional Grasshopper project. Instead they've spent hours in dramatic play, acting out vividly imagined scenarios, everything from *Aladdin* to *Cinderella* to original stories. Dramatic play sounds formal—parents envision a director, costumes, scripts—but in reality it's a fluid form of social interaction for four- and five-year-olds, a kind of ongoing conversation that can take place in the kitchen, at the art table, in the loft, on the playground, even sitting on a bus.

The most popular scenario this year has pitted the boys—the "princes"—against the girls—the "princesses." Each prince has several princesses, whose duties seem to include chasing and kissing the boys. The Grasshopper teachers—Amy Schuster, Janet Grady, and Emily Lyman—have watched this game develop in amazement and amusement. Many of these kids have parents who take great pains to break down gender stereotypes, to instill a sense of egalitarian feminism in their children. From their perspective this game seems both atavistic and incomprehensible. But games like this are how four- and five-year-olds make sense of the world.

"Dramatic play is their time to work out the things going on in their heads, things they're curious about or that trouble them," explains Amy. "At this age they're moving out of the egocentric phase. They're beginning to realize how things affect them and other people, and it's scary. They have to find some way to work it all out, and that's how they use dramatic play." The prince-and-princesses game, she says, probably grows out of the children's understandable confusion about their sexuality and gender, their place in the world. "We see them constantly playing games like princesses, cops and robbers, prisoners, being kidnapped, being lost, thrown in jail," says Amy. "All of those are big issues that they hear about but don't really understand. The dramatic play is their way of trying to understand."

This morning Emily Lyman, who's normally here afternoons, is subbing for Amy. Emily sits crosslegged on the floor in the hallway, her brown hair piled in charming disarray on top of her head, shouting to make herself heard over the loud whir of a fan. This is one of several transitions the Grasshoppers make during the day, in this case between breakfast and going outside to the playground. Slightly off-key, Emily sings to the kids, "Under the spreading chestnut tree, I played my banjo on my knee, I was as happy as can be, under the spreading chestnut tree." Each line has its own hand gesture, which Emily demonstrates as she sings. "OK," she says loudly, "do you want to take one out?"

This is a game the children know and love. This time through, instead of singing "Under the spreading chestnut tree," Emily and the Grasshoppers sign it, bringing their hands together in a point over their heads for *under*, bringing their hands down and around their bodies for *spreading*, then shouting out the rest of the song in a ragged chorus. "What should we take out next?" asks Emily. "I play my banjo on my knee!" calls Gracie. She has short straight brown hair, a bowl haircut with bangs. The Grasshoppers add the appropriate gestures, wringing their hands up and down in an approximation of strumming. "There's only one part left," says Emily, smiling at a small girl with curly dark hair. "Do you want to take it out, Cory?"

Cory nods, a loose-jointed, rolling motion that makes her round blue glasses slide down her nose. "Which part?" asks Emily, and Cory holds one hand to her forehead, palm down, the edge of her hand just under her hairline. "I don't know that sign," says Emily. "It's . . . it's . . . it's a haircut!" Emily grins, a bit sheepish that she doesn't understand Cory's sign, then brings her closed hand to her heart, the sign for *happy*, standing for the last bit of the song left to be taken out. This time the Grasshoppers go through the song in complete silence; only their arms, sweeping through the air grandly, shaping the signs, keep time to the tune they hear in their heads.

Cory can hear it too, but she can't sing. Nor can she talk, although she can produce some sounds and say a few short words like *up*. Cory has a kind of cerebral palsy, probably caused by malnutrition or injury before or during birth. Her birth mother died in childbirth. Cory's adoptive mother, Jenny, first

It's hard to say who's more into the story, Emily or the children—Jacob, Lateef, and Lydia

laid eyes on her when she was about a month old, in a refugee camp on the border between Burma and Thailand. In the late summer of 1991, Jenny was 26, living in Bangkok, working for an international relief organization. She was touring a camp for refugees from the Karen tribe, one of Thailand's oppressed ethnic minorities. As she walked through the compound of bamboo houses on stilts with the camp leader and his wife, Lulu, a midwife came up to them and spoke in the Karen language. Lulu turned to Jenny. "The woman said she delivered a baby a month ago and the mother died and the baby's dying," Lulu told her. "The father tried to give the baby away to her, and she couldn't take it. She wants to know if I could take it, and I said no. I told her to bring the baby to you."

Two years earlier, while working in a hospital in Thailand, Jenny had become fond of an infant, Lena, who was ill with pneumonia and encephalitis. After Lena was discharged from the hospital, her birth mother sold her to a childless couple for four dollars. The couple brought her back to the hospital because she wouldn't eat; she was defective merchandise, and they returned her.

At almost a year, Lena weighed 10 pounds. Her illnesses had left her with serious neurological damage. It was clear to Jenny that either she could take care of Lena herself or send her home again, this time to die. "I didn't know how I was going to feel about myself when I looked back in 10 years," says Jenny in her precise, ironic voice. Her hair is cut short, showing small earrings. Her chin comes to a point, giving her face a determined air. "I was scared because I didn't think I would be a very good parent. But then I thought, There are lots of bad parents, and I can do at least that well, and maybe it beats starving in a corner of a hut."

When Jenny first brought Lena to America, the girl refused to pick up food, to touch anyone, to use a tool. It took Jenny a while to realize that Lena had been slapped or beaten when she used her hands. For months Lena wouldn't put her hands near her mouth, wouldn't hold her own bottle, wouldn't feed herself. "And one day I was standing in the doorway, she didn't know I was watching," remembers Jenny, "and I saw her pick up a bit of cereal and slowly, slowly, slowly put it in her mouth. And I cried."

For the rest of that summer day in 1991, as she and Lulu walked around the camp, Jenny waited for the midwife to bring her the dying baby. Dark was falling, and she had a long drive ahead over roads muddy and torn up from the seasonal rains. She was about to get into her truck and start for home when a woman ran up and handed her a tiny, filthy bundle of rags. A crowd gathered quickly. Someone took the bundle from Jenny and opened it, and in the candlelight Jenny got a glimpse of "something batlike." Lulu looked up grimly and said, "You better go right now."

Jenny found herself and her Karen guide, a woman named Lydia, riding hell-for-leather in a truck toward town, an hour away. Lydia held the baby on her lap while Jenny drove. "I kept saying, 'Is she alive?' and she said, 'I don't know, but she's still warm,'" remembers Jenny. When they got to town, Jenny opened the cloth bundle and saw Cory for the first time. "Her eyes were rolled up in her head, and I thought, Oh great, she's blind," says Jenny with a wry laugh. "Then I thought, OK, we can live with that." Later that night, after Jenny had fed the baby and cleaned her up—she had never been bathed, and Jenny had to oil her and literally scrape the dirt off—Cory opened her eyes, and Jenny realized that she wasn't blind after all. Her eyes had been rolled back because she was so close to death.

Five years later Cory is small but sturdy, with a legendary appetite and the will to match. Because of the brain injury her muscle tone is poor, so she's been late to reach physical milestones like sitting, standing, and walking. As an Elephant and Bumblebee she used a low wooden cart, the kind sold by baby catalogues, to help her stand and walk. But now, amazingly, Cory can do most of the physical things the other Grasshoppers can — not as quickly, not as smoothly, but she can do them.

Except for talking. Cory started to say a few words sometime in her third year. And then one day Jenny, in an effort to encourage her to talk, told the girl she wouldn't pick her up until she said "Up." "Cory quit talking for months and months," Jenny remembers. "She's always been like that. When she was a tiny baby, if her bottle was the wrong temperature, she would rather starve than give in. I wanted her to drink room temperature stuff, but nope, she would rather die. She *will* not be pushed around." She grins. "Everybody knows she's bullheaded, and that makes it hard to know what else is going on."

By the time Cory was three, it was clear that she needed some other way to communicate with the people around her. Her cerebral palsy seems to affect her most from her nose to her chest; her neck is weak, she chokes frequently, she has trouble controlling the movements of her tongue. Jenny had to accept the possibility that Cory wasn't just being stubborn, that her daughter might never speak like other people.

Like many young children, Cory was very good at nonverbal communication — pointing, leaning, smiling, grunting, and otherwise using her body to show other people what she wanted. But there's only so much that can be expressed without words. So at age three, Cory started learning American Sign Language (ASL), the language of gestures used by many deaf people in this country. ASL is not an easy language for Cory; her lack of muscle tone makes it difficult for her to move her fingers with precision, so many of her signs are hard to understand. Over the last two years some of the teachers at Red Caboose — notably Carolyn, Crystal, and Amy — have taken classes in sign language so they could communicate with Cory. Many of the other children have learned some signing, too.

But it's not enough. By age five, children are putting fairly complex thoughts and feelings into words and games, games that are the basis of their learning and social interaction. Clark says, "Our job in the Bumblebee Room is play." The same is true in the Grasshopper Room. A child like Cory, who can't enter into dramatic play as the other kids do, who can't spin her own tales or add her own elaborations to the group story, is left out more and more. Not because other kids are mean or exclusionary, but because in the most basic sense they can't talk to her.

And it's not for lack of trying. It's hard to know what Cory's experience would have been at another center, but at Red Caboose teachers and kids and parents go out of their way to include her. At calendar time, for instance, Amy and Janet try hard not to overlook Cory as the other kids "read" the calendar, bring in show-and-tells, and choose what they'll do for the rest of the morning. In the Grasshopper Room more than in any of the other rooms, the children learn academics, specifically those things that kids in public kindergarten are expected to know: how to recognize the letters of the alphabet, upper- and lower-case; how to recognize numbers up to 20; how to write their own names; their address and phone number; and, maybe most important, the social rules of functioning in a group—raising hands, taking turns, participating. The teachers spend a lot of time and energy preparing the kids for kindergarten, both academically and emotionally. The closer it gets to the beginning of public school—only seven weeks away now—the more anxious the kids become. Many of them don't remember going through a transition this big before, especially those who have been at Red Caboose since they were toddlers.

This morning Janet helps settle the children on the floor in the book area and then stands beside a large, hand-drawn calendar on the wall. Janet is a round woman with a pleasant face and a kind voice. She's heavily pregnant, due at the end of August; her four-year-old daughter, Megan, is enrolled part time. The Grasshopper Room is actually two rooms, connected by an open doorway. The Dinosaur Room, named for its dinosaur wall hanging, is where the sign-in sheet and log book are. It also houses the play kitchen area, with a toy refrigerator and stove and realistic-looking vegetables and fruits. There's a tiny bathroom off the kitchen area, with one toilet and sink. Across from the kitchen area is the loft, an elaborate two-story space reached by climbing up a wooden wall with variously sized foot- and handholds. Next to the loft is a computer, and next to that is the book area, a small carpeted corner with a chalkboard and a rack of books. Near a door into the Moonshine Room is a corner with Legos and other building toys, and across from that are a couple of low tables and chairs and a sink. A guinea pig lives in a cage in the far corner.

Through the open doorway near the tables is the Busy Room, with another group of long, low tables and chairs. Like the Bumblebees, the Grasshoppers eat breakfast and lunch in small groups, half in the Dinosaur Room with Amy and half in the Busy Room with Janet. The Busy Room has a carpeted corner with dollhouses and other toys, a low table with leaves, snakeskins, and

A view from the Busy Room into the Dinosaur Room

other interesting objects, another computer, and a door leading into the back hallway.

"OK," says Janet. "Who remembers what we said about the calendar on Friday? What was going to happen today?" "Take 'em off!" chorus the children. "All the numbers come off," confirms Janet, pulling the Velcro numbers off the June calendar page. "It's a new month. Brad, do you know what month it is?" Brad looks down and thinks. His blond hair is cut short on top, with a long tail in back. "It's not June anymore," Janet reminds him. "July!" cries Brad, looking up triumphantly. Janet smiles. "We have a birthday in July," she says. "Does anyone remember who it is?" "Cory!" says Lateef promptly. Since moving up to the Grasshopper Room, Lateef has appointed himself Cory's protector and best buddy. "Yes," says Janet. "Cory's birthday is July 17th. Very soon, Cory. Let's see. You're going to be seven? Eight?" Cory holds up five fingers, her mouth wide open in a grin, her glasses sitting crooked, as usual, on her nose. "Five? Am I being silly?" asks Janet.

Emily sits down on the floor with the children, and immediately Onawa sits down next to her. Onawa is a Bumblebee, but she's here this morning visiting Emily, who besides being a Grasshopper teacher is also her stepmother. Lydia and Claire sit together; Claire, in a pink tutu, is also a visiting Bumblebee.

"Does anyone know what letter July starts with?" Janet asks the Grasshoppers. Cory lifts her pinkie in the air and loops it down and around, signing the letter *j*. But as hard as Janet tries to watch Cory, to be aware of her responses, she doesn't notice. "G," guesses Lateef. "J," Janet corrects him, pronouncing the letter with great clarity. "J. Ju-ly. July." She holds up a rectangular card with the word *July* hand-printed on it. "What letter is this?" she asks, pointing to each letter in turn, and the children chant them together: J-U-L-Y. "How many letters is that?" asks Janet. "Cory, how many letters is this?" Cory holds up four fingers, just as Gracie blurts out the answer.

Janet Velcros the July card to the appropriate spot on the calendar and moves on to the day of the week, holding up the card labeled "Monday" and asking the Grasshoppers to spell the word together. Cory signs along as the others say the letters out loud. Finally Janet changes the date, sticking the number 1 up on the calendar. Today is Monday, July 1st.

The calendar took longer than usual this morning, so show-and-tell is brief, just a peacock feather and a pheasant feather that Gracie absolutely can't wait to show the others. She runs to her locker to get them, and while the group waits Janet says conversationally, "Lateef is just back from his vacation. He went where?" "My grandma's house," says Lateef. "And where was that?" asks Janet. "Pittsburgh," answers Lateef. "And Marley just came back from her vacation, and you were where?" continues Janet, and answers herself. "In Door County at your dad's."

Gracie's feathers are much admired. She lets some of the other kids touch them, holding the feathers out to them so that the polish on her nails is clearly visible. When she's done, Janet asks, "Who's ready to make choices?" Cory raises her hand. "OK, Cory, what is your choice?" says Janet. "Are you going to get Dyna to tell me?" Cory gets up and half-skips, half-toddles to the art corner, where she leans over and tugs at a long plastic handle attached to a green cart on wheels. The cart is wedged between the wall and the easels, and it takes Cory a bit of maneuvering to turn it around, pull it out, and wheel it to the waiting group. She flips a switch on the cart and waits for Dyna to boot up. The rest of the Grasshoppers watch her silently, waiting for the conversation to resume. After a minute or two Dyna's screen begins to glow, revealing a row of computer icons in boxes. Finally Janet says, "OK, what is your choice, Cory?" Cory presses an icon, and a flat, childlike voice issues from the machine, saying, "I would like to play in the kitchen."

"OK," says Janet patiently. "Is there someone you would like to play in the kitchen with? Can you tell me who?" Cory lifts her hand, palm out, and pulls her fingers and thumb back so they're bent at the first knuckle, signing the letter E. "Erick?" asks Janet. Cory has developed special signs for some of the kids and teachers, and the rest she refers to by the first letter of their names. Now she repeats her sign and points, away from Erick. "Oh, Emily?" says Janet, getting it. "I'll meet you in the kitchen, OK?" says Emily. Cory beams. She carefully maneuvers Dyna over to a wall, where it won't be in the way, and heads for the kitchen.

Dyna is new in Cory's life, on loan from the public school district. The Dynavox, as it is officially named, is a voice output machine, a computer designed to speak for someone who can't. The district hopes Dyna will help Cory function in the mainstream world. While its technology is amazing, the machine is at best a cumbersome replacement for speech, a sloth in a world of cheetahs. Dyna is most useful in the large group, when Janet and the other teachers can give Cory a chance to get the machine, turn it on, and push the right buttons. The time lag is awkward but not impossible. But in the flurry of normal social interaction, kids shouting questions, correcting one another, telling a story, expressing a feeling, Dyna is virtually useless. By the time Cory can find the right icon and press it—*if* it exists, if her mother has programmed Dyna with exactly the right phrase or story or sound—the conversation has swept past her. Very few five-year-olds have the patience to hold a conversation with Cory and Dyna.

There are other drawbacks, too. In a crowded room, with lots of background noise, even grown-ups have trouble understanding Dyna's uninflected words. On the playground on a summer day, the machine is practically unintelligible. And bright lights and sunlight create glare on the screen, making it hard for Cory to find the right icon. All in all, Jenny's not sure whether the limited range of expression Dyna gives her daughter is an asset or a liability. She was thinking about Dyna on the day she went to speak to a second-grade class at Midvale, a public school on the near west side, where Cory's cousin goes. The kids there had heard about the cousin who didn't speak, and they wanted to know more. Jenny used her visit as an opportunity to educate the kids—the hard way.

"I made all the kids put tape over their mouths," she explains. "I knew one kid had a pet rat. So I asked him questions about his pet rat, and I deliberately called it a *he* when I knew it was a *she*. I could see and hear some of the kids talking around their tape, trying to tell me it was a *she*, and I ignored that. I talked to them later about how frustrating it is when someone gets something just a little bit wrong, but you can't get past that. I want Cory to be in places sometimes where she can get away from that, where she can just say, 'Look, the rat is a *she*,' and move on."

Jenny is an ardent supporter of Red Caboose—both of her children have gone there—but she's had to face the fact that for Cory, at age five, Red Caboose is not ideal. There's no way someone can always be watching Cory, helping her express herself, facilitating her play with the other kids. In a group this size it's too hard to catch the important interactions, to be there when it matters for the kids. Janet and Amy and Emily do their best, but they can't give Cory constant one-on-one attention. Not that Jenny expects that; she just wishes Cory's road wasn't always so hard.

This morning at choice time Gracie and Marley, who have been best friends for almost two years, decide to paint together. They stand side by side, each with a sheet of yellow construction paper clipped to her easel, carefully adorning their pages. Janet, helping Claire on with her shoes, stops to watch them for a minute. "You have different color grasses," she says to the girls. "There *are* different colored grasses, depending on where you live. I like both of them." She admires the paintings silently. "What are you putting on top of your grass, Gracie?" she asks. "A rainbow," explains Gracie, carefully adding purple and orange stripes. Marley pulls at the back of her dress and studies Gracie's painting intently for a minute; then she asks Gracie for the pink paint. "Can I please have the yellow, Marley?" Gracie answers politely, and they exchange colors and keep on painting.

During choice time Wendy appears in the Grasshopper Room on a mission of—not mercy, exactly. More like public health. One of Wendy's areas of expertise is checking for head lice, a plague common in preschools and public schools, and she's just learned that a child who slept over at Onawa's house has them. She stands Onawa between her knees, near a window where the light is good, and begins combing through the girl's hair with her fingers, looking for signs of lice: tiny white egg cases sticking to individual hairs, or (much, much worse) small brown insects leaping across the scalp. Emily watches Wendy check her stepdaughter. "I really don't want to get lice," she says. "She better not have it." Cory taps Emily on the shoulder to get her attention and hands her a plastic doll. The doll is naked, an anatomically correct boy, and Emily dutifully pulls on the clothes Cory hands her. When she's done, she hands the doll to Cory and says, "Babies need a lot of hugs." Cory cuddles the doll to her chest and smiles.

Wendy stands up and tousles Onawa's hair, setting her free. "You're fine," she tells the girl. "Yes!" cries Emily. Now she *won't* have to go home and vacuum the sheets. Now she can turn her full attention to the Grasshoppers. "Is your baby getting ready to go out somewhere, Cory?" she asks. Cory closes one hand into a loose fist, palm outward, and wags it up and down, the sign for *yes*. Todd, who's recently moved up from the Bumblebee Room, pretends to give Cory's doll a shot with a toy syringe. "This baby doesn't like shots," says Emily. "You know what happens when he gets shots? He cries. Do you cry when you get shots?" "I don't get shots," says Todd slowly. At this age kids often *don't* remember getting shots, unless they've just gotten their kindergarten shots. "Give medicine to my baby," he says, holding up a doll. Emily takes the doll—another boy—and cradles it, then hands it back to Todd, who squirts imaginary medicine into the doll's mouth.

Lydia brings her doll over for some medicine, too. Cory wanders toward a pile of old keyboards, calculators, and telephones, regards them for a moment, and wanders off. It's hard to tell, watching her, how much intention is behind her movements; her lack of muscle tone gives her a shambling, wandering gait no matter how purposefully she moves. Still, she's come a long way. Two years ago, when she had just started walking unassisted, her gait was slower, more meandering; she always looked as though she were walking underwater, against some invisible resistant force.

Emily is now the subject of much medical attention in the kitchen area. Lydia wraps one of her legs with an ace bandage while Onawa Velcros a strap around her stepmother's wrist, where it dangles uselessly. "What's that going to do for me, Onawa?" asks Emily. "It's *not* gonna fix your heart up," says Onawa mysteriously. "Emily, can you help me get down?" calls Claire from above. She and Lydia have been up in the top loft, and now Claire is a little nervous about climbing down the side of the wall. She's used to going up and down the stairs to the Bumblebees' loft.

Emily *could* reach up and pluck Claire out of the loft, but instead she talks her down, directing her to turn around, now lower her foot to the next hole, now move her right hand. Finally Claire reaches the bottom, having climbed the whole six feet or so by herself. "Good job, Claire," praises Emily, and Claire beams, justifiably proud of her prowess. The Grasshopper teachers spend a lot of time fostering independence, encouraging kids to "do it myself" whenever possible, helping them figure out how when they're stuck. Cory watches this whole process intently; the upper loft is one of the few places she can't get to on her own. Maybe she's plotting a way to haul herself up and down without asking a teacher for help. That would be like Cory, to surprise everyone one day by just appearing in the loft, grinning her mischievous grin.

By 10:50 the kids are starting to wind down. Grace and Marley are still at the easels, where they've been painting steadily for 45 minutes, demonstrating one of the tenets of High/Scope—that kids can and do concentrate for longer than 20 minutes at a stretch if they're doing something they want to do. The girls' papers are completely covered with layers of paint, clumps and swirls of color. Now they're giggling, starting to lose their focus, dotting different colors of paint across their pictures, chanting, "Raindrops! Raindrops!" Emily, admiring them, says, "Grace and Marley, can you put your names on them? We can hang them up on the wall." "There's no room on mine," complains Gracie. "Five minutes, Grasshoppers," calls Janet. "In five minutes we'll start cleanup."

These days the Grasshopper Room is calmer than it's been for a while because some of the more "challenging" kids have left. Rayshaun, Tony, Ayesha —all were kids who came to Red Caboose for the first time as four- and five-year-olds. All have left within the last few weeks for one reason or another, and Emily worries about what will happen to them now. "They needed us," she says. "It's sad, because they actually improved a lot since they were here, and they really needed us. But in some ways I think everybody's relieved."

The conflicts these days are more the usual kind: Tantrums, though they're rarer here than in the rooms downstairs. Hurt feelings. Sharing. This morning, for instance, Lydia and Skye are arguing over who's going to put away a tub full of colorful wooden puzzle pieces—not over who *has* to put it away but who *gets* to put it away. "Emily," calls Lydia, possessor of the tub, "she's not letting me put it away!" Skye, grabbing for the tub, says with the frankness of a four-year-old, "But it looks so good!" "Why don't both of you take one end and you both walk over there?" says Emily, pointing to a toy shelf. "I want to do it by myself," insists Lydia. She and Skye each have one end of the tub, and neither is budging an inch. "Can you think of a way that will make you both happy?" asks Emily.

The girls glare stubbornly at each other. Lydia's delicate features are set in a frown. Skye's expression is more phlegmatic; she shakes her head, her ribboned braids bouncing behind her. When no solution is forthcoming from the combatants, Emily offers one. "How about if Lydia carries it this far, and Skye carries it from there?" she asks. Lydia shakes her head no. "You need to think of something that will make Skye happy too," presses Emily. Lydia, who's normally quite congenial, turns to Skye and says clearly, "It's not OK with me for you to help me." Emily laughs in surprise. "Well, I see Skye is willing for both of you to carry it," she says, "and I think that's the only thing that you both will do."

Skye in the Grasshopper Room loft

But at the prospect of sharing the glory, Lydia gives up. "I'm not gonna carry it," she says, dropping her end of the tub and walking away. Skye catches the tub and puts it away with alacrity, conscious only of her victory and not of the snub. Lydia and Claire, meanwhile, are carefully, reverently, carrying a box marked "The Chicken Game" the two feet or so to the shelf. Tenderly they slide it into place and scoot off together.

Sometimes it seems that as kids get older they become meaner and more hurtful to one another. The us-against-them mentality, the excluding behaviors that begin in the Bumblebee Room intensify at age four and five, and this group has been particularly prone to them. Hurt feelings have abounded this year in the Grasshopper Room. At least once a day, and sometimes more, someone says, "I'm not gonna like you if you do this or that." Threats of no invitations to birthday parties appear regularly and carry a lot of weight. Wearing the wrong kind of shoes can be grounds for being left out of a game or group. Conformity is all-important to four- and five-year-olds emerging from the egocentric stage. Erick, for example, always holds his hand out for sunscreen when the other Grasshoppers get it, but for a long time the teachers didn't give him any; his skin, after all, is too dark to burn. But Erick pleaded and insisted, and finally his mother signed a permission slip so he, too, could get sunscreen. "This is the age where they really start noticing that stuff," explains Amy. "What's really different? Colors of the skin. What you wear. What your mommy and daddy do. I've personally had a lot of discussions about things like Gracie's got two mommies, and I've got a mommy and daddy, someone else has a mommy, that kind of thing."

"And I've been hearing Lateef saying that Erick is his brother and Erick has to do things just with him because their skin color's the same, and Erick should choose Lateef to be his friend before he chooses anyone else," puts in Janet. "And Erick doesn't see it that way at all. He just chooses a friend. If it's someone he likes to play with, it doesn't matter what color his skin is or whether they look the same as he does." "Lateef has a little more black pride," says Emily. "He says things like, 'Erick and I are the same color.' He's more prideful."

Emily is less disturbed than Amy and Janet at the occasional callousness the Grasshoppers dish out, maybe because she hasn't been teaching as long as they have. "The kids are trying to see how far they can take it," she says. "They're thinking, If they tell me *stop*, can I keep doing it and see what happens after that? They're trying different methods as an experiment, the same way adults experiment with people's responses sometimes. I don't know if it means you're going to be a ruthless person."

Down the hall and around the corner from the Grasshopper Room, Wendy is sitting in the office, ruminating on enrollment, W-2, and other issues of importance. Opponents to W-2 got a boost recently when the archbishop of Milwaukee, Rembert Weakland, publicly urged President Clinton to reject the program on the ground that it would "inflict children with hunger in order to infuse their parents with virtue."[1] The archbishop went on to say that W-2 is welfare repeal rather than reform. Governor Thompson responded by attacking the archbishop. "If you look at the Christian doctrine, there is a thing in the Bible that says people should learn to take care of themselves and have a little bit of personal responsibility," Thompson told reporters. The governor's spokesman added that the archbishop was "a talker, not a doer, on the matter of helping the poor."[2]

Maybe the archbishop's comments will rally W-2's despairing opponents.

Look Ma, no feet: Erick hangs out on the playground

Or maybe that's a naive hope. Either way, Wendy feels fairly confident that at the moment, anyway, Red Caboose is not in imminent danger. "There was a time when we had 30 families on funding," she says. "*That* would have been — let's just say I would not be so calm." In fact, the number of families on funding is down to about 10 percent of Red Caboose's families. For months the board has been discussing ways to attract more low-income families. Wendy thinks it's probably a function of fiscal policy; there's a two-year waiting list right now for county assistance, so many low-income families who want care can't afford it. By the time some of those families get to the top of the list, their kids will be in kindergarten.

Recently a Red Caboose parent who works for the county told Wendy about a way to beat the waiting list: if someone applies for AFDC and then turns it down, they are then automatically offered child-care funding. "You don't want to *tell* somebody to go apply for welfare," says Wendy. "It's such a personal thing. But we had a parent here who was desperate, a teenage parent with a one-year-old, and we told her about this. She called right from here, went down there and got the application form. She applied for AFDC and turned it down on a Wednesday. By Friday she had child-care money." Wendy shakes her head, lifting a handful of heavy dark hair back over one shoulder. "What a stupid system," she continues. "All she needed was child-care funding, not AFDC. It just doesn't make sense."

On a sunny, unseasonably cool morning in mid-July, the Grasshoppers get ready for a field trip. All the kids except the Turtles go on a few field trips each summer, and the Grasshoppers travel most extensively. Besides the usual trips to the zoo and the library, they venture out into the real world as much as possible, all part of their ongoing quest to get ready for kindergarten and "real" life. Last month, for instance, they visited a wildlife center about 45 minutes north of Madison. Today they'll visit Tenney Park and eat lunch at a Mexican restaurant owned by one of the Grasshopper parents.

The kids are so excited they're bouncing around the room—without trampolines. Even Cory, the heartiest eater in the bunch, barely touches her French toast and applesauce. Her mom, Jenny, is here, sitting in a little chair beside her daughter, eating breakfast with the children. Cory is having what Jenny calls a cling-on day. When Jenny steps out of the room for a minute, Cory falls apart, tears cascading down her cheeks. Erick, who like Lateef has taken a special interest in Cory this summer, asks, "What's the matter, Cory?" She ignores him, looking for Jenny. When she spots her by the office she stumbles into her mother's strong, slender arms.

When the rest of the Grasshoppers pile out onto the playground to line up, Jenny carries Cory downstairs and outside. She puts her daughter down in the line, leans forward until their foreheads touch, and rubs noses with her. Cory smiles, her tears drying on her cheeks, and manages to wave as Jenny leaves. She's distracted from her grief by the arrival of the bus, a small yellow schoolbus with the rounded green seats of schoolbuses 30 years ago. Amy stands by the parking lot fence, counting heads as the Grasshoppers board, something she and Janet will do many times before the morning is over. There *are* a few things worse than leaving a child behind, but not many.

The children buckle their own seat belts, and Janet, in a pink maternity top and jeans, squeezes her way down the narrow bus aisle, checking everyone. Then the bus is off, heading east on Washington Avenue, down Baldwin Street, driving through a neighborhood of attractive houses with porches to Tenney Park. Once there, the Grasshoppers sit at one end of the parking lot, waiting for the teachers to regroup. Erick, sitting next to Brad, leaps up suddenly. "Oooo!" he shouts, pointing. "He farted!"

Everyone gets a partner for the walk to the playground: Meghan and Daniel, Laila and Meghan M., Mirko and Todd, Gracie and Marley, and a threesome at the back, Brad, Erick, and Lateef. Cory holds up her hand to Amy, asking to be partners. Over a bridge they walk, passing ducks and red-winged blackbirds — a far cry from the pigeons found in big-city parks. When the playground comes into sight, the children rush it like bees rushing their hive, with Cory following slowly but steadily behind them.

Meghan finds the monkey bars, a series of high metal loops, and is swinging her way across them, hand over hand. "You can do it, Meghan!" says Amy, giving her a high five when the girl reaches the end. Erick and Brad head for a pair of child-size steam shovels in a sandy area, the kind with a seat and two levers for moving the shovels up and down and scooping sand. Todd pumps his legs on a swing shaped like a horse. Cory and Mirko sit on a tire swing while Janet pushes them around and around. Cory smiles, showing all of her very white teeth. Her dark curly hair is pulled into a ponytail on one side of her head. She wears long pants in bright Caribbean colors and a long-sleeved green and white shirt to keep away mosquitoes.

Across the playground, Meghan M., Gracie, Anna Y., and Laila huddle in a little plastic tunnel, engrossed already in their latest fantasy. "I'm going to the big bad wolf's house!" says Laila, popping out and hopping across a little drawbridge. "Anna, come on, let's go to the big bad wolf!" On the other end of the play structure, Cory climbs an arched metal ladder. The ladder isn't very high, only about three feet off the ground, but her apparent lack of coordination makes it scary to watch her climb. Neither teacher makes a fuss or rushes over, but Amy keeps an eye on the girl. Steadier than she looks, Cory makes it up easily. "I'm much more confident of her than I used to be," comments Amy, watching Cory tumble through the structure. "She knows what she can and cannot do. I don't think she'd do the firefighter's pole, for instance. But climbing up and down, that's no problem." Cory runs to her and points up toward the monkey bars, and Amy lifts her up until Cory, like the other Grasshoppers, can hang high above the ground, held only by her own two hands.

Across the playground, Amy spots Seth and his father heading toward the group. They got to Red Caboose late and missed the bus, so Seth's dad drove him here to meet the Grasshoppers. You wouldn't know from looking at Seth that he's partly blind. No one knows how impaired his vision is, only that he has trouble seeing both close up and far away. But he maneuvers almost as well as any of the other five-year-olds, zooming around the center at top speed, only occasionally bumping into people or things.

Amy suggests a game of duck-duck-goose, and the Grasshoppers sit in a circle in a field dotted with clover. The sky is furring up with clouds, but the field is still lit in spots with shafts of sun. In the traditional version of this game, one child walks the outside of the circle, tapping the others lightly, naming them "Duck, duck, duck." When she taps someone and says "Goose!" that child is supposed to leap up and chase her back around the circle, catching her before she can sit down in her spot.

But the Grasshoppers like to play it their way, each picking her own code word to replace *goose*. Gracie goes first. After much deliberation she picks *horsie*, and then moves around the circle, touching each head in turn. "Elephant," she says, "rhino, hippopotamus, giraffe, duck, goose, horsie!" At *horsie* she touches Erick's head and begins to run. Erick, not quite sure whether *horsie* is the signal, sits still for a minute, then springs up and races around the circle. On his turn, he chooses the word *ninja*. "White," he says, touching Daniel's head, "red, goose, red, white, yellow, ninja!" He taps Brad's head and races away.

As the game goes on, each child in turn picks someone different. Brad picks Lateef, Lateef picks Meghan, Meghan picks Mirko, Mirko picks Gracie. It's as though they're making sure everyone gets a turn, though Amy hasn't asked them to do that. Maybe all those years of teachers urging empathy and compassion are beginning, at age five, to pay off. The teachers would like to think so. Then Cory wanders over. She wants to play, too, but how can she? How could she articulate the words? She stands outside the circle, unusually still, watching. Before she can do anything a couple of rowdy ducks fly by and the game comes to a sudden halt. The circle dissolves; the children chase the male ducks across the field until they take indignantly to the air.

When it's time to head for the restaurant, the Grasshoppers walk through a cloud of gnats, back toward the paved path that leads to the parking lot.

The bus rumbles out of the park, past the Tenney Lock and Dam. The five-year-olds take great delight in saying the word *dam* and getting away with it. Heading down North Sherman Avenue, the bus passes Magic Penny, another nonprofit child-care center. "I went there," says Marley excitedly. "I went there when I was four years old!" A lifetime ago. Past the Respite Center, past an apartment complex. "Meghan," says Amy, "is this where your dad lives?" "Yes," says the girl proudly, "right in the front one there." Amy points through the bus window. "I live in this building," she tells the kids, and they stare at it out the window as if this makes it very special indeed.

The bus pulls into the parking lot of a small shopping mall and stops in front of Pedro's. The Grasshoppers file out of the bus and into the restaurant, where Meghan M. detaches herself from the group and flings herself into the arms of a smiling man in a suit. "You're here!" says her father, and steps forward to greet the rest of the children.

The restaurant's white stucco walls are covered with Mexican rugs and portraits of bull fighters. There are plants and cages with brightly colored toy parrots. Meghan's dad, Jim, has set aside a long table for the Grasshoppers, with a balloon tied to the back of each chair and a plastic cup at each place with a strawberry "margarita" in it. The children take over the bathrooms, washing their hands; Janet goes in with the girls, Jim with the boys. He comes out again a minute later with one of the boys. "Accident in his pants," he says to Janet. "OK," she says, and takes the boy into the women's room; she'll take off his underwear and clean him, but she has no spare pants. "You OK?" Amy asks Janet when they emerge a few minutes later. "Yeah," says Janet heavily. Cleaning a five-year-old's poop—especially when you're eight months pregnant—is *not* the best part of the job.

Amy and Janet make a good team, working so well together that they can almost read each other's minds. Janet's strong points are her experience and her kindness, her calm air of motherliness. She grew up in Madison and started working at Red Caboose 13 years ago. Her concern for the kids is evident in the way she pays attention to little things—brief interactions, subtle feelings, the seemingly small things that make up so much of a child's life. The only time anyone has seen Janet's composure slip was last winter, in the early months of her pregnancy, when she wasn't feeling well and showed it. The rest of the time she is a rock, steady and well rooted.

Amy, 27, is representative of a newer breed of teacher: younger, hipper, more ambitious. She has a degree in elementary education and intended to teach in the public schools. She wound up at Red Caboose instead. The kids adore her, admiring her many earrings and rings, the small yin-yang symbol tattooed on one ankle, her short smooth blond hair. Amy's good at analyzing what's going on with five-year-olds, helping them put feelings into words for themselves and for one another. She's also a lot of fun, playing games with the kids, encouraging their dramatic play, singing funny songs with them, more like a cool older sister or aunt than a mother.

Jim leads the children into the dining room for a demonstration of the tortilla machine, which looks like a cross between a conveyor belt and a spiral staircase. Each child will get a turn to make a tortilla, placing a ball of dough into a little silver cup, which carries it into the machine where it's flattened and cooked as it flips from level to level. The Grasshoppers line up for their turns in making this magic. Meghan M. goes first, since it's her family's restaurant; then the rest of the kids take turns. After that they gather around the table and begin chowing down on hot tortillas with butter.

Meghan—the *other* Meghan, not Meghan M.—her mouth full of tortilla, looks up long enough to ask, "Is this a fast food restaurant? Fast food isn't really healthy for you." "Isn't it?" says Janet, trying not to laugh. One of the best parts of working with kids this age is their honesty, the way they come right out with what they think and feel. Often these opinions emerge in very grown-up ways, as if they originally came straight from the mouths of parents—which in this case is probably true.

The rest of the food comes out quickly, meat and bean and cheese burritos, big plates of vegetables. The kids eat hungrily. There's even a surprise after lunch: a scoop of vanilla ice cream with chocolate sauce drizzled on top. The Grasshoppers are on their best behavior, and it shows. Not one voice has been raised; no one has gotten cranky or angry or possessive. As the meal comes to an end the noise level rises slowly, the kids getting a little restless at last. Time to go. Jim helps Janet and Amy snip the balloons off the backs of chairs and retie them onto each child's wrist, a buoyant souvenir of the morning.

As the Grasshoppers are leaving, Jim squats and Meghan M. runs to him. His arms around her, he talks softly into her ear. Gracie grabs her balloon near the top of its string and bumps it into Marley's balloon. Cory joins in, whapping her pink balloon into the other girls'. Marley looks disturbed for a minute, then grins along with Cory. It's one of the few times Cory has been able to make a joke—and that's a real loss for a kid with a devilish sense of humor. Most of the time she can't get across anything more than the basics, certainly not with the other Grasshoppers, because the repertoire of signs that she can make and that they can understand is limited—yes, no, play, with,

Lateef, Cory, and Anna in front of the Moonshine Room mural

little, girl, boy, and various names. A few kids understand more signs, and so does Amy, who's taken some signing classes. But that's pretty much it.

Even with her limited vocabulary, though, Cory manages to convey something of her personality. The way she signs *no*, for instance. The sign for *no* is made by holding the palm of the hand facing out and bringing the index and middle fingers sharply together with the thumb, in a kind of snapping motion. When Cory's feeling emphatic — which is often — she brings her whole hand down, not just those two fingers, the signing equivalent of a decided shake of the head. When she's feeling playful, she might close her fingers around someone else's nose as she signs *no* — especially her mom or one of the teachers. Or she might turn her back, walking away from the conversation, then casually flip her hand over one shoulder—an offhand, sly *no* that connotes a raised eyebrow, a half-smile.

Otherwise, she's limited to grinning at other people's jokes. Like the day Jenny sat in the playground with Cory in her lap, talking with a few of the teachers. In an effort to practice her own signing, Jenny is signing along as she speaks. "On my birthday," she says and signs, speaking for Cory, "my mom was not very happy. She thinks I'm too big." "That's right," says Janet, looking at Cory, "you're supposed to be getting smaller, aren't you? We're not supposed to feed Cory, so she doesn't get any bigger. No more lunch for Cory." Cory, grinning widely, signs, "No, no, no!" "We'll just give you some milk," continues Janet. "Or some baby food." "Right," says Jenny fondly. "Mushed carrots, or rice." She rolls her daughter over in her lap and presses her face to Cory's. "Right?" Jenny asks, kissing Cory on the nose. Cory reaches out and pinches her mother's nose in a *no*, then cuddles contentedly.

Sometimes Jenny wonders if she made a mistake in leaving Cory at Red Caboose this year. Up until last summer, when Cory was a Bumblebee, Jenny's feelings about the center consisted mainly of gratitude for the way everyone went out of his or her way to accommodate Cory, physically and otherwise. Then the parents of another Bumblebee forced the question on her in a way she couldn't ignore. One afternoon when they had come to pick up their daughter, they happened to observe her take a tumble, unnoticed by any of the teachers. They told another teacher they felt that their daughter was being ignored and that Carolyn, the Bumblebee teacher, was paying too much attention to Cory.

The parents who complained were voicing a concern felt by many parents of "normal" children who go to school with "special-needs" kids. It's a natural worry, and it has some basis in reality. There's only so much teacher time and attention to go around. For every child like Cory there are 19 more who *aren't* getting as much attention as they otherwise would. Maybe Cory needs it more than they do; maybe it's good for them to learn to be independent; maybe they gain more than they lose by having a child like Cory in their group. These arguments all have validity. But the fact remains that there is a trade-off, there is a loss involved, and some parents find this unacceptable.

And maybe some parents don't understand the trade-off. For 23 years Red Caboose has consciously sought out all kinds of families and children. The play structure in the Moonshine Room was the first wheelchair-accessible indoor play structure in the county, maybe in the state. The "normal" kids get a lot out of the arrangement, too, everything from the tangible—learning

some sign language — to the intangible: Learning to accept kids who are different. Learning to relate to all kinds of children, not just those like themselves.
Learning compassion and empathy. These, too, are important lessons for preschoolers. Maybe even more important than learning to spell their names.

The complaint threw Jenny off balance for many months, through Cory's
surprisingly easy transition to the Grasshopper Room. "That was the beginning of a very difficult time for me as a parent," she remembers, running
her fingers through her cropped brown hair. She's the antithesis of the stage
mom, the last person in the world to demand or expect special privileges as
her child's due. "First of all I was trying to defend Carolyn, who was the center of Cory's universe at the time," she explains. "Carolyn was a very special
person to Cory because she *always* took the time to understand her, and she
always seemed to understand her. Especially early on it was not an easy thing
to understand what Cory wanted. Carolyn had a knack for doing that and
also had the patience for it. So she and Cory had a very special bond. It bothered me that someone might not appreciate what she meant to Cory. I wanted
people to understand what Cory was up against. In trying to express it to
someone else I had to really look at it carefully."

To help articulate the dilemma, Jenny decided to write a letter describing
what life at Red Caboose was like from Cory's point of view. She began to set
down some of the things she'd observed. They weren't easy things to think
about. "I remembered in the Elephant Room," she explains, "the kids used
to chant to parents, 'Hi Cory's mom, hi Cory's mom, hi Cory's mom.' They
would do it until they were acknowledged. And Cory would be waving during this, and no one would ever see her and no one would ever acknowledge
her. She knew who everybody was, she knew everybody's siblings, she knew
the whole web of Red Caboose. But people wouldn't see her greeting them or
saying good-bye to them, and it broke my heart."

Jenny also began to realize the extent to which Cory was left out by the
other kids — not because they were mean or heartless, but because they were
four-year-olds with their own interests and priorities, and Cory couldn't keep
up. Not being able to talk gave Cory a kind of invisibility, especially since many
of the other children were very verbal. They couldn't or didn't take the time
to include the largely speechless Cory in their games. When they did, says
Jenny, they often made her the baby. "And I think she excludes herself because
she doesn't want to be the baby, she doesn't want people putting words in her
mouth, telling her what she would say," says Jenny fiercely. There isn't a four-
year-old on the planet who wants to be the baby in a game played with other

four-year-olds. What Jenny saw was that for Cory, the wish to be treated as a "big girl" outweighed the wish to be accepted by her peers; she paid, and still pays, a very big price for her independence.

The more Jenny thought about all this, the more she realized she had to go outside Red Caboose to get Cory what she needed. Cory was already in an early childhood program for kids with special needs. Jenny put the word out that she was looking for playmates, especially kids who signed. She took Cory to the circus one day and saw a mother signing to her young daughter. "I followed them into the bathroom and asked if they would come over and play," says Jenny with a laugh. She hired a teacher to come to the house once a week and teach sign to Cory and Lena and herself; eventually her sister, mother, niece, and many neighbors sat in, too.

So now, thanks to Jenny's efforts, Cory has a core group of friends who are more like peers. She goes to a playgroup that includes kids who are fluent signers. Slowly but surely she is acquiring a home in the world, a growing number of places and relationships in which she can be herself, say what she means and be fully understood, where her curiosity and intelligence and humor are not truncated by the limitations of her body. The complaint about Cory and Carolyn turned out to be a blessing in disguise, at least for Cory.

What it means for the center is less clear. How many resources can a place like Red Caboose devote to a couple of high-needs kids? How far can the center reasonably be expected to go in order to accommodate them? Maybe the real issue is whether a place like Red Caboose can *ever* go far enough. School boards across the country, faced with the prospect of mainstreaming children with many types of special needs, wrestle with this same issue. In the world of good intentions, places like Red Caboose get high marks for trying, and the trying makes them better places for all children. But trying isn't enough. Who knows how Cory's life would be different, now and in the future, if she had spent the last year in a place where she was really, fully understood?

On a Wednesday afternoon in late July, the Grasshoppers are getting ready for nap. The five-year-olds nap in the Moonshine Room, their cots spread out under the wooden play structure, next to it, and, in a few cases, at the very top, near the side-by-side sliding boards. For most of them the hour between one and two o'clock is a rest time, but a few of the kids still sleep, still *need* to sleep. Morgan, who's usually quite poised and unflappable, stands beside Amy, sobbing hysterically. "I miss Mommy," she says between gulps. "She said she would call me half an hour after she left." Amy scoops Morgan up and carries her to her cot, soothing her with words and with the comfort of her arms. "It hasn't been half an hour yet," she reassures the girl, laying her on the low cot. Lately Morgan has been spending more time with her father because of a new custody agreement between her parents. Her father may be glad to have more time with her, but Morgan is paying the price, at least right now. She's not used to being apart from her mother, and it hurts.

From the hall outside the Moonshine Room comes more crying, this time Janet's daughter, Megan. Janet rocks the sobbing girl against her pregnant belly and sighs. Megan has been coming to the center a few mornings a week, and some days leaving is just too hard, even though she's going home with Janet's sister. Amy goes into the office to ask Kathi to be sure and get Morgan to the phone when her mother calls. If she misses her mom's call she'll be heart-broken; she's going to her father's house tonight, and won't see her mother again for several days.

By one o'clock Denice is settled in the Moonshine Room, rubbing backs. On Wednesday she covers the nap room so the three Grasshopper teachers can have their weekly meeting, where they talk about room issues large and small: enrollment, relationships among children, how specific kids are or aren't adapting. Each room in the center has a staff meeting once a week, and the four lead teachers meet weekly, too. Communication is the grease that keeps the center's wheels turning smoothly.

Downstairs in the kitchen, Amy puts a Healthy Choice pepperoni pizza into the microwave. Emily, wearing pink shorts and a bright yellow T-shirt, opens a chocolate bar, Janet a can of soda. Emily is talking about her new role as stepmother to Onawa and her brother. "When I first started living with them, I felt more like a day-care provider," says Emily, peeling the paper off a Kit Kat bar. "As I get more and more part of their lives, I feel more like a mom and less sure of myself. Now I can see what goes on with parents a little bit more easily. Why you can be the sucker. But I feel embarrassed about it. I feel like I should know better."

Amy, who has no children, neatly cuts her pizza into pieces and begins to eat. Janet puts her soda down on the shabby kitchen table and leaves the room. As lead teacher she feels a special responsibility to the Grasshoppers, and with all the earlier chaos upstairs, she wants to make sure everything's OK. While they wait for her, Amy and Emily discuss kindergarten anxiety and how it's affecting the Grasshoppers. Madison public school starts the third week of August, so the five-year-olds have only a month to go. Most of them have some anxiety about the coming change, and it shows up differently in each child.

"Some kids have a harder time saying good-bye to Mom and Dad," says Amy. "We also see baby things coming back, baby talk, sucking thumbs, wetting pants, things like that. One parent told me her child started asking for a bottle again." She takes a bite of pizza. "This group, though, is so ready for kindergarten, intellectually, emotionally, all of the above. More than other groups. They're really verbal, very willing to participate in things. Always willing to listen to what the teacher has to say."

Janet comes back into the kitchen looking pained. "Morgan's mom called, Morgan's crying again, and I needed to pull myself together after Megan's little scene out in the parking lot," she says, referring to the tantrum Megan threw when her aunt came to pick her up. "Megan *never* acts like that. She's usually like, 'Oh, Aunt Carol!' Not today." She pulls out a chair and sits down, catching her breath, then launches without preliminaries into the meeting. "Wendy still doesn't know what she's going to do to cover my maternity leave," she says. "I know it's my responsibility, because it's my hours, but I want to say, 'Don't tell me because I don't need any more stress this week!'" She's laughing. Sort of. Emily, who works the fewest hours of the three, has agreed to take Janet's hours three mornings a week, which leaves two mornings and five early afternoons to cover. Janet mentions a new sub who came from Children's House.

"She's really good," says Emily, her mouth full of chocolate. "She went to high school with me."

Janet's maternity leave couldn't have come at a more awkward time of year. She'll probably miss the last week or two of kindergarten anxiety, and she'll certainly miss the settling-in period for the new crop of Grasshoppers. But babies don't come when it's convenient. The teachers and the new Grasshoppers will just have to cope. "Why can't Emily take all my hours," asks Amy now, "and find an LTE to cover Emily's shift?" Amy will be lead teacher while Janet's gone, so it would make sense for her to work Janet's schedule.

The trouble with that, says Janet, is that Emily is one of two teachers who closes the center each night, and Wendy doesn't want to give an LTE that kind of responsibility. Late afternoon is one of the craziest times of the day; for the last half hour two teachers care for all the Elephants, Bumblebees, and Grasshoppers left at the center. "I guess I could come back for a couple hours every day," jokes Janet. "Strap the baby on with that little pack."

Cheryl wanders into the kitchen and out again, then Sue. This is the quiet hour, the time of day when the grown-ups take over, moving for the most part freely and without encumbrance through the center. Janet shuffles some papers in a blue folder and picks one out to show the other teachers. "This let-

Ride 'em, cowgirls: Rocio pedals while Lydia and Emily sit back and enjoy the ride

ter on safety concerns went out to parents," she explains. "Last night, when I was here till six, a Grasshopper parent went to her car and just left her child here on the playground, because the child was giving her a hard time. The child let himself out the gate when he realized his mother was serious." Normally, children are not allowed to open the playground gate, which leads right onto the parking lot.

"I caught an Elephant out in the parking lot the other day," puts in Amy. "She was only two feet out, but still."

"There are people who use our parking lot, thinking it's for the Gateway Mall next door, and they drive in there fast," says Janet.

Next comes a brief discussion of fall enrollment. "We talked a lot about this at our lead teacher meeting this week," says Janet. "It's gone up by, I think, two heads. One is a four-day, and they have a sibling in the Elephant Room. The other one is Jacob, who has a sibling in the Turtle Room. They weren't going to start till fall, because they're moving here from Waukesha, but the parents already bought a house and they both found jobs, so he's starting here on August 5th. And so we're gonna be real over that week." Over the usual ratio, she means.

Usually the new Grasshoppers come in as the old ones leave. In this last summer before kindergarten, the kids tend to peel off one at a time; most take vacations with their family or at least a few quiet days at home between the end of Red Caboose and the beginning of kindergarten. The schedule of who's leaving when is so confusing that Janet has written out a calendar of last days. Gracie will be the first to leave, then Daniel, then Anna Y. and Morgan. Fiona leaves the next week, Meghan M. the week after that. Marley, Brad, Erick, and Cory stay until August 23rd, the last Friday before public school starts. Mirko will stay another week because he's moving, and his school starts a week later. That first week of kindergarten consists of very short days, and Rocio will come to Red Caboose after school lets out. What do most parents do that week? Hers have to work full days, no matter what the public school schedule.

"Oh, and Emerson's last day is the 21st," says Janet, checking her list again. "And that's all I know about enrollment. I'm trying to get everything organized so you don't have a lot to worry about while I'm gone."

"I have a question about Arika," says Amy. Arika, who's a Bumblebee, has cerebral palsy and is confined to a wheelchair. "Are we going to meet with any of her support staff before she moves up? I remember when Cory and Seth came, we had all these meetings months before they came. Remember how Cory's mom was before she moved up?" Amy grins, then quotes Jenny. " 'Just wanted you to know that three months from now, Cory's going to be a Grasshopper!' " She laughs. All the teachers are fond of Jenny, in part because of her tigerlike devotion to her daughters.

"I've talked with Arika's mom quite a bit," says Janet. "I pointed out to her that I'm not going to be here when she moves upstairs. They'll start moving a few kids up the week of the 16th, and the rest the 23rd. Last year we found there were lots of problems with the transition, as children were leaving their friends."

"I also don't know much about what support Darrin has," says Amy. "Or if he has any at all." Darrin has been diagnosed with attention deficit disorder, ADD. He's known as a child who pushes the envelope, really tests the limits, over and over.

"I think the family is working with Rainbow now," says Janet. Rainbow is a local organization that does family therapy. Over the years, quite a number of Red Caboose families have worked with Rainbow's therapists, both at the center and otherwise.

Now Emily wonders whether Darrin is ready to be moved upstairs; he and Clark are just beginning to establish a bond, and to move him now might be hard on him and on everyone else. Amy and Janet have been having Darrin visit the Grasshopper Room in the mornings, getting him used to the routines and expectations of the older group. "I think he's beginning to realize he has to listen to us," says Janet optimistically.

Amy reminds her of what happened when another "wild" boy came into the room not long ago. "We were really good with being firm," she reminds Janet, "and sticking to our guns, and letting him know, 'These are the kinds of things we expect from you, and these are the things we know you can do.' I think we were very successful with him. Not that Darrin's like him, but—"

"It's the idea of having high expectations," finishes Janet, "of saying, 'This is what we expect from you as far as behavior goes.'" Amy nods. Some kids come into the center at age three or four without ever having had much expected of them in the way of listening or communicating. But in general, children rise to the occasion. "I think part of the Bumblebees' fear is that there are so many little kids coming in there," continues Janet. "A lot of those little Elephants moving up could be very terrified of Darrin."

Janet looks through her folder and begins jotting notes on a piece of paper. Sue comes in with Roberto on her hip, getting him a drink of water. He clutches her, one-armed, around the neck; his eyes are puffy with sleep, a wary look on his face. He looks much older, graver, not a baby anymore. Some of that change is normal, the shift from infancy to toddlerhood, but some comes from stress. In the late spring his father, Hakki, had a stroke and almost died. Hakki's still in the hospital. Roberto's too little to understand what's happening, but he knows that his father is gone and that something's terribly wrong.

At last Janet puts down her pencil and pushes her paper into the middle of the table. This is the enrollment list that will cover the time she's away—she hopes. "We'll be at 16," she tells the other teachers. "We're down two openings, but if the four-day-a-weeker comes we'll end up being over on a few days. And if I have to increase Megan's schedule—I have to figure out something. She's got to go *somewhere*. My sister quit on Monday." Megan can probably increase her time at Red Caboose, but someone has to take care of the new baby, too, or Janet won't be able to come back to work. Figuring out her own child care, plus figuring enrollment for the Grasshopper Room, plus saying good-bye to the current Grasshoppers—no wonder Janet is feeling overwhelmed.

"When I lived at home," says Janet, "my mom used to go away on the last weekend before public school started, because she couldn't stand to be around me. That last day I would just come home crying. My babies all left! And yet I'm so excited for them, and that's all I keep telling them. 'It's gonna be so much fun, I'm so excited for you, call and let us know what it's like.' I *have* had a couple of them call me at home that first Monday night and tell me what they did during the day." Wondering what their days will be like is a huge source of anxiety for the five-year-olds. The teachers try to prepare them for what's coming, but no two kindergartens are exactly alike. A lot of Red Caboose kids go to Lapham, an east side school that has kindergarten through second grade, but not everyone. This year there are four Grasshoppers going to Franklin, one to Thoreau, and one—if all goes well—to Glendale.

For months Jenny has been waging an all-out campaign to get Cory into Glendale, the only school in Madison with a program for hearing-impaired kids. Jenny believes that Glendale is the *only* school where Cory will have a real chance to fit in, but so far the school district is unconvinced. "I'm worried that the district thinks that Cory has this voice output machine, so they can put her in a classroom and she'll be fine," says Jenny. "When in fact that's nowhere *near* what she needs. She needs to be surrounded by people sometimes where she can just communicate, where she doesn't have to go get the box and turn it on and find the right page. I want her to have a place where she can go and not have to work so hard and be misunderstood and frustrated. She has a lot to say, so I'd like her to be able to be fluent in something that works for her." Many of the kids and teachers at Glendale are competent signers. There, thinks Jenny, Cory could finally catch up, could begin to learn real communication instead of the halting phrases and single words she's limited to now.

But Cory doesn't live in the Glendale district, so the principal there has to approve her transfer. And the principal has been walking the fence all summer. So Jenny took Cory over to Glendale one day and, as she put it, ambushed the principal. "I pretended I didn't know the decision was actually stuck with her," she tells Amy out on the playground. "I told her I didn't know where in the process it was, that we just came to see because we *hoped* it would be that school and I wanted Cory to look around."

"And while Cory was there she just happened to charm the pants off the principal, right?" asks Amy.

"Actually, we went twice, 'cause the first time the principal wasn't there," Jenny admits, and Amy bursts out laughing.

After everything Jenny's been through with Cory, she's not *about* to give up now; she's not about to settle for anything less than the best Cory can do. She'll never forget taking Cory to a neurologist when she was two and being told that Cory's floppy muscles could well stiffen into the more rigid form of CP, permanently locking into one position. By the time Cory was five, said the neurologist, she could be much, much worse.

"I said, 'OK, thank you very much,' and we left, and I was busy," remembers Jenny. "And a couple of days later it hit me, what he meant. She has such a wonderful smile, and I thought, 'She's gonna lose it, she's gonna be so frustrated.' I'm imagining wheelchairs, and people I think of when I think of CP. I was sitting on Bascom Hill between my classes and crying, trying to be stoic." Jenny knew from her experience with Cory's eyes — she had strabismus, crossed eyes, and had surgery and then glasses to correct the condition — that a physical disability could lead to being shut out in other ways, too. "I did *not* want her isolated from other people because of the condition of her body," she says. "When she was cross-eyed, people didn't come up and talk to her like they would normally. Eye contact is very, very important, and so are physical things in general."

Jenny spent a miserable week imagining Cory's bright spirit and infectious grin imprisoned in a stiffening, spasming body. Then, at a medical school dinner, she met a well-known pediatric neurologist and, in despair, asked her advice. "Cory was sitting at the table with me, shoveling her face with cookies and hamburgers," recalls Jenny, "and I told this woman the story, and I said, 'I don't know what to expect.' She asked, 'Well, does she sit up?' And I said, 'She's right here,' and pointed to her." The neurologist watched Cory sit at the table eating, zoom around with the help of her cart, and she told Jenny, "This child will have no problem. She'll never regress. She'll only progress. It's never going to get worse." Jenny continues, "And then she turned back to her friends at the table, and I tapped her on the shoulder and said, 'Excuse me, you just changed my life!'"

After all that, a stonewalling principal isn't going to stop Cory's progress if Jenny can help it. Nothing and no one will get in her way. Cory's lucky, so lucky, to have a mom like Jenny.

The Grasshopper room meeting is over by 2:30, and the teachers head upstairs. Janet's shift is over, but she has some paperwork to take care of up in the office. In the Dinosaur Room, Gracie sits at a low table, drawing a flower with orange and green and pink markers on a stiff white card. "This is a card for Morgan," she announces. "Sometimes she's real mean to me, so I decided to make a present for her so she might be a little nicer." "Do you think that might work?" asks Emily, raising one eyebrow. Fiona and Rocio are up in the loft, giggling together. In the play kitchen area, Skye, Kylis, Lateef, and Lydia are amusing themselves with toy food.

A few minutes later Cory, waking up from her nap, heads for the office next door to the Moonshine Room, wearing just her blue jeans. She takes one look at Wendy and bursts into tears, making heart-wrenching, guttural sounds. Janet, who's sorting through some papers, explains to Wendy, "Her mom was here when she fell asleep." "You're really sad, aren't you?" says Wendy, gently putting one arm around Cory and shepherding her over to Janet.

Laila stumbles out of the Moonshine Room rubbing her eyes, her shoes in one hand. Her T-shirt has a drawing of Jasmine, a character from the Disney movie *Aladdin*, a movie that her Saudi Arabian father finds racist but that Laila adores. "Do you need a hug?" asks Amy. Laila nods, walking around the table to lay her head on Amy's shoulder. "Everybody needs hugs, don't they?" asks Amy softly. Morgan and Rocio sit together at another low table, poring over a tub full of yarn scraps. Laila sits down near them and watches. Cory, who has stopped crying, hands her glasses to Janet, who washes and dries them, a task she does at least several times a day. When Janet hands them back, Cory puts them on and walks unsteadily to the book area, where she sits down on the floor with a book in her lap. Lateef plunks down next to her and puts his arm around her, and they look at the book together. Mirko, passing by, says to Cory, "Do you ever go to the library?" She makes her hand into a fist and waggles it, the sign for *yes*.

At three o'clock Emily asks the Grasshoppers to do cots, a regular after-nap ritual. The children drag their cots into one corner of the Moonshine Room, where Emily stacks them in a neat pile. Laila says to Morgan, "Do you want to play with me?" Morgan, still clutching her naptime quilt, ignores her; maybe she doesn't want to play, maybe she isn't quite awake yet. But Laila immediately gets upset. "She doesn't like me playing with her because I haven't seen her for a while," she complains to no one in particular. "I say, 'Can I play with you?' and then she says, 'No, I'd rather play with Rocio more than you.'"

Laila seems heartbroken and furious and bitter, all at the same time. She turns toward Emily, who's watching this exchange, then comes back to Morgan, ready to plead her case again. "Every time I play, you play with me," says Morgan, finally rising to the bait. "Every single time!" "I haven't even seen you," protests Laila. "You were away on vacation and I didn't even see you." "Well, most of the time I play with you and not my other friends," says Morgan in a reasonable, only slightly whiny voice. "Laila, sometimes I need to play with my other friends, too." "You go play by yourself with Rocio," commands Laila, her voice breaking pitifully. "I'll just stay here by myself."

"You don't need to get so upset, I'm just telling you," says Morgan, beginning to relent. "Want to hold my dog?" She holds out a stuffed animal, but Laila shakes her head violently. "Another day like this," says Morgan, sound-

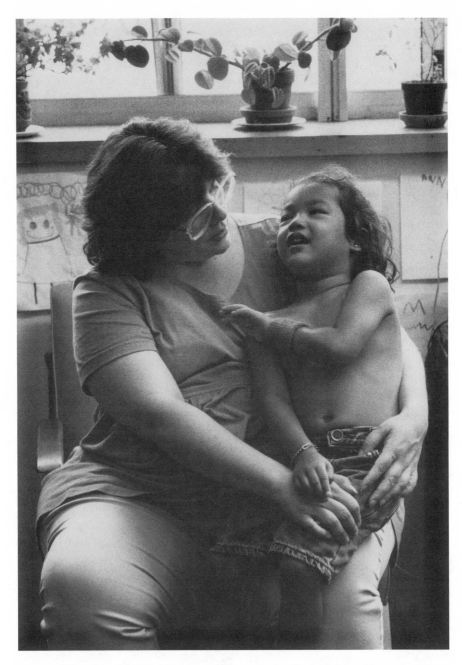

When Cory wakes up crying, Janet cuddles her in the office until she's smiling again

ing like a tired, exasperated parent. She's beginning to get upset herself, her voice taking on a defensive tone. "Laila's upset because every day I'm here she wants to play with me, and I can't play with her all the time I'm here." "Well, I didn't even see her," says Laila tearfully to Emily. "And I really missed her."

At this point Emily decides it's time to step in. This is a judgment call, and she's judging a situation that is quite different from, say, two Elephants arguing over a truck. Laila and Morgan have been doing a good job of telling each other how they feel, so Emily didn't need to facilitate in the way that Clark or Denice often do. But now the girls are stuck. They're telling each other how they feel, but that's not solving anything. Laila still feels hurt and Morgan still feels put-upon. Now what?

"Have you been missing Morgan 'cause she's been gone?" Emily asks Laila, who nods. "Did you tell Morgan that you missed her?" In fact Laila hasn't, at least not in those words. But as she opens her mouth to speak, Morgan breaks in, talking to Emily rather than to her friend.

"I told her that sometimes I need to play with my other friends," says Morgan. This is one reason why Emily has waited this long to get involved; as soon as a grown-up steps in, the children stop talking to each other and talk to the grown-up. Emily wants them to turn back toward each other with more understanding. So she says to Morgan, "Why don't you tell Laila that you hear what she's saying, and you'll play with her when you're done playing with Rocio?"

"I'll play with you when I'm done playing with Rocio," says Morgan to Laila. Emily persists. "Can you tell her that you hear what she said?" she says to Morgan. "I hear what you said, OK?" says Morgan unhappily. "But I don't want to play with you right now."

Gracie, meanwhile, stands on the edge of the group, listening. Now Laila turns to her. "I want to play with Gracie," she says, a bit sullenly. But Gracie isn't buying it. She sidesteps Laila and blurts out to Morgan, "I tried to make a present for you, 'cause lately I've really wanted to play with you, too, the same way as Laila." "You two," says Morgan, a bit desperately. Rocio, who's waiting for Morgan to resume their game, suggests, "How about we all play together?" "Silly Rocio!" says Morgan fondly, and the two of them walk off together. Gracie and Laila lag forlornly behind. Emily, watching them trail away, shakes her head. "Why is Morgan the sought-after one?" she asks rhetorically. "Morgan isn't any better than them in verbal skills or making up games, so what is the reason behind that?"

The drama continues to unfold, with Emily watching. Morgan and Ro-

Guardian angel: In the Grasshopper Room, Lateef hovers protectively beside Cory

cio, in the kitchen area, are making pineapple pizza with some of the extremely realistic toy food there. Laila and Gracie hover nearby, watching, and Meghan M. drifts over and tries to join them. Laila puts her hands on her hips and turns her back on the newcomer. "Gracie, know what?" she says. "Meghan just breaks on through. I want to have some time alone with you, and now Meghan has to break into the game." Laila is demonstrating all too vividly the principle of doing unto others what has been done to her. Morgan calls over, "Tell Meghan how you feel, Laila." But Laila stalks angrily away. From across the room she watches the other Grasshoppers playing together: Morgan and Rocio wipe the inside of a pizza pan with a paper towel, Meghan and Lydia wrap a cast around Amy's leg, Cory and Lateef giggle in front of the full-length mirror in the kitchen. Emily, observing Laila, sighs. It seems to be an unwritten rule that the Grasshoppers always and only want to play with the person who doesn't want to play with them. Four- and five-year-olds, testing their limits in a different way, figuring out where they fit in.

Laila watches disconsolately until Amy calls, "Grasshoppers, it's cleanup time! After we clean up, we can go outside and have snack!" Then Laila, like everyone else, begins putting away toys and tidying the room. Gracie, standing beside the art table, bursts into tears. "Do you miss your mom all of a sudden?" asks Emily. Wailing, the girl nods. Gracie's family is getting ready to move to California. One of her moms is already out there; Gracie and her other mom will be leaving in a few weeks. "There's nothing I can do right now, but she'll come soon," promises Emily, putting her arm around Gracie. Gracie shrugs it off. "I don't want a hug, I want my mom!" she sobs. The other children are cleaning up around her, a point that is not lost on Emily, who lays one hand briefly on the girl's neck. "Feel better?" she asks. Gracie shakes her head. "I just want to call my mom," she says with a whine. "Gracie, you can use the bathroom," says Emily firmly, sending her back into the afternoon routine.

One by one the kids finish cleaning up and wash their hands, then line up in the hallway to go outside. Emily walks from child to child, asking each one what he or she did that afternoon, writing each response in the log. When she gets to Cory, she asks, "You wanna go into the room and get Dyna and show what you played with?" Instead, Cory steps into the room and points up at the loft. "You played in the loft?" asks Emily, writing it down. Cory hasn't played in the top loft before. "Who'd you play with?" Cory steps back into the hall and looks down the line of children, hoping to find the right person and point to him, but she doesn't see him. If she could spell, she could tell Emily, but being preliterate is a distinct disadvantage with sign language. Eventually she gives up, and Emily moves on, asking Gracie the same question. "Can't remember," says Gracie lethargically.

The rest of the Grasshoppers are anything but lethargic. The line is dynamic, full of wiggling, giggling, fidgeting, wandering, chattering children. Amy sits beside Cory and begins a song, one of the Grasshoppers' favorites. "Two little blackbirds, sitting on a gate," she chants, "one named Curvy and the other named Straight." As she says each name she raises an index finger, each one a blackbird. "Go away, Curvy," she continues, making one finger curve through the air and behind her. "Go away, Straight." This one flies straight behind her back. "Come back, Curvy. Come back, Straight," she finishes, and the children clap. The next variation is "Two little blackbirds sitting in the snow, one named Fast and one named Slow." This, too, is a favorite, maybe because

"One named Quiet and one named Loud." In the hall outside the Grasshopper Room, Amy and the kids shout it out.

five-year-olds know what it's like to dawdle. Fast goes and comes quickly, but Slow's progress is long and drawn-out. "Come back, Slow!" shouts Laila happily. After Fast and Slow come Quiet and Loud, and the children take great pleasure in shouting Loud home.

On the playground, the Grasshoppers eat graham crackers and apples in the mild sunshine while Darrin screams behind the shed. Crystal has him by one hand, trying to shepherd him gently into the center, but he's fighting her every step of the way. He grabs the metal edge of the water table as he goes by, and Crystal has to pry his hand loose and lift him bodily through the door, screaming the whole time. Nearby the Bumblebees, too, are eating their snack, sitting on the low rubber edge that lines the asphalt walkway. Wendy comes out, staying with the Bumblebees while Crystal deals with Darrin in-side. After a few minutes Darrin comes out and sits down with the other Bumblebees, calmer now, and Wendy goes back inside.

After snack, the Grasshoppers spread out to play. Fiona walks the rub-ber edge as if it were a balance beam. Skye skips to the sandbox. A freight train rumbles by, giving its frantic call. Tiny sparrows flitter and light, picking up graham cracker crumbs. Cory tosses her paper plate into the garbage and runs toward Lateef, who runs away playfully. He clambers up into the square plastic climbing cube and somersaults down its plastic slide. Cory climbs up into the cube and watches. "Cory, come down here and sit on my lap!" orders Lateef, sitting on the wood chips below her. She climbs down the side of the cube. "Wanna sit on *my* lap, Cory?" asks Erick hopefully.

After a short struggle, Erick runs out of the cube toward Emily. "Lateef's making unfair of me!" he says. "I want Cory to sit on my lap, and he's making unfair of me!" Emily comes over to see how she can help. "Be quiet!" shouts Lateef. Erick starts to cry, perched on top of the cube now. "Lateef, I want you to come here and listen," says Emily. "I'm listening!" he insists. "No, I want you to come here and really listen," she says. She carries him over to Erick, so the two boys stand face to face.

"Now, I want you to listen to Erick," she says to Lateef. After a moment, Erick says, "I don't like when you're unfair to me." "Know what he's talking about?" prods Emily. Lateef nods. "What do you have to say back to him?" "Sorry," says Lateef. "Is that good enough, Erick?" she persists. Erick shakes his head. "I want you to shake his hand," says Emily. Lateef sticks his hand out, and Erick shakes his head. "What's the matter?" asks Emily. "Why won't you shake his hand?" Erick just stares. Words can't convey what he's feel-ing, at least not yet. "Maybe when you're ready you can shake Lateef's hand," says Emily.

"He's mad 'cause Cory wouldn't sit on his lap," says Lateef loudly. He's right, as it happens, but that's no longer the point. "You're lying!" protests Erick. "You made fun of me!" "No, *you're* lying!" shouts Lateef. The accusations fly back and forth until Lateef breaks the stalemate by announcing, "You're a booty-head!" Emily, hoping to dispel the rising tension, says to Lateef affec-tionately, "*You're* a booty-head!" but the damage has been done. Erick starts to howl. Emily looks helplessly from one boy to the other. She doesn't know what to do, so finally she obeys her instinct, flipping Erick into her arms and cuddling him fiercely. He puts his arms around her neck, tears staining his face. Emily rubs her cheek on the top of his head, where the hair is soft and

A tender moment on the playground: Emily comforts Erick

tightly curled. They sit quietly like this for a while, and then Emily whispers into his ear, "You're a good guy, Erick. It looked like you were trying to talk with Lateef and he wasn't understanding. Do you want to play with someone else?" "I want to play with Brad," he says, and, as if a great burden has been lifted, which it has, he slides off her lap and runs across the playground.

Toward the end of July, rumors are buzzing again about W-2. In recent weeks the House and Senate have each passed a version of welfare reform, and if they can work out a compromise the federal government will enact its own welfare reform. The Senate version is more family-friendly; for instance, it guarantees child care to poor mothers with kids age six and under. But it has flaws. As Barbara Reisman of the Child Care Action Campaign told me back in June, "The Senate bill doesn't say anything about what child care means. It doesn't set any kind of minimal health and safety standards, doesn't say anything about quality."

Like other children's advocates, Reisman is disappointed in this round of welfare reform. "It creates the potential for kids to be in very dangerous environments," she explained. "It will be a challenge for centers to maintain quality in the face of cutbacks. They've got to figure out a way to make it clear to the entire community what benefits they're providing, and why it's important to the entire community to support it." In other words, as economists would say, the community must recognize that child care is a social good, a service that benefits the wider community as well as the individuals who pay for it.

Until federal welfare reform stands or falls, President Clinton is not going to issue waivers to Wisconsin or any other state. And W-2 can't be implemented until the waivers come through. Meanwhile, life at Red Caboose goes on as usual. Haley's last day in the Elephant Room comes and goes; her mom, Kirsten, lost her funding, so for now Haley is at home with her. In the Grasshopper Room, the talk is of kindergarten and other increasingly complex subjects. One day at lunch, for instance, a spoonful of spaghetti sauce sparks a lively conversation about family. The sauce lands on Rocio's dress, much to her dismay. She scrubs at it with a paper towel, but the stain remains. "My mom can wash it," she says resignedly, then perks up. "My dad used to do the wash, but he's not allowed to anymore. He might shrink stuff, 'cause he just leaves it there till it shrinks. He doesn't even pick it up. He just leaves it there with a towel on top of it."

"My mom and dad are better washers than that," says Mirko. "Cory, who does the laundry at your house?" asks Amy. While the kids eat Max's spaghetti and meatballs, Amy's eating a plate full of salad and a few crackers. Cory points to herself. "You do the laundry?" asks Amy incredulously. "Nooo," says Mirko. "Do you help fold sometimes?" asks Amy. "I do," says Gracie. Seth says, "I help my dad turn on the washing machine and the dryer." Seth's mom, Karen, is blind—not that that stops her from doing household chores. She navigates the sighted world quite competently, thanks to her guide dog.

The discussion continues, from who does the laundry to who can be a mom. "You're not a mom if you don't have kids, right?" says Erick. "What if

she's pregnant?" asks Mirko. Erick says, as if in response, "My mom said someone who's not pregnant and doesn't have a kid, guess what? You can still be
a mother." "You mean a grandmother?" says Mirko inspiredly. "No, a *mom*,"
insists Erick. Rocio puts in, "You can have a stepmom. You can have a magi-
cal friend." There is some controversy over this mysterious statement, which
Rocio settles by stating majestically, "You can have adoption papers. I was
adopted." This is hardly news to anyone at the table; the subject of Rocio's
adoption has been discussed many times, sometimes quite fancifully. "Did you
hear that, Erick?" says Amy. "Rocio found a way that could happen. If somebody adopts a kid." "I want to adopt some kids," says Erick. "Why can't men
have babies?" asks Gracie thoughtfully. Uh-oh. The dreaded question—well,
one of them. But Amy is ready for it. "Women's bodies are made to have
babies," she explains. "Your mom has a uterus in her body. Men don't have
a uterus." The kids accept her explanation in the spirit in which it is offered.
The only response comes from Gracie, who asks, "Can I have some bread?"
with no apparent sense of anticlimax.

August

The first few days of August bring big news to the child-care community, most
of it depressing. Magic Penny, one of the three nonprofit centers left on the
east side, is closing. Even though Red Caboose may get some of Magic Penny's
children, the closing of a nonprofit is still bad news. Who will be the next
to go?

There's always the worry that it could be Red Caboose. Wendy talks to
a few people around town, hoping to get the lowdown on what happened
at Magic Penny. She hears that the center wasn't able to meet its last three
payrolls, that it had been plagued with poor financial management and high
turnover in directors. Sad for Magic Penny, but reassuring for Wendy because
none of these is true of Red Caboose. According to scuttlebutt, Magic Penny
had even been reduced to "borrowing" the staff's union dues, which are de-
ducted from their paychecks, and then not paying the union—a real no-no, a
felony, in fact, if you "borrow" more than $1,000.

Meanwhile, in Washington, President Clinton is ready to sign the federal
welfare reform bill at last. While the *New York Times* and other national papers
are busy praising Clinton for this "master stroke" in his reelection campaign,
the people who will see the day-to-day results of this legislation are in shock.
Wendy's only comment is, "Pretty revolting." This is why she doesn't pay attention to politics, much less get involved in them.

The good news at home is that Governor Thompson has decided to suspend the W-2 child-care copayments, pending "further study." The copays lasted exactly one day; they went into effect on August 1 and were suspended the next day. Somehow the message got through that the copays were (a) unrealistic and (b) jeopardizing child care for everyone. Thompson is quoted in a local newspaper as saying, "Despite what the critics say, I'm determined to make W-2 a program that ultimately does a lot of good for the children of this state. And if we have to make changes in order to have it work, I'm not afraid to do it."[3] In the same article, State Representative Rebecca Young wondered whether the governor's squabble with the archbishop of Milwaukee had something to do with his change of heart. "Perhaps he's been reading his Bible," she said. "I think that, after his tiff with the archbishop, the governor is trying to make up for his loose lips and save his sinking ship of W-2." Whatever the reason, the state will work on revising the copays; in the meantime, the old reimbursements apply.

There's more good news, too. On a Friday morning in early August, on a sweltering hot day, Janet gave birth to a healthy baby boy, two weeks early. In a way the timing was good; Amy had a few weeks to get used to being in charge before the changeover of children. Still, those last weeks before kindergarten have been emotional. Kids who have known each other since age one hold hands or walk with their arms around each other. For these last weeks, at least, the Grasshoppers are a group, holding fast to one another before the bonds of the last few years, the long years of early childhood, are loosened for good.

Gracie leaves first, in mid-August, heading for a new life in California. Everyone cries, even the teachers. "She's the first kid I really had to say goodbye to whom I'll never see again," explains Amy. Today, the Tuesday before kindergarten starts, is Seth's last day. On the playground Cory pedals a trike, looking more coordinated than she does walking. Clark, catching sight of her, engages her in an elaborate pantomime, stopping, staring, looking toward her and finally leaping over, making a tunnel out of his long legs. She laughs silently, letting her head loll back.

From the sandbox comes the sound of Kenny sobbing. Clark goes to see what's wrong. Lateef, standing nearby, points helpfully and says, "Darrin hit him." Darrin strikes an aggressive pose. "Darrin, tell us what happened," says Clark. "A punch went in his face," says Darrin slowly in his thin child's voice. "A punch from you?" says Clark seriously. "My hand hit him," explains Darrin. Clark pulls Darrin closer, so the boys are standing face to face. He turns to Kenny. "So what do you think happened?" he asks. "He punched me," says Kenny softly. "Do you know why he punched you?" asks Clark. "What made him so mad at you?" "I pushed him," says Kenny, even more softly. Clark turns to Darrin. "Is that what made you so mad, because he pushed you?" "Yeah," mutters Darrin. "And why do you think he pushed you, Darrin?" presses Clark. Silence. Then, "I saw the caboose of the train, but it got gone," says Darrin.

Clark turns to Kenny, now sitting in his lap. "And why don't you tell me why you pushed Darrin?" he says. "'Cause he punched me in the nose," says Kenny, deliberately clouding the issue. "I want to talk about punching *and* pushing, if you don't mind," says Clark. It's quite a funny line, but he manages to keep a straight face. "What could you have done instead of pushing?" "Tell a teacher," says Kenny promptly. "That's one thing," agrees Clark. "What could you have told Darrin?" "Don't do that," says Kenny. Clark turns back to Darrin. "And Darrin, what could you have done besides punching? Is punching an OK thing to do when someone's pushing you?" "No," says Darrin, looking away. Clark takes Darrin's chin in his hand and gently turns the boy's head to face himself. "We're almost done," he says. "We're almost ready to go play, so look at me." When Darrin's attention is as focused as it's going to get, Clark says slowly, enunciating each word, "Don't—punch—anymore. You must talk. You're a big boy, you need to be a talker." "OK," says Darrin. "And you, young man," says Clark to Kenny, "you do not push. All right? Talk, don't push." He chucks Darrin under the chin, and Darrin reaches up to hug Clark around the neck. Clark hugs him back, and then gives Kenny a hug, too. "Don't be a forgetter, either, remember that," he says. "It's gonna save you a lot of tears and unhappiness." He releases both boys and stands watching them run away. "I'll be doing it again in five minutes," he says to himself. From the other end of the playground comes the sound of Kylen's voice, shouting, "Clark, he pushed me!" Clark sighs, shakes his head, and heads toward the inevitable.

Some of the Grasshoppers are playing a game called statues with Emily—not Emily Lyman but a sub who's covering for Janet. The kids are frozen into various positions on the playground and Emily walks lightly among them, touching each one and giving them an occupation. She taps the top of Cory's head. "This statue is a beautiful ballerina," she says. Cory pivots and grins. "This statue," Emily continues, tapping Mirko, "is a Kung Fu man. This statue"—she taps Carlos—"is a princess. This statue"—she taps Todd, then steps back to study him for a minute—"is doing tai chi." "This is what an ice skater does," explains Todd. "That's exactly right, an ice skater!" exclaims Emily.

After an hour on the playground, the Grasshoppers come inside for calendar time. "Grasshoppers, if you want to take off your shirts or your dresses, that's OK," says Amy. "It's pretty hot." Years ago, the kids at Red Caboose were allowed to get naked in really hot weather, but now they have to keep their underwear on. Most of the boys immediately strip to their underpants. Rocio and Meghan run to their lockers to change into bathing suits. For the girls, at least, sexual modesty has begun. "Elias is wasting water," says Meghan when she comes back. Amy ignores her. There's a difference between tattling and telling a teacher when you need help. Amy tries to reinforce that difference by responding when it's appropriate and ignoring when it's not.

Emily looks at Rocio and Meghan in their bathing suits and smothers a laugh. "There's down home," she says, referring to Meghan's red and white gingham tank suit, "and there's kowabunga." Rocio's wearing a bikini in fluorescent shades of orange and green, which nicely sets off her caramel-colored skin. "I have my boxers on under here," says Lateef to Amy, sweaty in his long pants, shirt, and vest. "I know, honey, but your mother wants you to keep your clothes on," Amy says kindly.

After calendar, the kids make their choices. Today Rocio, at Amy's invitation, acts as the teacher, calling on kids one at a time and asking what they want to do. She starts, predictably, with her brother. "Carlos, what do you want to do?" she asks primly. "Play in the loft with the dress-ups," he answers, "with Meghan, Marley, and you." "OK," says Rocio, moving on to Seth and Elias. Then she comes to Cory. Cory's response to the question is to make fists out of her hands, with the thumbs and pinkies sticking out, and wiggle them, then point to Mirko. "What's she saying?" asks Rocio, looking to Emily. It's disheartening that even Rocio, one of the brightest kids in the group, doesn't understand the sign for *play*, which Cory uses several times a day.

Cory and Mirko sit down together in front of the antiquated computer. Carlos floats by, wearing a sheer white negligee, underpants, and a lacy orange cape. Emily manages to set up the game Mirko wants to play, despite the fact that the software is 11 years old and cranky. The screen shows an image of Snoopy lying on his doghouse, and then breaks it into squares and mixes them up. The object of the game is to put them back into the right order, like doing a puzzle on-screen. Mirko takes the first turn, clicking the mouse and pressing the space bar to arrange the pieces on the screen. Then he tries to help Cory, but she lifts his hand off the mouse. Just because she can't talk doesn't mean she's a baby. She knows how to do this puzzle just as well as Mirko does.

Mirko loses interest and wanders away, but Cory sits in front of the screen, clicking the mouse over and over. She tries a piece in one place, then in another, working the patterns until they come right. Just as she finishes, Todd pulls up the empty chair beside her and starts to sit down. Cory puts her hand on it to stop him, but he ignores her, or maybe doesn't notice her body language, and sits down anyway. She puts her hands up to the screen, covering it, but he just sits patiently beside her. Finally she brings the side of her right hand down perpendicular into her left palm, the sign for *stop*, and Todd notices what she's doing for the first time. "Stop," he says, and obediently gets out of the chair. Relieved, Cory clicks the mouse and begins another puzzle.

In the corner behind Cory, Seth sits by a pile of Legos and sobs — no, wails, words garbled with tears, the volume rising quickly. "He said, 'Stop it,' when I wasn't doing anything!" he manages to get out, pointing to Elias, a new Grasshopper. "He was putting Legos in here!" says Elias in a tone of outrage. "They're not supposed to go in here!" Amy unravels the story: Elias was building a castle of Legos, and Seth started adding to the building. "Whose castle is this?" she asks the two boys, plus Brad, Lateef, and Kenny, who are all listening. "It's Red Caboose's. And who gets to use this castle? Everybody, right? Who gets to use this part right here?" She points to the parts of the castle, one by one, reiterating that everyone can use them. Seth, who had quieted momentarily, is working his way back to hysteria. He throws a handful of Legos violently onto the ground. "You're throwing your toys," Amy says calmly. "I would like you to be in a place where I know you won't hurt anyone. You can come with me, or I will help you." "I don't want to leave!" whines Seth. Amy bends over and lifts him off the floor, bending her knees to save her back; he's the heaviest of the Grasshoppers. "Later we can talk about this, when you're not crying or throwing things and you'll be able to listen to me," she says in a reasonable voice as she leads him into the Busy Room.

It's not surprising that Seth is feeling fragile today. Like the other five-year-olds, he's facing two scary transitions: saying good-bye to the known and saying hello to the unknown. He cries in the next room for a few minutes, winding down slowly. Amy brings him back into the Dinosaur Room and sits him at the lunch table for a few minutes, making sure he's calm. Then she leads him unresistingly to a corner where there are lots of toy race cars, which he usually loves to play with, giving him a chance to settle down completely before having to interact with any of the other kids.

Cory, sitting at the computer, bangs her hand in frustration; the mouse is stuck again, a constant problem with this ancient equipment. Amy comes over and eventually manages to shake it out of its lethargy. The noise level in the room is louder than usual. The new Grasshoppers are arriving, more each day, and the old ones are growing more and more anxious as their last days approach. "This year is as bad as it's ever been," says Amy, cracking a smile. Janet's absence, plus the parade of subs to cover her hours, plus the usual upheaval at this time of year makes for a pretty chaotic environment. By chance, most of the Grasshoppers who have left have been girls and most of the new ones have been boys. Today, for example, there are 11 boys and only 4 girls in the room—another reason, maybe, for the unusual noise and confusion.

By this age there are real distinctions between boy culture and girl culture. Even the most politically correct parents have to acknowledge this. Nancy, Brad's mother, stands watching the action in the Dinosaur Room, her hands in the pockets of her shorts, shaking her head. "I want so much for there to be no difference between girls and boys," she says. Why those differences exist, whether it's genetics or socialization or both, is a question no one can answer. But no matter how hard the teachers try to minimize the differences, gender roles are very much a part of life in the Grasshopper Room. Now, for instance, Rocio and Meghan M. sit at the lunch table, weaving brightly colored yarn scraps. Working together, they tape one end of the yarn to the table to hold it steady. Behind them, Erick and Lateef set up a racetrack for toy cars. Erick grabs some pieces of track away from Lateef, causing a huge argument to erupt.

It's not that the girls don't fight; they do, and they need to, just as all kids this age need to figure out the rules and how far they can go with one another. And it's not that the boys don't work together, because of course they do that, too. But the overall picture is different. The boys tend to be rowdier, more physically active, more actively confrontational; the girls tend to be quieter, better at concentrating, weaving and braiding and making things. When they fight, the aggression comes out differently—playing emotional games, excluding each other, threatening to withdraw friendship or invitations to parties.

Seth's parents show up while the children are eating lunch, to memorialize their son's last day. Seth's dad, David, pulls a camera out of a bag and snaps a picture of Seth eating beets and cheese. Seth's mom, Karen, stands beaming in the doorway, one hand on her guide dog's harness. Seth will spend the next few days at home with his parents, getting ready for his transition to the "real world." But isn't Red Caboose part of the real world? When kids start at the center—especially the littlest ones, the one- and two-year-olds—Red Caboose certainly *seems* like the real world to their parents, the big bad real world where not everybody loves you and things don't always go your way. But for the Grasshoppers, Red Caboose has come to feel like a protected, sheltered little world, a place where everybody knows you and at least some of them love you. A place to cling to in a storm of change.

That change is coming no matter how the kids and their parents feel about it. For the moment, though, the only future the Grasshoppers are interested in are the treats Karen and David have brought. Amy takes the children down the back stairs and around to the back door to go outside. Emily Lyman carries a big bowl of grapes, part of the treat, and offers one to Wendy, who's just finished saying good-bye to prospective parents here for a visit. Life goes on, after all, and luckily fall enrollment looks good. "Is this a special treat?" she asks, surveying the Grasshoppers. Her voice rises a bit on the last few words. Usually Wendy talks to children in the same reasonable tone of voice she uses with grown-ups, but even she falls victim to the squeaky-voice syndrome occasionally.

Now she squats beside Seth, who's visibly basking in the warmth of so much attention. Emily opens the tub and passes out chocolate chip cookies. "I'm gonna miss Seth!" exclaims Wendy. "Yesterday I told Seth I wasn't gonna miss him because he's gonna come back a lot," says Emily. "That's good," says Wendy. Emily asks Seth which kindergarten he's going to. "Lowell," he answers. "Right around the corner," explains his father. "Does that mean that you're not gonna take a bus, that you're gonna get to walk, with patrols and crossing guards?" says Wendy. She has the ability to make even the most mundane scenario sound as exciting as a three-ring circus.

One by one, the Grasshoppers finish snack and run off. "Thank you, Seth," shouts Rocio as she heads for the swings. Wendy strolls the playground, checking things out. She pauses by the metal slide, which is attached to the oldest playground structure, the one built by neighborhood carpenters 20-some years ago. The center sent out fund-raising letters to grandparents a few months ago and raised $1,500, which was earmarked for a new slide. But the contractors Wendy called refused to replace the slide because the spot doesn't meet the new regulations for playground safety. The slide should be eight feet away from the wall, but it's much closer than that. So now Wendy's considering replacing the whole structure, either bit by bit or all at once. It's time, anyway. After 20 years, things are starting to go.

On Friday afternoon, the last Friday before school starts, the mood in the Grasshopper Room suddenly lifts. The gloom and anxiety are gone, replaced by a feeling of holiday freedom. A frenetic undercurrent runs through the

You can't catch me! Anna, Lydia, Mirko, and Rocio clown around with Amy. And no, they aren't usually allowed to stand on the picnic table.

room. Many of the Grasshoppers have already left: Gracie, Anna Y., Laila, Daniel, Seth, Fiona, Cory. Cory is going to Glendale after all. Jenny called the school and said, "Since I haven't heard otherwise, and since I have to make some after-school plans, I'm going to go ahead and assume that Cory will be at Glendale." Maybe she had gotten in already; maybe Jenny's chutzpah gave the principal a little push. Jenny doesn't care how it happened, as long as it did.

The logbook is filled with good-bye notes from parents. "Thank you all for the amazing job with Seth," wrote Seth's dad. "Brad and his family can hardly imagine life without Red Caboose," wrote Nancy, Brad's mother. "Brad will miss his old friends. The adults will miss the teachers who taught us so much about parenting." There's a long note from Jenny. Gillian, Marley's mom, stands in front of the log with a pencil in her hand; today is Marley's last day, and she's come with the obligatory treat and to bring her daughter home. It's a day that has special resonance for Gillian, since she was a Red Caboose kid herself more than 20 years ago.

Rocio is in the book area with Lateef, listening to a tape Lateef brought in from home. "Go, go, Power Rangers!" sings a tinny, evil-sounding voice. "Uh-uh-uh-uh-uh, catch me if you can." The two of them are doing a stylized dance to the music, a cross between karate and modern dance, slowly swinging their arms and legs to the music. Emily the sub, who's in for Amy this afternoon, stands watching them. "You're doing *capoeira!*" she exclaims, referring to the Brazilian martial art she studies. She faces them, as a gym instructor would, and begins demonstrating capoeira moves, legs apart, swinging her weight from side to side. The kids follow her movements as well as they can. Suddenly Lateef drops to the floor, rolls toward Emily, and karate-chops at her leg. "No, no, no!" she scolds. "In capoeira you never touch anybody!"

At three o'clock Emily Lyman calls out, "Grasshoppers, let's go get our cots!" and the children run into the Moonshine Room to retrieve their cots for stacking. "Marley, don't go, don't go," laments Rocio. Emily squats beside a cot where Joseph, newly moved up from the Bumblebee Room, is still asleep, mouth open, arms and legs wrapped around a multicolored quilt.

By 3:30 everyone's awake and the cots are put away. The children have washed their hands and are sitting in a circle on the floor. A fan by the window blows warm air through the already warm room. Finn, a new Grasshopper, sits beside Mirko. Emily Lyman passes out the Red Caboose snack first, apple slices and cups of peanut butter for dipping. Gillian sits on a little chair, Marley on the floor beside her. As the kids eat, Emily Lyman says, "We have a special guest today. Marley, will you introduce our guest?" "Chocolate chip cookies," says Marley. The Grasshoppers giggle. After a little coaxing Marley introduces her mom. "Today's a special day for Marley, 'cause it's her last day," Emily tells the kids. This is the prompt for a by-now familiar ritual. "Happy last day to you, happy last day to you," sing the Grasshoppers to the tune of "Happy Birthday." Marley's going to the after-school program at Lapham, and she'll see some of the old Grasshoppers there. But it won't be the same.

While Marley passes out cookies, Emily Lyman sits down to tell a story. "Once upon a time, a long, long, long time ago, there lived a king," she begins, hardly pausing between words. "And this king was a very very great king, but he was getting old. And one day he was lying on his deathbed; that's where you lie before you die. And he called his daughter to him. And his daughter's name was Rocio. And he said, 'Rocio, I think I'm preparing to die. But I want to tell you three things before you rule this kingdom. The first thing I want you to do is always wear this heavy gold crown on your head. The second thing is always rule with an iron fist. And the third thing to remember is always drink from this side of the royal golden goblet. Can you remember that?'" Emily's voice, when she speaks for the king, is deep and heavy. "And Rocio said, 'I can remember that.' She became queen after he died, and she was a great queen because she always remembered the three golden rules. And she lived for a long time, but one day she too was on her deathbed preparing to die. And she called her son to her, and her son's name was Brad. She said"—her voice goes high and dainty—"'I'm getting ready to die. I've been queen for a long time, but soon you'll be king, and I want you to remember the three rules that my father told me before he died. The first rule is always wear this heavy gold crown on your head. And the second rule is always rule—'" Emily pauses, waiting to see if anyone remembers, and the real Rocio pipes up, "Always rule with an iron fist."

"'Always rule with an iron fist,'" Emily agrees. "'And the third rule is always drink from this side of the royal golden goblet.'" Emily sips from a paper cup of water to demonstrate. The story goes on through several more kings and queens reigning, passing along the three golden rules, and dying, and then Emily comes to the last queen, and names her Marley. The children are spellbound, their eyes bright, trying to figure out how the story will end. "And the king said, 'Marley, you will be queen, and I'm gonna tell you the three rules that my mother told me and the three rules that her father told her before, so you can be a good queen. The first rule is'—what?" A number of Grasshoppers chant slowly, "Always wear this gold crown on your head." "And the second rule is—" prompts Emily, her fist in the air, and the Grasshoppers obligingly recite, "Always rule with an iron fist." "And the third rule—" says Emily, and back comes the answer: "Always drink from this side of the royal golden goblet."

"And he said, 'Can you remember that?'" continues Emily. "And Marley said, 'I can remember that, but there's one thing I don't understand. Why should I do those things?'" A few of the Grasshoppers giggle uncertainly, not sure where this is leading. "And her father said, 'Well, you have to wear this gold crown because'—why should she wear the gold crown?" Rocio calls out, "So everybody knows that she's queen." Emily nods and goes on. "And always rule with an iron fist because why, Carlos?" "Ummm," says Carlos, and Rocio jumps in to help him: "So people will know that she rules the kingdom." Emily nods again and goes on. "And the third thing," she says brightly, the story obviously winding up, " 'Why should I always drink from this side of the cup?' And her father said, 'That I don't know.' And he thought for a minute and said, 'The reason why you should always drink from this side of the royal golden goblet is because if you drink from the other side of the royal golden goblet, what would happen?' " Emily stands up, walks to the garbage can, brings the far side of the paper cup to her lips and drinks, dumping the whole cup of water over herself and into the garbage. The Grasshoppers sit, dumbfounded, and then crack up.

It's a wonderful story, with a subtext that rings true to these children on the verge of change. The old king dies and the new queen is crowned. The old life is over and the new one begins, full of pomp and mystery and humor. By telling the story, Emily is marking the solemnity of the occasion and reminding them that life goes on, and it's just as often silly as it is serious.

Emily knows some of these kids better than any of the other teachers. She was an LTE in the Turtle Room for six months back in 1992, when some of the children now going off to kindergarten were Turtles: Anna Y., Mirko, Laila, Cory. Emily has watched them grow up and wonders what their lives will be like now. "Red Caboose teaches the kids to be sensitive, to care about other people's feelings," she says as the Grasshoppers finish their snack and line up to go downstairs for movies. Their world is changing, but it's still movie day. "And now they're going to go into a world where one thing is definitely clear: the more ruthless you are—especially the girls—the more popular you're gonna be," continues Emily. "They'll have to deal with the self-esteem problems you feel if you're on the outs because you're a nice kid. It's gonna be tough."

Emily has more to say, but she doesn't get the chance to say it. From across the room she spots Brad and Joseph whacking each other, and she calls out, "Brad and Joseph, I don't want to see any more of that! That's unsafe! It's scary for me to watch!" Erick comes up to her, holding out one arm, showing her a tiny crack in the smooth dark skin of his elbow where a drop of blood wells up from a scratch. "I want a Band-Aid," he says. "Let's go get one," she replies, and they do.

Epilogue

On a rainy Saturday afternoon in April 1997, some of the parents and teachers of Red Caboose have gathered at Luke House, a local soup kitchen. Most of the board members are here, along with an ex-board member, Lynn, and a number of teachers—Gary Dosemagen and Cheryl Heiman from the center, Neil Skinner and Lee Lohr from after-school. And, of course, Wendy.

They sit, for once, in adult-size chairs at round tables in a room where meals are served each week to some of Madison's poor and homeless. Everyone's brought something to eat, from bagels and cream cheese to nori rolls. The center is celebrating its 25th anniversary this year, and the subject of today's discussion is where Red Caboose should be heading—philosophically and practically—over the next 25 years.

Twenty-five years is cause for celebration, but it's no guarantee for the future. The problems faced by centers like Red Caboose today—how to pay teachers a living wage, how to keep the quality of care high, how to stay affordable for parents—will become more acute, not less, in the years to come. Welfare reform in Wisconsin and nationwide will make finding and paying for good child care even more challenging than it is now for the poor and the working poor.

In my year at Red Caboose, I learned about what makes a good child-care center successful and what obstacles it's up against. At first, each day I spent observing was exciting. Then it became tedious, the same routines over and over. Toward the end of my time in each room a whole new level of experience opened up. Once I got past both the novelty and the boredom of life with young children, I came to care much more than I thought possible about the way those lives were being shaped, right before my eyes.

The most important thing I came away with was the abiding sense that what happens day in and day out at a place like Red Caboose matters. All the rhetoric in the world is nowhere near as convincing as the experience of watching young children every day. And *if* it matters, we have to say so. We have to acknowledge that each day in the life of a child is meaningful, and then we have to confront the uncomfortable fact that as a society we treat our youngest children as throwaways even while we pay lip service to the notion of education. It is profoundly ironic that we obsess about the physical dangers of child care—the rare instances of abuse or neglect—but turn a blind eye to more common consequences: Lack of compassion. Inability to care about others. Low self-esteem. Apathy. Despair.

We know what good child care looks like: well-paid, well-trained teachers, low staff turnover, good teacher-child ratios, small group sizes. We know what it takes to create good child care: more money than parents can pay. And we know that millions of American kids, caught in the political crossfire, don't have it. The Left touts child care as an ideal, ignoring the reality that much of that care is not good enough. The Right touts stay-at-home moms, ignoring the fact that many parents *have* to work. This country will never embrace a national model of child care, writes psychologist Sandra Scarr, "largely because mothers are not to be encouraged to work."[1]

Red Caboose and other centers succeed in doing good work with children *despite*, not because of, the decisions and policies we as a nation have put in place. With the things I had seen and learned fresh in my mind, I went to the experts for their solutions, their vision of where we could and should go next.

British pediatrician Penelope Leach is an outspoken critic of child care as it exists today, especially for the "under-threes," infants and toddlers. In her book *Children First*, Leach envisions a "child-place" in every community, where parents could drop by with infants and get to know other at-home parents, where toddlers and preschoolers would be cared for and educated, where school-age children could spend the hours between school dismissal and parents' arrival home. Children could make friends of all ages; grown-ups could find the companionship and stimulation to make them better caregivers for their own and other people's children; single parents and families could find support and community at a crucial time in their lives, the years when they raise young children.[2]

Leach's vision reads like a fairy tale, idyllic and unrealistic. But other countries have incorporated many of these elements into their real-life child-care systems. Nursery schools in Japan are so well respected that stay-at-home mothers take jobs just so their children can enroll—and then quietly quit those jobs. A typical Japanese family pays about $200 a month for child care, about one-fifth the cost of providing the care; the government pays the rest.[3] In France, early childhood education has been in vogue since the 1880s, when the laws setting up a system of public schools mentioned the *école maternelle*, or nursery school, as the first level of public schooling. Today, 96 percent of all three-year-olds in France are enrolled in one of these public nursery schools.[4]

We have nothing like this level of care in America. Our unstated national policy is *not* to help families and children.[5] The closest we come to the European model is a handful of high-quality centers run by businesses that subsidize the cost of care for their workers as an employee benefit. But this kind of care is for the lucky few. To achieve something close to the Japanese or French models, or something approaching Leach's vision, government and individuals in America would have to undergo a radical change in attitude. We would have to make the ideal of community a national priority. We would need to acknowledge that despite the myths of self-sufficient pioneers and rugged American individualists, no family can or should have to go it alone—a notion as revolutionary as democracy in the 1700s.

In their 1991 book *Child Care Choices,* Edward Zigler and Mary Lang agree that radical change is necessary. Their solution to the child care crisis is the "School of the 21st Century," what many in the field have come to see as the only viable option: subsuming child care into the public-school system. They envision year-round care, in school buildings whenever possible, for children ages three through six; before-, after-school, and vacation care for elementary-school kids; and outreach services for all families within the school district.[6]

The under-threes, once again, have no place in the School for the 21st Century. Parents would get a yearly stipend for each infant and toddler, to help pay for child care or for a parent to stay home. Such a stipend would be financed by expanding Social Security, an idea Zigler and Lang justify by arguing that most people who collect Social Security are senior citizens, and more children than seniors are living in poverty right now.[7]

Many of the professionals who work in child care are ambivalent about this idea. On the one hand, public schools do have established funding sources and credibility; they're both economically and morally defensible. Most people, even those without children, acknowledge the need to pay for public schools. On the other hand, public schools are both far from perfect and famously inflexible, resistant to change in any form.

Wendy tells a story about the time 19 years ago when her son André was in elementary school, when she and a few other parents tried to reform the hot lunch program. They made an informal study of what was served, and discovered that fresh fruit was served several times a month, desserts often doubled up, and fried foods were served frequently. They surveyed parents about changes they'd like to see, and then Wendy went to the district with her findings, sure that with the evidence in hand she could effect change. "I was told things like 'Canned peaches aren't a dessert; they're part of the fruit and vegetable food group,'" she recalls. "Or 'Kids don't eat beets, so we have to hide them in chocolate cake.'" She ran smack up against the long-entrenched school bureaucracy. If the public schools are so intransigent about lunch, imagine how they'd react to more substantive change.

"The government in America tends to do everything badly," writes Anne Roiphe in her book *Fruitful: A Real Mother in the Modern World.* "Child care that ran like the motor vehicle bureaus in most states would indeed be a nightmare. All our children would be victims of friendly fire. But good, small child-care centers, professionalized, with communal commitment to quality, might be possible."[8] I would hate to see good centers like Red Caboose swallowed up by the public schools. But I also worry about the children who aren't in places like Red Caboose. The public schools would almost certainly raise the *overall* quality of care for *most* American children. The good of the many versus the good of the few. Like Wendy, I wish there were a way to combine the best of both worlds.

Meanwhile, in the absence of significant government funding or corporate support, centers like Red Caboose have to make their own long-term stability. For more than an hour, the parents and teachers at Luke House brainstorm ideas to keep Red Caboose thriving into the next century. The ideas range from the practical to the pie-in-the-sky: Provide child care during basketball games and symphony concerts. Rent the center's kitchen to a caterer. Start an infant-care room. Do evening care for the growing number of second-shift workers. Build a parking garage under the center and rent out spaces. Host pancake breakfasts and spaghetti dinners. Produce a Red Caboose instructional video. Package some of Max's most popular dishes and sell them. This last suggestion causes a ripple of laughter, mostly at the thought of finding "Max's Own Lasagna" in the freezer case at local grocery stores.

Each idea raises a whole series of other questions and issues. How can Red Caboose survive financially *and* stay true to its mission? How can the center keep reaching out to low-income families, keep its population diverse, serve those who need it most? How can more money be brought into the center from outside the traditional source—parents' pockets? How will welfare reform affect the children of Wisconsin?

One year after I finish observing at Red Caboose, W-2 is about to take full effect. The copayment schedule has been revised for the better; instead of paying up to 42 percent of their gross income for child care, families now pay up to 16 percent.[9] About 700 people in the state have been certified as provisional caregivers. It's too early to know what the long-term results of such care will be. But look at what happens already in licensed care: A convicted sex offender looks after a toddler while the family provider sleeps. A mother finds a used syringe in her six-month-old daughter's snowsuit. Teachers at a center refuse to let a dizzy girl off a spinning tire swing, then make her clean up her own vomit and laugh at her while she does.[10] True stories, all of them. If these things happen in licensed care, where teachers have some training and education, what will happen in places where caregivers have no training?

As I write, another nonprofit center in Madison has closed, the latest victim of financial mismanagement. Red Caboose, meanwhile, has just celebrated its 25th anniversary with a big party at Olbrich Gardens. At the party, Wendy got up in front of several hundred parents and children, past and current, and wished the center another 25 years, knowing full well that wishes alone won't make it so.

Action is what is needed. What will it take to make us act? And who is *us*, anyway? I have come to believe that *us* is parents. We are our children's most passionate advocates. We alone can convincingly muster the moral and economic arguments that will bring about change. Think of it as a kind of revolution, a bloodless coup: If even half the working parents in this country rose up, forced the debate on child care into the headlines and political back rooms, change would follow. Who knows what form that change would take? Parent allowances, so new parents could stay home with babies? Leach's "child-places" in every community? National standards for child care? Government subsidies for accredited centers?

Here's to the revolution.

NOTES

Notes

Prologue

1. U. S. Department of Education, National Center for Educational Statistics, *National Household Education Survey* (Washington, D.C., 1995).

2. National Commission on Children, *Beyond Rhetoric: A New American Agenda for Children and Families,* the final report of the National Commission on Children (Washington, D.C., 1991).

3. U. S. Department of Education, National Center for Educational Statistics, *Access to Early Childhood Programs for Children at Risk* (Washington, D.C., 1994), p. 9.

4. William Carlos Williams, *Collected Poems: 1909–1939, Volume I* (New York: New Directions Publishing Corp., 1938).

5. Cost, Quality and Child Outcomes Study Team, *Cost, Quality, and Child Outcomes in Child Care Centers, Executive Summary,* 2d ed. (Denver: Economics Department, University of Colorado at Denver, 1995), p. 9.

Chapter 1. Fall: The Bumblebee Room

1. William T. Gormley, Jr., *Everybody's Children: Child Care as a Public Problem* (Washington, D.C.: Brookings Institution, 1995), p. 31.

2. Carnegie Corporation of New York, *Starting Points: Meeting the Needs of Our Youngest Children,* the report of the Carnegie task force on meeting the needs of young children (New York, 1994), p. 55.

3. Ellen Galinsky, "The Cost of Not Providing Quality Early Childhood Programs," in *Reaching the Full Cost of Quality in Early Childhood Programs,* ed. Barbara Willer, pp. 28–38 (Washington, D.C.: National Association for the Education of Young Children, 1990).

4. Burton, Whitebook et al., *Valuable Work, Minimal Rewards: A Report on the Wisconsin Child Care Work Force,* prepared by the National Center for the Early Childhood Work Force and the Wisconsin Early Childhood Association (Washington, D.C., 1994), p. ii.

5. Diane Adams and George Hagenauer, "1994 Child Care Survey Report: City-Certified Child Care Programs," Community Coordinated Child Care (4-C), Madison, Wis., 1994, typescript.

6. Marcy Whitebook et al., *National Child Care Staffing Study Revisited: Four Years in the Life of Center-Based Child Care*, the Child Care Employee Project (Oakland, Calif., 1993), p. 1. Also see Burton et al., *Valuable Work, Minimal Rewards*, p. 32.

7. Margaret O'Brien Steinfels, *Who's Minding the Children? The History and Politics of Day Care in America* (New York: Simon and Schuster, 1973), p. 106.

8. Nancy Balaban, "The Role of the Child Care Professional in Caring for Infants, Toddlers, and Their Families," *Young Children*, July 1992, p. 66.

9. National Commission on Children, *Beyond Rhetoric*, p. 269.

10. Barbara Willer, "Estimating the Full Cost of Quality," in *Reaching the Full Cost of Quality in Early Childhood Programs*, ed. Barbara Willer (Washington, D.C.: National Association for the Education of Young Children, 1990), p. 61.

11. Adams and Hagenauer, "1994 Child Care Survey Report."

12. Gormley, *Everybody's Children*, p. 122.

Chapter 2. Winter: The Turtle Room

1. Edward F. Zigler and Mary E. Lang, *Child Care Choices: Balancing the Needs of Children, Families, and Society* (New York: The Free Press, 1991), p. 93.

2. Steinfels, *Who's Minding the Children?* p. 78.

3. National Institute of Child Health and Human Development (NICHD), preliminary results of the Study of Early Child Care, presented at the Society for Research in Development, April 4, 1997, Washington, D.C.

4. Alison Clarke-Stewart, *Daycare: The Developing Child* (Cambridge, Mass.: Harvard University Press, 1982), pp. 67–70.

5. David P. Weikart, "Quality Preschool Programs: A Long-Term Social Investment," Occasional Paper 5, Ford Foundation Project on Social Welfare and the American Future, Ford Foundation, New York, 1989, p. 7. Birth rates cited are per 100 women; the percentage 117 includes women with more than one child.

6. Clarke-Stewart, *Daycare*, pp. 74–75.

7. Mary Dublin Keyserling, *Windows on Day Care: A Report Based on the Findings of the National Council of Jewish Women* (New York: National Council of Jewish Women, 1972), p. 1.

8. U.S. Department of Education, National Center for Educational Statistics, "Statistics in Brief," October 1995, Table 1.

9. Willer, "Estimating the Full Cost of Quality," pp. viii–ix.

10. Maris A. Vinovskis, "Early Childhood Education: Then and Now," *Daedalus* (Winter 1993), p. 154.

11. Zigler and Lang, *Child Care Choices*, pp. 29–30.

12. Vinovskis, "Early Childhood Education," pp. 157–158.

13. Zigler and Lang, *Child Care Choices*, p. 31.

14. Vinovskis, "Early Childhood Education," p. 160.

15. Steinfels, *Who's Minding the Children?* p. 68.

16. *A Teacher's Guide: Assistant Child Care Teacher*, Wisconsin Department of Public Instruction (Madison, 1990), p. 2.

17. Steinfels, *Who's Minding the Children?* p. 73.

18. Sandra Scarr, *Mother Care Other Care: The First Authoritative Guide to Child Care Decisions that Takes into Account the Child's Needs and the Working Mother's Dilemmas* (New York: Basic Books, 1984), pp. 57–58.

19. Zigler and Lang, *Child Care Choices,* p. 15.

20. Angela Browne Miller, *The Day Care Dilemma: Critical Concerns for American Families* (New York: Plenum Press, 1990), p. 21.

21. James Daniel, "Day Care: How Good for Your Child?" *Reader's Digest,* August 1971, p. 137.

22. Ibid., p. 138.

23. Steinfels, *Who's Minding the Children?* pp. 247–248.

24. Sheila B. Kamerman and Alfred J. Kahn, *Starting Right: How America Neglects Its Youngest Children and What We Can Do about It* (New York: Oxford University Press, 1995), p. 133.

25. Clarke-Stewart, *Daycare,* p. 34.

26. Keyserling, *Windows on Day Care,* p. 3.

27. Although this story was reported to me as having actually happened at Red Caboose, the same story appeared as a Doonesbury cartoon during the 1970s.

28. Vinovskis, "Early Childhood Education," p. 155.

29. Kamerman and Kahn, *Starting Right,* p. 8.

30. Ibid., p. 11.

31. Ibid., p. 130.

32. Cost, Quality and Child Outcomes Study Team, *Cost, Quality, and Child Outcomes,* p. 2.

33. Ibid.

34. Penelope Leach, *Children First: What Our Society Must Do—and Is Not Doing—for Our Children Today* (New York: Alfred Knopf, 1994), p. 97.

35. High/Scope Educational Research Foundation, "Significant Benefits: The High/Scope Perry Preschool Study through Age 27," quoted in *Working for Change,* a publication of the Child Care Law Center (March 1995), p. 18.

36. National Commission on Children, *Beyond Rhetoric,* p. 12.

37. Gormley, *Everybody's Children,* p. 51.

Chapter 3. Spring: The Elephant Room

1. *National Child Care Staffing Study* (Oakland, Calif.: Child Care Employee Project, 1989).

2. Brenda Eheart and Robin Lynn Leavitt, *Toddler Day Care: A Guide to Responsive Caregiving* (Washington, D.C.: Lexington Books, 1985), p. 114.

3. Margaret Boyer et al., eds., *Between a Rock and a Hard Place: Raising Rates to Raise Wages* (Minneapolis: Child Care Workers Alliance, 1991), p. 44.

4. Scarr, *Mother Care Other Care,* p. 49.

5. Ibid., pp. 49–50.

6. Zigler and Lang, *Child Care Choices,* pp. 9–10.

7. Scarr, *Mother Care Other Care*, p. 270.

8. Mary L. Culkin, Suzanne W. Helburn, and John R. Morris, "Current Price versus Full Cost: An Economic Perspective," *Reaching the Full Cost of Quality in Early Childhood Programs* (Washington, D.C.: NAEYC, 1990), p. 13.

9. Ibid., pp. 13–14.

10. Ibid., p. 16.

11. Ibid., p. 24.

12. Telephone conversation with author, June 1, 1995.

13. Cost, Quality and Child Outcomes Study Team, *Cost, Quality, and Child Outcomes*, p. 9.

14. Susan Dynerman, *Are Our Kids All Right? Answers to the Tough Questions about Child Care Today* (Princeton, N.J.: Peterson's, 1994), p. 35.

15. Maurice Sendak, *Chicken Soup with Rice* (New York: Harper & Row, 1962).

16. Charlotte Zolotow, *The Old Dog* (New York: Harper Collins, 1995).

17. Dorothy Conniff, "Child Care—You Bet! Quality . . . Doubtful to Below," *Wis-Kids Journal*, May-June 1997, p. 5.

18. National Commission on Children, *Beyond Rhetoric*, p. 12.

Chapter 4. Summer: The Grasshopper Room

1. *Capital Times*, Madison, Wis., July 5, 1996, p. 1.

2. *Capital Times*, Madison, Wis., July 9, 1996, p. 1.

3. *Capital Times*, Madison, Wis., August 3–4, 1996, p. 1.

Epilogue

1. Scarr, *Mother Care Other Care*, p. 269.

2. Leach, *Children First*.

3. *New York Times*, February 1, 1995, p. A4.

4. Ian McMahan, "Public Preschool from the Age of Two: The *Ecole Maternelle* in France," *Young Children*, July 1992, pp. 22–28.

5. Miller, *The Day Care Dilemma*, p. 52.

6. Zigler and Lang, *Child Care Choices*, pp. 198ff.

7. Ibid.

8. Anne Roiphe, *Fruitful: A Real Mother in the Modern World* (New York: Houghton Mifflin, 1996), p. 251.

9. *Capital Times*, Madison, Wis., December 12, 1996, p. 1.

10. *Capital Times*, Madison, Wis., August 21, 1997, p. 8A.